365 Ultimate Fish Recipes

(365 Ultimate Fish Recipes - Volume 1)

Jennifer Wilson

Content

CHAPTER 3: MAHI MAHI RECIPES 62

CHAPTER 6: SWORDFISH RECIPES..... 152

CHAPTER 7: SOLE FISH RECIPES........159

Chapter 1: Flounder Recipes

***

1. Almond Stuffed Flounder Recipe

Serving: 2 | Prep: | Cook: 15mins | Ready in:

Ingredients

- 2 4-ounce flounder or sole fillets (1/4 to 1/2 inch thick)
- 1/2 cup shredded swiss cheese (2 ounces)
- 2 tablespoons chopped almonds
- 1 tablespoon snipped chives
- 2 tablespoons margarine or butter, softened
- paprika
- 1/4 cup dry white wine
- 1/4 cup shredded carrot
- 2 teaspoons all-purpose flour
- 1/8 teaspoon dried tarragon, crushed
- Dash salt
- Dash white pepper
- 1/2 cup milk
- 1 cup hot cooked wild rice
- Fresh tarragon (optional

Direction

- Rinse fish; pat dry with paper towels. Set aside.
- For stuffing, in a small bowl combine half of the Swiss cheese, the almonds, chives, and 1 tablespoon of the margarine or butter.
- Spoon half of the stuffing onto one end of each piece of fish. Roll up fish around the stuffing. Place fish, seam side down, in a small baking dish. Sprinkle with paprika.
- Pour 3 tablespoons of the wine into the dish.

- Bake, uncovered, in a 375 degree F oven for 15 or 20 minutes or until fish flakes easily with a fork.
- While fish is cooking; in a small saucepan cook carrot in the remaining margarine or butter for 3 to 4 minutes or until tender.
- Stir in the flour, tarragon, salt, and white pepper; add milk all at once. Cook and stir until mixture is thickened and bubbly. Stir in remaining Swiss cheese and remaining wine.
- To serve, place fish rolls atop hot cooked wild rice; top with sauce.
- Garnish with fresh tarragon, if desired. Makes 2 servings, 4 with another side or salad.

2. Alton Browns Baked Stuffed Flounder Recipe

Serving: 8 | Prep: | Cook: 25mins | Ready in:

Ingredients

- 2 tablespoons unsalted butter
- 1 medium onion, chopped
- 1/2 teaspoon kosher salt, plus extra for the sweat and for seasoning fillets
- 1 clove garlic, minced
- 1 (10-ounce package) frozen chopped spinach, thawed and squeezed dry
- 1 lemon, zested
- 1/4 teaspoon freshly ground black pepper, plus extra for seasoning fillets
- 2 tablespoons chopped fresh parsley leaves
- 1 cup heavy cream
- 1/4 cup white wine
- 10 ounces grated Cheddar
- 1 1/2 to 2 pounds flounder fillets
- 3 cups leftover cooked rice

Direction

- Preheat the oven to 350 degrees F.

- In a medium sauté pan over low heat, melt the butter; add the onion and a pinch of salt and sweat until translucent. Add the garlic and continue to cook for another minute. Add the spinach and lemon zest and cook until just heated through. Season with the salt and pepper, add the parsley, and stir to combine. Remove from the heat and keep warm.
- Place the heavy cream and wine into a saucepan over medium heat. Once the mixture begins to simmer, gradually add the cheese and stir until melted. Set aside and keep warm.
- If the fillets are large, cut in half. Season each filet on both sides with salt and pepper. Divide the spinach mixture evenly among the fillets and roll the fish around the mixture. Place the rice into a 2 1/2-quart casserole dish and spread evenly. Place each roll on top of the rice, seam side down. Pour over the cheese sauce and place in the oven for 25 minutes. Allow to cool for 5 minutes before serving.

3. Asian Style Flounder Packets Recipe

Serving: 4 | Prep: | Cook: 8mins | Ready in:

Ingredients

- 2 large green onions
- 2 Tbl. soy sauce
- 2 Tbl. seasoned rice vinegar
- 4 flounder fillets (about 6 ounces each)
- 2 tsp. grated, peeled gingerroot

Direction

- Cut tops of green onions crosswise into 2-inch pieces, then cut each piece lengthwise into thin strips; reserve for garnish. Thinly slice white part of green onions.
- In small bowl, mix soy sauce and rice vinegar.
- Preheat oven to 425 degrees.

- From roll of foil or cooking parchment paper, cut four 15" by 12" sheets.
- Arrange 1 flounder fillet on half of each piece of foil; spread each with 1/2 tsp. ginger. Spoon 1 Tbsp soy sauce mixture over each flounder fillet; top with sliced green onions. Fold other half of foil over fish. To create sealed packets, fold edges of foil over about 1/2-inch all around, overlapping folds.
- Place packets in 15 1/2" by 10 1/2" jelly-roll pan.
- Bake packets 8 minutes.
- To serve, with kitchen shears, cut an X in top of each packet to let steam escape before serving. (When packets are open, check that fish flakes easily when tested with a fork.)
- Garnish fish with reserved green onion strips.

4. Baked Flounder Fillets In Lemon Soy Vinaigrette

Serving: 0 | Prep: | Cook: 10mins | Ready in:

Ingredients

- two 6-ounce flounder fillets
- 1 garlic clove
- 2 tablespoons fresh lemon juice
- 2 teaspoons soy sauce
- 1/2 teaspoon sugar
- 1/2 teaspoon salt
- 2 tablespoons olive oil

Direction

- Preheat oven to 450°F.
- Arrange fillets in a ceramic or glass baking dish just large enough to hold them in one layer. Mince garlic and in a small bowl combine with lemon juice, soy sauce, sugar, and salt. Whisk in oil until emulsified and pour vinaigrette over fish.
- Bake fish in middle of oven until just cooked through and no longer translucent, 5 to 7 minutes.

- Per serving: 285 calories, 16 g fat (2 g saturated), 81 mg cholesterol, 1014 mg sodium, 3 g carbohydrates, 0 g fiber, 32 g protein

5. Baked Flounder With Minced Clams Recipe

Serving: 4 | Prep: | Cook: 25mins | Ready in:

Ingredients

- 1 1/2 lbs. flounder fillets
- 1 onion, finely minced
- 1 c. dry white wine
- 1 1/2 TB flour
- 2 TB butter, melted
- 1 c. hot cooking liquid
- 1/2 c. heavy cream
- 1 (8oz.) can minced clams, drained

Direction

- Arrange fillets in a shallow baking dish; add minced onion and dry white wine. Bake the fillets in a preheated 325° oven until they are just done or for 15 to 20 minutes.
- Transfer the fillets carefully to a heatproof serving dish and keep them warm. Reserve 1 c. cooking liquid.
- Make a sauce with the flour blended with melted butter. Gradually add the 1 cup of hot cooking liquid. Simmer the sauce, stirring often, until it is smooth and thickened, then, add heavy cream and minced clams. Taste the sauce for seasoning, stir it until it is hot but not boiling, and pour it over the fish fillets.
- Put the dish under a broiler for a few minutes until the sauce bubbles and begins to glaze. Serve while hot.

6. Baked Flounder With Crabmeat Stuffing Recipe

Serving: 4 | Prep: | Cook: 25mins | Ready in:

Ingredients

- 1/2 small onion, minced
- 1/2 small red pepper, finely chopped
- 3/4 tsp Old Bay Srasoning
- 1/4 tsp salt
- 2/3 c light cream
- 8 oz. imitation crabmeat, finely chopped
- 3 tsp chopped parsley
- 4 flounder fillets(about 4 oz. ea)
- 3/4 c white wine or water
- cooked rice(optional)

Direction

- Heat med-size nonstick skillet over med. heat. Coat pan with nonstick spray, then add onion and red pepper and coat generously with spray; cover and cook 4 mins or till softened, stirring occasionally. Remove cover and stir in 1/2 tsp of Old Bay, 1/8 tsp of the salt and the light cream.
- Increase heat to med-high and bring to boil; cook for 1 min or till reduced and thickened. Gently fold in crabmeat and 2 tsp. of the parsley; refrigerate 30 mins.
- Heat oven to 400 degrees. Coat 13x9" baking dish with nonstick cooking spray. Place one of the flounder fillets, skinned-side up on work surface, then spoon 1/2 c crab mixture onto end of fillet; roll up, creating small bundle. Repeat using remaining fillets and crab.
- Transfer bundles to baking dish, seam side down and sprinkle with remaining 1/4 tsp Old Bay, 1/8 tsp salt and 1 tsp parsley. Add wine or water to pan; transfer to oven.
- Bake for 20 mins or till fish is solid white and flakes easily with a fork.
- Remove to plates with large spatula and serve with rice, if desired.

7. Baked Flounder With Scallop Stuffing Recipe

Serving: 6 | Prep: | Cook: 20mins | Ready in:

Ingredients

- 1/2 cup butter
- 1 clove garlic, minced
- 1 small onion, finely chopped
- 1/2 pound scallops, chopped
- salt and pepper
- dry white wine
- fine dry breadcrumbs
- 6 flounder fillets (5-7 oz)
- 1/4 cup butter, melted
- 1/2 cup hot water
- White Sauce:
- 2 tablespoons butter
- 2 tablespoons flour
- 1 cup milk
- salt and fresh ground pepper
- dry white wine

Direction

- In a 10 inch skillet, melt the 1/2 cup of butter. Add garlic and onion and sauté until onions are translucent. Add scallops and cook 2 or 3 minutes. Season with salt, pepper, and white wine to taste. Add sufficient bread crumbs to prepare a moist stuffing.
- Place each flounder fillet dark-side-up on a flat surface. Placing the scallop stuffing in the center of each fillet, divide evenly among the fillets. Fold both ends of each fillet over the stuffing, overlapping the ends.
- Pour the melted butter and the hot water into a 9x12 inch baking dish. Transfer the stuffed fillets to the baking dish and bake 20 minutes while you prepare a white sauce.
- WHITE SAUCE: In a small saucepan, melt butter, then whisk in flour. Cook over low heat 2-3 minutes, whisking constantly. Then add milk, and salt, pepper, and white wine to taste.

Increase heat to medium, whisking constantly until the sauce is thickened. Cook several minutes over low heat, stirring.
- When the flounder has baked 20 minutes, pour the white sauce over the stuffed fillets. Return the baking dish to the oven briefly and heat until the sauce begins to bubble.

8. Baked Paprika Flounder Recipe

Serving: 4 | Prep: | Cook: 10mins | Ready in:

Ingredients

- 4 to 5 small flounder filets
- butter cooking spray
- salt
- pepper
- Italian herbs
- paprika

Direction

- Preheat oven to 400 degrees.
- Spray baking sheet with cooking spray. Place filets on baking sheet and spray them lightly.
- Sprinkle coarse salt, ground pepper, Italian herbs and paprika to taste. It's good with a lot of paprika.
- Bake at 400 degrees for ten minutes or until white and flaky.

9. Baked Stuffed Flounder Recipe

Serving: 4 | Prep: | Cook: 30mins | Ready in:

Ingredients

- 1/2 cup chopped celery
- 2 Tbsp chopped parsley
- 1/2 cup chopped green onions with tops
- 1/2 lb shrimp, boiled and chopped
- 1 (or more) clove garlic, minced

- 1 egg, slightly beaten
- 3/4 cup butter
- 1-1/2 cups moistened unseasoned croutons
- 1/2 cup crabmeat
- salt, pepper and cayenne pepper
- 4 medium sized flounder, washed,scaled, with heads removed..

Direction

- In a large skillet or saucepan, sauté celery, onions, and garlic in 1/4 cup butter over low heat.
- In a large bowl, mix bread cubes, shrimp, crabmeat, parsley, and egg well.
- Season to taste with salt, black and cayenne pepper. Set aside.
- Split the thick side of the flounder lengthwise and crosswise forming a cross; loosen meat from bone to form a pocket for stuffing.
- Melt 1/4 cup butter the brush fish well with the melted butter, salt and pepper.
- Fill flounder pockets with seafood stuffing mixture.
- Melt remaining 1/4 cup butter in shallow baking pan. Place fish in pan, making sure not to overlap.
- Cover with foil and bake at 375 degrees for 25 minutes, until fish flakes easily with a fork.
- Remove foil and bake another 5 minutes.
- Enjoy!

10. Battered Flounder Bites Recipe

Serving: 10 | Prep: | Cook: 15mins | Ready in:

Ingredients

- Sauce:
- 1 cup mayo
- 2 Tbs chopped shallots
- 1 tbs chopped jalepeno peppers
- 2 tsp hot sauce
- 1 tsp lemon juice
- 1/4 tsp salt

- dash red pepper flakes
- Fish:
- 1, 8 oz pkg hush puppy mix
- 3/4 cup milk
- 1 1/4 lb flounder fillets cut into 1/2 inch pieces
- 2 cups of oil to fry
- 1 cup flour to dredge fish

Direction

- Combine sauce ingredients and cover and chill.
- Prepare fish:
- Heat oil to 350F.
- Combine hushpuppy mix and milk into a batter.
- Dip fish into flour and then into batter.
- Fry golden about 3 to 4 minutes per side.
- Serve with sauce.

11. Broiled Flounder With Warm Orange Glaze Recipe

Serving: 4 | Prep: | Cook: 15mins | Ready in:

Ingredients

- 4 (6oz) flounder fillets (thawed if frozen)
- 1 tbsp butter or margarine, melted
- 1/2 tsp seasoned salt
- 1 cup orange marmalade
- 1/4 cup fresh orange juice
- 2 tsp grated fresh gingerroot
- 1/4 tsp pepper sauce
- 2 naval oranges, sectioned
- orange sections and chives (optional)

Direction

- Preheat broiler. Coat broiler rack with non-stick cooking spray. Place fillets on rack. Brush with melted butter and sprinkle with seasoned salt. Broil 4 inches from heat until fish flakes with a fork, about 8 minutes.

- Meanwhile, in a saucepan, combine marmalade, orange juice, ginger, and hot pepper sauce. Heat and stir. Serve over flounder. Garnish with orange sections and chives, if desired.
- Note******Flounder, with its firm, white, finely textured flesh, may be cooked many ways. The tangy orange sauce gives zest to this mild-flavored fish.

12. Broiled Flounder With Pineapple Salsa Recipe

Serving: 4 | Prep: | Cook: 8mins | Ready in:

Ingredients

- 4 (4oz) flounder fillets
- butter-flavored spray
- 2t lemon-herb seasoning, salt-free
- 1/4t salt
- 1 (8oz) can crushed pineapple in juice, drained
- 3 green onions, sliced
- 1/3c radishes, chopped
- 1/3t dried crushed red pepper

Direction

- Place fish on rack of a broiler pan coated with butter spray. Coat fish with butter spray; sprinkle with lemon-herb seasoning and salt.
- Broil fish 5 1/2" from heat 8 minutes or until fish flakes easily when tested with a fork.
- While fish broils, combine pineapple and remaining ingredients. Top each fillet with 1/4 cup pineapple salsa.
- 132 calories, 12% from fat.

13. CRISP CRUSTED SOLE OR FLOUNDER Recipe

Serving: 4 | Prep: | Cook: 8mins | Ready in:

Ingredients

- 4 sole fillets
- COLD salted water
- 2 beaten eggs
- Crushed cornflakes... about 2 cups
- Salt
- lemon wedges

Direction

- Soak fish in COLD salt water for 5 minutes...
- Drain WELL.
- Dip in egg.
- Dip in crumbs and pat into the fish.
- Place on platter and let stand for a few minutes until breading sets.
- Heat equal parts oil and butter in a heavy fry pan.
- Add fish and brown quickly on one side.
- Turn over, salt and brown.
- Serve immediately with Lemon wedges and tarter if wanted!
- Easy... Enjoy!

14. Cascades Baked Stuffed Flounder Recipe

Serving: 6 | Prep: | Cook: 30mins | Ready in:

Ingredients

- 6 baby flounder, boned, or
- 6 flounder fillets
- seafood Dressing (see below)
- salt and pepper to taste
- 3 tablespoons lemon juice
- 1 cup fine bread crumbs
- 1/3 pound butter, melted

Direction

- Preheat oven to 375°F.
- Grease shallow baking pan.

- Stuff each fish with 4 to 6 tablespoons of Seafood Dressing, or spread the same amount of dressing over each fillet. Roll and fasten with toothpicks.
- Place in prepared baking pan, and season with salt, pepper, and lemon juice.
- Sprinkle bread crumbs over fish.
- Melt butter and pour over fish.
- Bake at 375° F. for 25 to 30 minutes or until fish flakes easily when tested with a fork.
- SEAFOOD DRESSING
- 6 tablespoons butter
- 1/4 cup celery, finely chopped
- 1/2 cup onion, finely chopped
- 1/4 cup green pepper, finely chopped
- 1/2 pound shrimp, cooked and diced
- 1 teaspoon parsley, chopped
- 1 teaspoon pimiento, finely chopped
- 1/2 teaspoon paprika
- 1 teaspoon Worcestershire sauce
- 1/2 teaspoon seafood seasoning salt to taste
- 1/8 teaspoon cayenne pepper
- 1/4 cup dry sherry
- 1 1/2 cups bread crumbs
- Melt butter, add the vegetables, and sauté until tender.
- (6 servings)

15. Cheesy Flounder Fillets Recipe

Serving: 4 | Prep: | Cook: 20mins | Ready in:

Ingredients

- 1/3 cup light mayonnaise
- 1/3 cup cheddar cheese, shredded
- 4 flounder fillets, 6-ounces each
- 1 package (6.1 ounces) tomato lentil couscous mix
- 1 box (10-ounces) frozen spinach

Direction

- Preheat oven at 400F.

- Spray a baking dish with nonstick cooking spray.
- Mix together the mayo and cheddar cheese. Place the fillets in the dish and fold in half. Evenly divide the mayo mixture over each and spread evenly.
- Bake fillets for 20 minutes or until fish flakes easily.
- While fish is baking, prepare couscous and spinach following package directions.
- Serve fillets with couscous and spinach alongside.

16. Cheesy Flounder Florentine Recipe

Serving: 4 | Prep: | Cook: 25mins | Ready in:

Ingredients

- 1 (9oz.) container fresh Alfredo
- 4 (5 ounce) flounder fillets
- 8 ounces spinach fettuccine
- 1 teaspoon Dijon mustard
- 1/4 teaspoon ground black pepper
- 1/3 cup grated Parmesan cheese, divided
- 1/3 cup shredded Gruyere cheese, divided
- 2 cups fresh spinach cleaned and chopped

Direction

- Preheat oven to 400 degrees F (200 degrees C).
- Fill a large pot with lightly salted water and bring to a rolling boil. Stir in the spinach fettuccine, bring back to a boil, and cook pasta over medium heat until cooked through but still firm to the bite, about 8 minutes. Drain and transfer into a 2-quart casserole. Toss fettuccine with 1 tablespoon butter.
- Warm Alfredo in a small saucepan, over low heat. Whisk in Dijon mustard, black pepper, 1/4 cup of Parmesan cheese, and 1/4 cup of Gruyere cheese.
- Spread spinach over fettuccine noodles; arrange fillets on top of spinach. Pour sauce

over the fish and sprinkle remaining Parmesan and Gruyere cheeses over the top.

- Bake in the preheated oven until sauce is bubbling, about 15 to 18 minutes, letting the cheese brown a bit on top. Serve on plates with a drizzle of lemon.
- Notes: You can use 1 to 1 1/2 pounds of firm white fish in this recipe.
- Tip: Aluminum foil helps keep food moist, ensures it cooks evenly, keeps leftovers fresh, and makes clean-up easy.

17. Crab Stuffed Flounder Recipe

Serving: 4 | Prep: | Cook: | Ready in:

Ingredients

- 1 lb. fillet of flounder or
- 1/8 c. chopped onion
- 1/8 c. butter
- 8 oz. crab meat
- 1 tbsp. parsley
- 1/4 c. crackers or bread crumbs
- 3 tbsp. butter
- 1 tbsp. flour
- salt and pepper to taste
- 1 c. milk
- 1/4 tsp. paprika

Direction

- Cook onion in 1/8 cup butter until tender. Stir in crab, crumbs, parsley, salt and pepper. Spread mix over fillets. Roll and place seam down in baking pan.
- In saucepan, melt 3 tablespoons butter, blend in flour. Add enough milk until mixture thickens (1 cup). Pour over fillets. Bake 25 minutes. Sprinkle with cheese and paprika. Bake for 10 minutes. Any white meat fish can be substituted.

18. Crispy Crusted Flounder Recipe

Serving: 4 | Prep: | Cook: 20mins | Ready in:

Ingredients

- 1 cup tomato, seeded, chopped
- 1 cup leeks, thinly sliced
- 1/2 cup green bell pepper, chopped
- 1 Tbs. garlic minced
- 4 flounder fillets (6 oz.each)
- 1/2 cup coarse bread crumbs
- 1/2 cup parmesan cheese, grated
- 1/2 cup plain potato chips, crushed
- 1/2 tps. paprika
- 1/4 tps. cayenne
- 2 Tbs. butter, melted
- 1 Tbs. scallion, thinly sliced
- lemon wedges

Direction

- Preheat oven to 450 F.
- Combine first four ingredients in a bowl. Spread on a baking sheet coated with cooking spray. Arrange fillets on top of vegetables; season with salt and pepper to taste.
- Combine crumbs and next four ingredients; toss with melted butter. Divide crumb mixture evenly over each fillet, pressing into the fish. Bake 20 minutes or until fillets flake easily when tested with a fork.
- Sprinkle with scallion and serve with lemon wedges.

19. Crispy Fillet Of Flounder With Almonds Recipe

Serving: 2 | Prep: | Cook: 18mins | Ready in:

Ingredients

- CRISPY FILLET OF FLOUNDER with almonds

- ~~~~~~
- 4 slices fillet of flounder (you may substitute other fish)
- 1/2 c. milk
- 2 c. corn flakes
- 4 tbsp. butter
- 1/4 Cup Chopped almonds
- salt and pepper and other spices to taste

Direction

- Preheat oven at 450 degrees.
- Rinse the fish with cold water.
- Use a glass baking pan or Corning Ware dish.
- (Spray well with baking spray).
- Roll the fish in the 1/2 cup milk so that breading will stick and will help keep the fish moist.
- Crush the 2 cups of corn flakes and roll the fish in it.
- (I coat the fish on a plate).
- Place in the prepared baking dish.
- Press almonds onto top of fish.
- Melt the 4 tablespoons of butter and pour over top of all.
- Place in preheated oven for 15 to 20 minutes, then serve
- We enjoy this with tartar sauce.
- THIS IS OUR TONIGHT'S 'SUPPER' WITH BROCOLLI AND CARROTS AND LIGHT HUSH PUPPIES.

20. Delightful Fried Flounder Recipe

Serving: 4 | Prep: | Cook: 20mins | Ready in:

Ingredients

- 4 flounder fillets
- 1/3 cup cornmeal
- 1/3 cup all-purpose flour
- 1 teaspoon salt

- 1/2 teaspoon paprika
- 1/4 teaspoon onion powder
- 1/8 teaspoon freshly ground black pepper
- 1 egg lightly beaten
- 1 tablespoon water
- 1/2 cup vegetable oil

Direction

- Rinse fish and pat dry.
- Combine cornmeal, flour, salt, paprika, onion powder and pepper on sheet of wax paper.
- Combine egg and water in shallow dish or pie plate.
- Dip fish in egg mixture then coat with cornmeal mixture.
- Heat oil to 365 in electric skillet or heavy skillet.
- Fry fish for 7 minutes on each side then drain on paper towels.

21. Doi Rui Recipe

Serving: 0 | Prep: | Cook: 1hours | Ready in:

Ingredients

- 500g Rohu fish, cut into medium-sized pieces
- 1 onion
- 1 bowl curd , beaten properly to avoid lumps
- 1 cup mustard oil
- 2 tbsp ginger-garlic paste
- salt, as per taste
- sugar, as per taste
- 1 tsp turmeric powder
- 1tsp red chilli powder
- 1 cup curd
- water
- 1 tsp cardamom(elaichi) powder (roasted dry and ground)
- 1 tsp cinnamon(dalchini) powder (roasted dry and ground)
- 1tsp cloves (laung) powder (roasted dry and ground)

Direction

- Fry the fish pieces in oil with salt and turmeric powder.
- Add oil to another pan and add ginger-garlic paste, salt, sugar, turmeric powder, red chili powder.
- Add curd and stir nicely. There should be no lumps. Add little water.
- When the gravy starts boiling, add the fried fish pieces.
- Add ground elaichi, cloves, cinnamon.

22. Flounder Florentine Recipe

Serving: 4 | Prep: | Cook: 40mins |Ready in:

Ingredients

- 1 lb flounder or sole fillets
- 6oz fresh mushrooms
- ½C swiss cheese (2oz)
- 16oz frozen spinach
- 1 T pimiento
- Dash salt
- 6oz (3/4C) evaporated milk
- 1/4 scant tsp ground nutmeg
- black pepper to taste
- Dash paprika

Direction

- Thaw fish if frozen. Set aside.
- Heat oven to 375. Line baking pan with foil and spray foil.
- Slice mushrooms and shred cheese.
- Toss vegetables with salt; spread in pan.
- Place fillets on top of spinach.
- In a saucepan, combine milk, cheese, nutmeg and pepper. Cook and stir over low heat until cheese is melted.
- Pour sauce over fish; sprinkle with paprika.
- Cover dish with foil and bake 40-45 minutes.
- Or you may cook it in the microwave:

- Cover with vented microwave-safe plastic wrap. Cook on 70% power (medium-high) for 8-9 minutes, giving dish a half-turn after 4 minutes.

23. Flounder Francaise Recipe

Serving: 1 | Prep: | Cook: 6mins |Ready in:

Ingredients

- Batter:
- 2 eggs
- 6 ounces parmesan cheese
- Pinch parsley
- 8 ounces milk
- Combine all ingredients and mix well.
- Sweet lemon Sauce:
- 2 cups chicken stock
- 1/2 cup lemon juice
- 1/2 cup sugar
- In saucepan combine all ingredients. Bring to a boil and reduce by 1/2.
- 4 (6-ounce) flounder fillets
- 12 (16/20 count) shrimp, cleaned and deveined
- butter, to taste
- lemon juice, to taste
- white wine, to taste

Direction

- Preheat Oven: 350 degrees. Dip fillets in batter and cook in a nonstick pan with a small amount of cooking spray. Cook on both sides until fillets are golden brown. Place fillets on oven pan and bake for 5 to 6 minutes. Sauté shrimp with a small amount of butter, lemon juice and white wine. Place on top of fillets and serve topped with sweet lemon sauce.

24. Flounder In Pecan Sauce Recipe

Serving: 6 | Prep: | Cook: 20mins |Ready in:

Ingredients

- 3 ounces ground pecans
- 8 cloves garlic peeled
- 1/2 cup flat leaf parsley chopped
- 1/2 teaspoon sweet Spanish paprika
- 2-1/4 cups fish stock
- 1/2 teaspoon salt
- 1/2 teaspoon freshly ground black pepper
- 1/4 cup olive oil
- 6 flounder filets
- 6 pecans coarsely chopped for garnish

Direction

- Process pecans, garlic, parsley, paprika, fish stock, salt and pepper in blender until smooth.
- Heat oil in a large skillet and sauté fish for two minutes on each side then add sauce.
- Cover and cook over low heat for 20 minutes.
- Put fish on a serving platter and pour sauce over top.
- Garnish with coarsely chopped pecans and serve immediately.

25. Flounder In Wine Sauce Recipe

Serving: 4 | Prep: | Cook: 30mins |Ready in:

Ingredients

- 2 pounds skinned flounder fillets
- 1-1/2 teaspoons salt
- 1/8 teaspoon freshly ground black pepper
- 3 tomatoes sliced
- 2 tablespoons flour
- 2 tablespoons butter melted
- 1/2 cup milk
- 1/3 cup dry white wine
- 1/2 teaspoon fresh crushed basil

Direction

- Sprinkle fillets on both sides with salt and pepper then place in single layer in greased baking dish.
- Arrange tomatoes over top of fish then sprinkle with salt and pepper
- Blend flour into butter then add milk and gradually cook until thick and smooth stirring constantly.
- Remove from heat and stir in wine and basil then pour sauce over top of tomatoes.
- Bake at 350 for 30 minutes.

26. Flounder Jardiniere Recipe

Serving: 6 | Prep: | Cook: 25mins |Ready in:

Ingredients

- 1/3 cup all-purpose flour
- 3 eggs, lightly beaten
- 2 tablespoons butter
- 2 tablespoons oil
- 6 fillet (about 1-3/4 pounds)
- 1 leek, cut in 2-inch pieces, thinly sliced lengthwise
- 3 carrots, cut in 2-inch pieces, thinly sliced lengthwise
- 1/4 teaspoon salt
- 1/8 teaspoon pepper
- 3/4 cup chicken broth
- 1/4 cup dry white wine
- 1 tablespoon fresh lemon juice
- 3 tablespoons capers, drained

Direction

- Place flour in small pan; place eggs in small bowl.
- Heat half the butter and oil in large nonstick skillet.
- Coat 3 fillets with flour; dip in eggs. Cook in skillet 2-1/2 minutes per side, until lightly golden.

- Remove to platter; keep warm. Add remaining butter and oil to skillet. Cook remaining fillets.
- To skillet, add leek, carrots, salt and pepper; sauté 4 minutes; if dry, add more butter.
- Add broth, wine, lemon and capers.
- Cover; cook 6 minutes, until carrots are tender. Spoon over fish.
- Makes 6 servings.

27. Flounder Milanese Recipe

Serving: 4 | Prep: | Cook: 20mins | Ready in:

Ingredients

- 4 (4oz each) skinless flounder filets
- pinch of kosher salt
- freshly ground black pepper
- 4 cups arugula
- 1 medium vine ripe tomato, diced small
- 1 teaspoon olive oil
- 1 lemon, halved
- 2 large egg whites
- 2/3 cup seasoned bread crumbs
- olive oil spray

Direction

- Season fish lightly with salt and pepper. In a medium bowl, combine the arugula, tomato, olive oil and the juice from half of the lemon. Season with salt and pepper, toss and set aside. Slice the other half of the lemon into 4 slices or wedges to serve with the fish.
- In a shallow bowl, beat the egg whites. Place the bread crumbs in another dish. Dip each fish filet in the egg whites, then bread crumbs.
- Heat a large sauté pan over medium heat. Spray a generous amount of olive oil spray on one side of fish and lay it in the pan, oil side down. Spray the other side of the fish generously to coat and cook for 4 to 5 minutes on each side, until the crumbs are golden and the fish is opaque and cooked through.

- To serve, place a fillet on each dish and top with arugula salad and lemon.

28. Flounder In Lemon Parsley Butter Recipe

Serving: 8 | Prep: | Cook: 10mins | Ready in:

Ingredients

- 1/2 cup butter melted
- 2 tablespoons cornstarch
- 3 tablespoons lemon juice
- 1 tablespoon chopped fresh parsley
- 2 pounds flounder filets
- 1/2 teaspoon celery salt
- 1 teaspoon freshly ground black pepper

Direction

- Melt butter in a large glass baking dish.
- Add cornstarch, lemon juice and parsley then stir to blend well.
- Dip each filet in butter sauce then arrange in baking dish butter sauce side up.
- Sprinkle filets with celery, salt and pepper.
- Cover loosely with clear plastic wrap and heat in microwave for 7 minutes.
- Let stand covered for 2 minutes to finish cooking then spoon sauce over each serving.

29. Flounder In Puff Pastry Recipe

Serving: 6 | Prep: | Cook: 50mins | Ready in:

Ingredients

- 1 lb fresh baby spinach
- 1/4 cup chopped onion
- 1 clove garlic minced
- 2 Tbs butter
- 1/2 cup sour cream

- 1/2 tsp salt
- 1/2 tsp pepper
- 1/4 tsp nutmeg
- 1 pkg frozen puff paste thawed
- 2 lb flounder filets

Direction

- Cook, spinach briefly, drain and pat dry
- Sauté onions and garlic in butter.
- Stir in sour cream, salt, pepper and nutmeg
- Unfold pastry sheets on lightly floured surface.
- On one sheet, Place spinach, onions, garlic in middle of pastry
- Place flounder fillets on top
- Place second pastry sheet on top and bring corners together gently pressing to seal
- Place on baking sheet
- Bake in a 400F oven until golden brown about 40 minutes
- Cut into 6 servings and garnish with fresh dill

30. Flounder With Tomato Onion Ragout Recipe

Serving: 1 | Prep: | Cook: 25mins | Ready in:

Ingredients

- 1-½ teaspoons olive oil
- ¼ medium red onion, thinly sliced
- ½ cup grape or cherry tomatoes, halved
- 1 to 2 teaspoons white-wine vinegar
- coarse salt and ground pepper
- 1 flounder fillet (5 to 6 ounces)
- 2 tablespoons chopped fresh parsley

Direction

- Tomato-onion ragout:
- In a 10-inch skillet, heat ½ teaspoon oil over medium. Add onion and cook, stirring occasionally, until light browned, 1 to 2 minutes. Add tomatoes and cook, stirring

occasionally, until slightly collapsed, 30 to 60 seconds.
- Remove skillet from heat. Add vinegar; stir to combine. Season with salt and pepper. Remove to a bowl; cover and keep warm.
- Flounder:
- Wipe skillet clean with paper towels. Place 1 teaspoon oil in pan, and heat over medium-high. Season fish with salt and pepper; place in skillet. Cook, until lightly browned, about 2 minutes.
- With a wide metal spatula, carefully turn fish over; cook until opaque throughout, about 1 minute. Transfer fish to a dinner plate. Spoon tomato-onion ragout over fish; serve with couscous or rice, if desired. Sprinkle parsley over top.

31. Foiled Flounder And Veggies Recipe

Serving: 1 | Prep: | Cook: 60mins | Ready in:

Ingredients

- 1 14 - 16 inch flounder headed and skined with dorsel fins removed
- 1 large red potato
- 1 large zucinni squash
- baby carrots chef's choice on the ammount
- salt
- ground black pepper
- cajun seasoning of your choice
- sliced lemons or oranges
- olive or vegtable oil

Direction

- Take prepared flounder and make several cross cuts to the bone on each side of flounder, season to your taste with Cajun seasoning, and rub in, then set aside.
- Slice potato and zucchini into ¼-inch slices, then set aside with baby carrots.

- Lay down 30 in. long x widest you can get heavy duty foil, shiny-side down.
- Coat the center of foil with oil at least 4-6 in. larger than the flounder.
- Lay down a layer of sliced potatoes 2-3 in. larger than flounder, in the oiled place, salt and pepper.
- Lay down a layer of zucchini on top of the potatoes, salt and pepper.
- Lay down a layer of baby carrots on top of the zucchini.
- Lay flounder on top of veggie stack topping with sliced lemon or sliced orange.
- Pull up sides of foil lengthwise and pull sides together and fold down to the flounder making a good seal in foil.
- Flatten ends of foil and fold back to the stack completing the seal.
- Place on grill over burner on low or in 250-degree oven for 45 mins.
- After cooking 45 mins, remove and open 1 end and pour out juices (be careful, extremely hot, use mittens or gloves).
- Reseal packet and place back on grill or oven for 15 mins to caramelize the bottom of the potatoes.
- Open carefully and eat right out of the foil packet, enjoy!

32. Fried Flounder Country Style Recipe

Serving: 6 | Prep: | Cook: 10mins | Ready in:

Ingredients

- 2 cups buttermilk
- 2 lb. flounder fillets, skinned
- 1 cup cornmeal
- 1/2 tsp. salt
- 1/2 tsp paprika
- 1/2 tsp pepper
- oil to fry

Direction

- Cut fish into serving size pieces.
- Soak in buttermilk for 1 hour.
- Remove from buttermilk.
- Mix cornmeal, salt, paprika, and pepper together.
- Coat fish in cornmeal mixture.
- Preheat iron skillet with 3 tbsp oil.
- Add fish and cook for 2-3 minutes.
- Turn and cook other side for 2-3 more minutes or until fish flakes easily with a fork.

33. Greek Flounder With Savory Pilaf Recipe

Serving: 6 | Prep: | Cook: 30mins | Ready in:

Ingredients

- 6 flounder filets
- 1 bag fresh spinach
- 3 scallions
- 1 bunch fresh dill
- 1/2 cup crumbled feta cheese
- 1/4 cup unseasoned bread crumbs
- 4 tablespoons butter
- 1/2 teaspoon salt
- 1/2 teaspoon freshly ground black pepper
- 1/4 teaspoon paprika
- 1 medium lemon
- Pilaf:
- 1 cup converted rice
- 1 cup chicken broth
- 1 cup water
- 1/4 teaspoon dried basil
- 1/4 teaspoon dried oregano
- 1/2 teaspoon freshly ground black pepper
- 1/2 teaspoon salt
- 3 tablespoons butter

Direction

- Chop spinach and dill then mince scallions and sauté scallions briefly in 1 teaspoon oil.

- Add spinach and dill and cook until somewhat limp then remove from heat.
- Rinse flounder under cold water then put on cutting board and squeeze lemon juice over each.
- Place some of the greens mixture on each and a teaspoon of the feta.
- Roll each fillet and place end side down in small baking pan.
- Continue with all filets until rolls are side by side in pan snugly.
- Sprinkle rolls with breadcrumbs seasoned with parsley, salt, pepper and paprika.
- Melt butter and pour over rolls then bake 25 minutes at 325.
- For pilaf sauté raw rice in melted butter until rice starts to turn golden brown.
- Add water and broth then bring to a boil and cover and cook 20 minutes.

34. L.I. Stuffed Flounder Recipe

Serving: 0 | Prep: | Cook: 40mins | Ready in:

Ingredients

- ingredients:
- 1/4 c. chopped onion
- 3 cloves garlic, minced
- 1/4 c. butter
- 1 small can mushrooms, save liquid
- 6 oz. pkg. frozen crab meat
- 1/2 c saltines (course)
- 1/2 tsp. salt
- Approx. 2- lb flounder
- 3 T. butter
- 3 T. flour
- 1/4 tsp. salt
- milk
- 1/3 c. white wine
- lemon
- paprika

Direction

- Preparation:
- Preheat oven to 400 degrees
- Cook onion in 1/4 cup butter until tender, add garlic and cook until you can smell the garlic, for about a minute. Stir in Mushrooms, crab meat, crackers and parsley. Spread over fish and roll with seam side down.
- Sauce:
- Melt 3 T. butter. Add flour. Add enough milk to mushroom liquid to make 1 1/2 cups. Add wine to saucepan and stir until thick and bubbly. Pour over fish. Bake 25 minutes. Remove and sprinkle paprika and squeeze the juice of one lemon on fish. Place in oven for 10 minutes.

35. Lemon Flounder With Roasted Vegetables Recipe

Serving: 8 | Prep: | Cook: 45mins | Ready in:

Ingredients

- For the flounder:
- 8 flounder filets, thawed
- 2 lemons
- coriander, salt & pepper
- fresh parsley
- For the vegetables:
- 1 green bell pepper
- 1 yellow bell pepper
- 1 large red onion
- 2 cups grape tomatoes
- 1 large garlic clove
- coriander, salt, pepper
- fresh parsley
- olive oil

Direction

- For the vegetables:
- Preheat oven to 450 degrees Fahrenheit.
- Heat olive oil in a heavy-bottomed pan. Chop up onion and garlic, add to pan. Slice bell peppers long-ways and add to pan. Halve

grape tomatoes, add to pan. Season each veggie with the spices as you add them to the pan. Sauté veggies until onion becomes translucent and tomatoes begin to lose their juices.

- Transfer veggies to a baking sheet and bake on top rack for 6-10 minutes. Make sure to leave the juices in the pan.
- For the flounder:
- Drench the filets in the juice of two lemons, then cover completely in coriander, salt, & freshly ground black pepper. Fry the filets 3-4 at a time, depending on the size of your pan, so that you have plenty of room to flip them over with a spatula. Cook on medium-high heat, about 3 minutes on each side.
- Serve flounder on a platter surrounded by the vegetables, and squeeze any remaining lemon juice over the top. Sprinkle with fresh parsley.

36. Lemony Stuffed Flounder Fillets Recipe

Serving: 4 | Prep: | Cook: 30mins | Ready in:

Ingredients

- 1/3 C butter
- 1/3 C celery, chopped
- 2 Tbl onion, chopped
- 1 Tbl parsley
- 1 C herb seasoned stuffing
- 1 Tbl lemon juice
- 1 tsp lemon peel
- 1/4 tsp salt
- 1/4 tsp pepper
- 1 lb flounder or other white fish
- 1/3 C butter
- 1/2 tsp dill weed

Direction

- Preheat oven to 350.
- In a 1-qt. saucepan, melt butter and sauté celery and onion until tender.

- Stir in stuffing, parsley, lemon juice and peel, salt and pepper; set aside.
- Cut each fillet to make 8 halves; place 4 halves in an ungreased square baking dish or pan.
- Top each with 1/4 C of the stuffing and top with remaining halves.
- Melt 1/3 C butter; stir in dill weed.
- Pour dill butter over fillets.
- Bake in center of oven 20 to 30 minutes or until fish flakes.
- Spoon sauce over fish and return to oven for an additional 5 minutes.

37. Light Spinach Flounder Pinwheels Recipe

Serving: 16 | Prep: | Cook: 10mins | Ready in:

Ingredients

- 1/2 cup frozen chopped spinach thawed and drained
- 1/3 cup soft whole-wheat bread crumbs
- 2 ounces sliced pimiento drained
- 2 tablespoons grated white onion
- 1 tablespoon chopped pecans
- 1 teaspoon lemon juice
- 1/4 teaspoon dried marjoram
- 1/4 teaspoon salt
- 1/4 teaspoon freshly ground black pepper
- 4 flounder fillets at 4 ounces each
- 1/4 cup dry white wine
- 1 teaspoon grated lemon peel

Direction

- Combine first nine ingredients in medium bowl then stir well.
- Spoon 3 tablespoons spinach mixture in centre of each fillet.
- Roll up jellyroll fashion beginning at narrow end then secure with a wooden pick.
- Place rolls seam side down in a rectangular baking dish.

- Combine wine and lemon rind then pour over rolls.
- Cover with heavy duty plastic wrap and vent.
- Microwave on high for 7 minutes then allow to stand one minute.
- Remove and discard wooden picks then slice rolls and transfer to serving plates.

38. New Bedford Flounder Roll Ups Recipe

Serving: 6 | Prep: | Cook: 25mins | Ready in:

Ingredients

- 6 large flounder fillets
- 4 strips of bacon
- ¼ C melted butter
- 3 C cornbread crumbs
- ¼ tsp chervil
- ¼ tsp dried tarragon leaves
- hot water
- butter

Direction

- Cook bacon until crisp; drain on paper towels
- Measure ¼ C bacon drippings and add to melted butter
- Combine cornbread crumbs, bacon, herbs and butter mixture; mix well
- Add enough hot water to make stuffing as moist as desired
- Place a spoonful of stuffing on each fillet; roll up firmly
- Place seam side down in a sprayed baking dish; dot generously with butter
- Bake at 375 for 25 minutes or until fish flakes easily with a fork

39. Oven Fried Fish Recipe

Serving: 4 | Prep: | Cook: | Ready in:

Ingredients

- 1/4 c. margarine, melted
- 1 tbsp. lemon juice
- 1/4 tsp. pepper
- 1/4 tsp. paprika
- 1/4 tsp. basil
- 1/8 tsp. garlic powder
- 1 lb. fillet or flounder
- 1/4 c. dry bread crumbs
- 2 tbsp. oil

Direction

- Combine margarine, lemon juice, pepper, paprika, basil and garlic. Dredge fish in margarine-herb mixture and roll in bread crumbs. Spread oil in shallow baking dish and arrange fish in one layer. Spoon remaining mixture over fish. Bake uncovered in 475 degree oven for 15 minutes or until fish flakes easily with fork.

40. Red Lobsters Country Fried Flounder Recipe

Serving: 6 | Prep: | Cook: 10mins | Ready in:

Ingredients

- * 2 pounds flounder fillets, fresh
- * 1 cup cornmeal
- * ½ tsp. salt
- * ½ tsp. paprika
- * ½ tsp. ground black pepper
- *1/2 tsp garlic powder

Direction

- Preparation:
- 1. Skin fillets and cut them into serving size portions.

- 2. Combine cornmeal with seasonings. Roll fish in cornmeal mixture.
- Pan Fry:
- 1. Place flounder in an iron skillet that has been preheated with about 1/8 inch of oil.
- 2. Brown on one side 2 - 3 minutes. Carefully turn and cook on the other side an additional 3 minutes, until fish flakes easily with a fork.
- 3. Serve with tartar sauce and coleslaw.
- Chef's Tip:
- Marinate the fish in buttermilk for one hour prior to frying for a moist, authentic taste.

- In the pan drippings quickly cook the fennel, onion and garlic with a touch of oil if it seems to dry, until just tender.
- Add vermouth, orange juice and reduce until there is only a tbsp of so of liquid.
- Add seasonings, olives, capers and tomatoes, heat thoroughly about five minutes to meld the flavors.
- Turn off heat, stir in butter to create sauce.
- Pour hot sauce over fish and serve.
- A dish of couscous is a delightful side, along with shredded zucchini in sour cream with nutmeg.

41. Riviera Flounder Recipe

Serving: 4 | Prep: | Cook: 15mins | Ready in:

Ingredients

- 8 small to medium flounder fillets (2 each)
- 1- 2 tbsp of mild veggie oil
- 1/2 to 3/4 cup of slivered fennel (bulb part on mandolin)
- 1 can of diced tomatoes, drained
- 1/3 cup or so of chopped green olives stuffed with pimentos
- 1/3 cup of white vermouth
- 1 onion sliced thinly lengthwise-mimic the fennel shape
- 1 garlic clove minced
- 5 strips of orange zest, julienned
- juice of one half of orange
- pinch or two of red pepper flakes, more if desired
- pinch of dried parsley flakes
- large pinch of dried tarragon leaves
- 1 tbsp of capers
- 1 tbsp of butter

Direction

- Heat oil in large flat skillet.
- Quickly sauté salt and peppered fish fillets. About 3 minutes per side. Reserve, tent with foil to keep warm.

42. Seafood Stuffed Flounder Recipe

Serving: 6 | Prep: | Cook: 30mins | Ready in:

Ingredients

- 2 lbs. skinless flounder 1/4 - 1/2 inch thick(can also use sole)
- 1 lb. sea scallops (can also use peeled cooked shrimp)
- 1 10 oz. pkg frozen chopped spinach, thawed
- 1 tbls. butter
- 1 onion, chopped
- 1 cup herb stuffing mix
- 1/2 cup sour cream
- 1/4 cup parmesan cheese
- 1 egg, lightly beaten

Direction

- Rinse fish and pat dry
- Cook scallops in boiling water 1-3 minutes or until scallops turn opaque
- Drain and cut into quarters
- Cook onion in butter until tender
- Squeeze water out of spinach
- Slightly crush stuffing mix
- In a mixing bowl, mix together onion, spinach, stuffing mix, sour cream, parmesan cheese, and egg.

- Carefully stir in scallops
- Preheat oven to 375
- Measuring length of fish to 6-7 inches, (overlap thinner ends of short fillets to make one)
- Spread about 1/2 cup of scallop mixture on top of each piece of fish
- Roll fish up starting at thin end and secure with a toothpick
- Bake for 20-25 minutes in a greased baking dish

43. Spicy Scallop Stuffed Flounder Recipe

Serving: 4 | Prep: | Cook: 60mins | Ready in:

Ingredients

- 4 small fresh flounder filets
- 1cup spicy bread crumbs
- 1/2lb fresh bay scallops
- 2 cloves minced garlic
- 1 egg
- 1 cup taco cheese
- 1tb olive oil
- 1tb oldbay seasoning
- 1tsp sea salt
- 1tsp black pepper

Direction

- In a medium bowl, combine all ingredients except old bay seasoning and flounder.
- Lay flounder filets flat and place 1/4 of the stuffing in each filet fold ends over and place folded end down.
- Line grill grate with aluminum foil spray with PAM.
- Place flounder fold sides down, sprinkle with old bay and grill at 375-400 for 35 mins.

44. Stuffed Flounder Fillets Recipe

Serving: 6 | Prep: | Cook: 20mins | Ready in:

Ingredients

- 1 pkg. (6 oz.) STOVE TOP savory herbs Stuffing Mix
- 1-1/2 cups water
- 1/4 cup (1/2 stick) margarine or butter, divided
- 6 flounder fillets (4 oz. each)
- 2 Tbsp. lemon juice, divided
- 1/4 tsp. paprika

Direction

- PREHEAT oven to 350°F. Prepare stuffing mix with the water and 3 Tbsp. of the margarine as directed on package.
- SPRINKLE fish evenly with 1 Tbsp. of the lemon juice. Spoon 1/3 cup of the prepared stuffing onto each fillet; roll up loosely to enclose stuffing, starting at one of the short ends. Place, seam-sides down, in greased baking dish; spoon remaining stuffing around roll-ups. Sprinkle evenly with remaining 1 Tbsp. lemon juice and the paprika; dot with remaining 1 Tbsp. margarine.
- BAKE 20 min. or until fish flakes easily with fork.

45. Stuffed Flounder Recipe

Serving: 4 | Prep: | Cook: 20mins | Ready in:

Ingredients

- 1 1/2 lbs. flounder fillets, 4 lg. pieces
- 1 cup backfin crabmeat
- 1 1/2 teaspoons chopped green pepper
- 1 1/2 teaspoons chopped pimiento
- 1/4 teaspoon dry mustard
- 1/4 teaspoon worcestershire sauce
- 1/4 teaspoon salt

- 1/8 teaspoon pepper
- 1/4 teaspoon Old Bay Seasoning
- dash ground cayenne, optional
- 4 saltine crackers, crushed
- 1 egg, separated
- 6 tbsp. mayonnaise
- 1 tbsp. chopped parsley
- 1/4 cup butter, melted
- 1/4 teaspoon paprika
- 1 teaspoon cider vinegar or lemon juice

Direction

- Rinse and dry the flounder.
- Remove the shell from crabmeat and add green pepper, pimiento, mustard, Worcestershire sauce, salt, pepper, Old Bay, cayenne, vinegar or lemon juice, and crackers.
- In a small bowl combine egg white and 1 tablespoon of the mayonnaise
- Add to crab mixture and toss until well blended.
- Brush fillets on cut side with melted butter.
- Place flounder in greased shallow baking pan and top each fillet with even amounts of the crab mixture.
- Drizzle remaining butter over top of stuffed fillets. Bake at 400° for 15 minutes.
- Combine egg yolk and remaining mayonnaise.
- Spread egg mixture on top of each fillet and sprinkle with paprika. Increase temperature to 450° and bake 6 minutes longer, or until golden and bubbly

46. The Baked Flounder Recipe

Serving: 4 | Prep: | Cook: 18mins |Ready in:

Ingredients

- * 2 lemons, sliced into 1/4-inch-thick rounds
- * 2 medium onions, sliced into very thin rounds (8 ounces ea.)
- * 4 tablespoons unsalted butter
- * 1 cup dry white wine
- * 1 teaspoon chopped fresh thyme, plus 4 sprigs
- * coarse salt and freshly ground pepper
- * 4 six-ounce flounder fillets (or other white fish)

Direction

- Preheat oven to 400°.
- Arrange lemons and onions in a 9-by-13-inch glass baking dish.
- Dot with butter; add wine and 1/4 cup cold water.
- Sprinkle with chopped thyme; season with salt and pepper.
- Bake until onions are soft and translucent, about 40 minutes.
- Remove baking dish from oven.
- Arrange fish fillets over lemons and onions.
- Season fillets with salt and pepper.
- Scatter thyme sprigs over fish.
- Baste fish with a little cooking liquid.
- Bake until fish is just opaque and cooked through 16 to 18 minutes.
- Do not overcook.
- Serve fish with cooked onions and lemons.

47. Walnut Flounder Ala Tramps Recipe

Serving: 6 | Prep: | Cook: 10mins |Ready in:

Ingredients

- 6 flounder fillets (about 5 oz. each)
- flour for dusting
- 1 c. plain breadcrumbs
- 2 c. walnuts: 1 1/2 c. finely chopped and 1/2 c. broken pieces
- 2 T. fresh parsley, chopped
- salt and white pepper to taste
- 6 eggs
- 1/2 c. freshly grated parmesan cheese
- 1/2 c. butter

- 3/4 c. vegetable oil
- 2 T. unsalted butter
- juice of 1 lemon
- parsley sprigs and 2 lemons cut into wedges for garnish

Direction

- Dust the fillets in flour, shaking off excess; set aside. Combine the breadcrumbs, walnuts, parsley, salt and pepper. Mix well and set aside. Combine the eggs and cheese in a bowl to make a batter.
- Preheat oven to 350.
- Dip the fillets into the batter, then dredge them in the walnut mixture, gently patting the nuts into the fish. In a large skillet, heat the butter and oil over medium-high flame until it starts to sizzle. Add the fish, reduce the heat to a simmer, and cook about 3 minutes on each side. Transfer the fish to a shallow and ovenproof glass baking dish (don't use a metal pan).
- Drain the oil and butter from the pan, then add the butter and lemon juice; cook over medium heat until hot. Pour the lemon-butter sauce over the fish and bake for 10 minutes.
- Transfer to heated platter, garnish with the parsley and lemon wedges and serve immediately.

48. Stuffed Whole Flounder Recipe

Serving: 2 | Prep: | Cook: 37mins | Ready in:

Ingredients

- 1 small flounder cleaned & butterflied
- 1/2 cup flakey crab meat
- 1/4 cup small shrimp shelled & deviened (raw salad shrimp)
- 1 cup herbed stuffing (bagged dry)
- 1 tbls. minced onion
- 1/2 tbls. minced green bell pepper
- 1 tsp. old bay

- 1/4 cup mayonaise
- salt &pepper
- butter

Direction

- In mixing bowl, combine all ingredients until smooth workable stuffing forms; salt & pepper to taste. Reserve butter & melt (1/4 stick +/-). Stuff flounder under each pouch and pile in middle cavity. Pour some of butter over entire fish and stuffing. Bake at 400 degrees in well-buttered pan until stuffing is done golden brown color; garnish with lemon slices and parsley. Serve.

Chapter 2: Bass Recipes

***

49. Baked Bluefish Recipe

Serving: 4 | Prep: | Cook: 30mins |Ready in:

Ingredients

- INGREDIENTS
- 2½ lb. bluefish fillets washed and patted dry. Cut into 4 or 8 pieces
- 4 medium potatoes (about 1 lb.) thinly sliced and blanched
- 4 tablespoons of olive oil
- 4 tomatos, coarsely chopped (about 1 lb.)
- 2 garlic cloves, finely chopped
- ½ cup of white wine
- ¼ cup of basil leaves, finely chopped
- salt and pepper to taste
- Pinch of hot red pepper flakes (Optional)
- basil leaves for garnish

Direction

- PREPARATION
- In a medium-sized bowl, combine the 2 tablespoons of oil, tomato, garlic, chopped basil, a pinch of red pepper (optional) and salt and pepper to taste.
- Put aside.
- Grease a baking pan with the 2 tablespoons of oil and spread blanched potatoes on it, sprinkle some salt and pepper.
- Place fish over potatoes, skin side down. Shake salt and pepper over fish fillets and cover the fillets with the basil- garlic-tomato sauce; pour wine over it. Cover with aluminum foil and bake at 400 degrees for 15 minutes, then remove foil and bake for an additional 15 minutes or until done.
- Transfer to a serving dish and garnish with basil leaves. Serve the potatoes as the contorno, "side dish".

50. Baked Sea Bass AllFreshSeafoodcom Recipe

Serving: 2 | Prep: | Cook: 20mins | Ready in:

Ingredients

- Chilean sea bass fillets
- 1 tsp basil, fresh
- olive oil
- 1 garlic clove, minced
- 1/4 cup diced red pepper
- 1/4 cup diced green pepper
- 1/4 cup diced yellow pepper
- 1 cup diced onion
- dash tsp salt, divided
- dash tsp black pepper
- 1 cup wasabi Crust

Direction

- Prepare the container by lining the bottom with the vegetables. Rub the sea bass with olive oil on both sides. Dip the sea bass into the salt and pepper, basil, then the wasabi crust. Bake at 350 for 20 minutes, or until sea bass is cooked.

51. Baked Sea Bass In Parchment Recipe

Serving: 4 | Prep: | Cook: 15mins | Ready in:

Ingredients

- extra virgin olive oil
- 2 to 3 cloves garlic, thinly sliced
- 2 - 4 very small fresh rosemary sprigs, plus extra sprigs for garnish
- 1 1/2 to 2 lb. sea bass fillet, in one piece, skin removed
- salt and freshly ground pepper
- 2 tbsp capers, rinsed and drained
- chopped fresh Italian parsley for garnish
- lemon wedges

Direction

- Position a rack in the middle of an oven and preheat to 425 degrees F. Cut a piece of parchment (baking) paper or aluminum foil that will enclose the fish fillet comfortably.
- Lay the sheet of parchment or foil on a flat surface. Brush an area in the center, about the size of the fish, with olive oil. Sprinkle with half of the garlic slices and top with 1 or 2 rosemary sprigs. Lay the fish on top and brush the top of the fish with olive oil. Sprinkle with remaining garlic slices and top with 1 or 2 more rosemary sprigs. Sprinkle to taste with salt and pepper.
- Enclose the fish in the parchment or foil by folding in the sides and the folding the edges together, sealing well.
- Place the packet on the baking sheet.
- Bake until the flesh is opaque throughout when pierced with the tip of a knife. 15-20 minutes depending on the thickness of the

fish. Plan on about 10 minutes per inch at the thickest part of the fish; do not overcook.

- Remove the packet from the oven, then open it up and carefully transfer the fish to a warmed serving platter.
- Top with capers and parsley. Arrange lemon wedges and rosemary sprigs around the fish. Spoon the juice from the packet over the fish and serve.

52. Baked Sea Bass With Rosemary And Garlic Recipe

Serving: 4 | Prep: | Cook: 15mins | Ready in:

Ingredients

- 1 large sea bass, about 1kg, scaled and gutted
- rosemary sprigs
- about 2 garlic clove thinly sliced
- lemon slices
- lemon juice
- small bunch basil leaves
- olive oil
- sea salt
- foil

Direction

- Preheat oven to 200C / gas 6.
- Stuff the cavity with lemon and some of the rosemary.
- Lay the fish on an oiled, foil-covered baking tray.
- Make about 6 slashes down its side.
- First lay the basil leaves over the slashes.
- Then poke the rosemary and garlic slices into the slashes.
- Drizzle with olive oil and sprinkle with sea salt and lemon juice.
- Bake for about 15 -20 mins.
- When fin pulls out easily then it's done.

53. Bass With Parsley Sauce Recipe

Serving: 4 | Prep: | Cook: 20mins | Ready in:

Ingredients

- 1 cup fresh parsley chopped coarsely
- 1 clove garlic chopped
- juice of 1 lemon
- 1/2 teaspoon salt
- 1 teaspoon freshly ground black pepper
- 4 bass fillets
- 3 tablespoons flour
- 1/2 cup olive oil
- 3 tablespoons onion chopped

Direction

- In food processor combine parsley and garlic with 2 tablespoons water and process until smooth.
- Thin mixture with an additional 2 tablespoons water and mix well.
- Add lemon juice and salt and pepper to taste then set aside covered
- On a flat plate combine flour with 1/2 teaspoon salt and 1/2 teaspoon pepper then mix well.
- Dip fillets into mixture coating well and shaking off any excess.
- In a large heavy skillet heat oil and fry fish until well brown on both sides.
- Transfer fish to a preheated serving platter and set aside to keep warm.
- Discard about half of the oil and in the remaining oil sauté the onions until golden brown.
- Add the remaining flour and over a low flame cook until mixture is light brown.
- Stir constantly then add parsley mixture and cook continuing to stir 3 minutes longer.
- Pour sauce over fish and serve immediately.

54. Bass With Tomato Cilantro Linguini Recipe

Serving: 4 | Prep: | Cook: 10mins | Ready in:

Ingredients

- 2 tablespoons olive oil
- 1-1/2 tablespoons fresh lime juice
- 1 tablespoon drained capers
- 4 small roma tomatoes seeded and chopped
- 2 garlic cloves minced
- 1/4 teaspoon cayenne pepper
- 1/3 cup fresh cilantro leaves
- 4 sea bass fillets
- 1/4 teaspoon salt
- 1 teaspoon freshly ground black pepper
- olive oil or cooking spray
- 10 ounces fresh linguine

Direction

- In a large bowl stir together oil, lime juice, capers, tomatoes, garlic, red pepper and cilantro.
- Set aside.
- Remove and discard any skin from fish then rinse and pat dry.
- Cut fish into 4 serving pieces then season with salt and black pepper.
- Spray a wide nonstick frying pan with cooking spray and place over medium high heat.
- Add fish and cook turning once for 8 minutes.
- Meanwhile in a 6 quart pan cook linguine in 3 quarts boiling water for 2 minutes then drain well.
- Set 2 tablespoons of the tomato mixture aside then lightly mix remaining mixture with hot pasta.
- Divide pasta among 4 warm plates and top each serving with a piece of fish.
- Top fish evenly with reserved tomato mixture.

55. Beer Sauce For Trout Or Bass Recipe

Serving: 6 | Prep: | Cook: 25mins | Ready in:

Ingredients

- 4 Tbsp of vegetable oil
- 1 large onion, chopped small
- 2 Tbsp of flour
- 1 1/2 cups of your favorite beer
- 2 Tbsp of light brown sugar
- 1/2 tsp of freshly cracked pepper
- 2 tsp of worcestershire sauce
- 3 pounds of trout or bass fillets, cut into 6 equal pieces

Direction

- This is great done outdoors under the summer stars in a big cast iron skillet, but in a pinch, use a large frying pan on your stove.
- Pour oil into the pan and sauté the onion until opaque. Add flour and stir continuously for about 2 minutes to make a light roux.
- Add the beer, brown sugar, pepper and Worcestershire sauce to the roux base. Cook and stir constantly until a nice sauce comes together, takes about 5 or 7 minutes.
- Add the fish fillets to the sauce and cook for about 10 minutes (maybe a little more, maybe a little less) until the fish flakes when prodded with a fork.
- Plate it up with fresh cooked rice and a salad. And maybe another beer on the side.

56. Black Sea Bass With Moroccan Vegetables And Chile Sauce Recipe

Serving: 4 | Prep: | Cook: 30mins | Ready in:

Ingredients

- Sauce

- 1 teaspoon olive oil
- 1 cup chopped leeks (or onions)
- 3 cloves garlic, chopped
- 2 teaspoons chopped fresh oregano
- 2 teaspoons curry powder
- 1 teaspoon allspice
- 1/8 teaspoon freshly ground black pepper
- 2 cups chopped fresh tomato
- 1 large green bell pepper, cored, seeded and thinly sliced
- 2 celery stalks, thinly sliced
- 2 tablespoons low-sodium soy sauce
- 1/2 cup low-sodium, fat-free vegetable stock
- fish
- 2 large carrots, peeled and thinly sliced
- 1 cup cauliflower florets
- 1 cup broccoli florets
- 1/2 cup low-sodium, fat-free vegetable stock
- 4 cups fresh spinach
- 2 large zucchini, cut into 1/4-inch chunks
- 4 fillets black sea bass (about 6 ounces each)
- 1 cup couscous
- 2 teaspoons pine nuts
- 1/4 cup fresh dill, chopped
- 1/4 cup crumbled feta

Direction

- Line a 9" x 12" baking dish with foil. Set aside. Heat oven to 400°F. Heat oil in a large saucepan over medium heat. Cook leeks, garlic, oregano, curry, allspice and black pepper until leeks become translucent, stirring, 2 to 3 minutes.
- Add tomato, bell pepper, celery and soy sauce. Cook until pepper softens, 2 to 3 minutes. Add stock. Simmer, covered, 25 to 30 minutes.
- Place carrots, cauliflower, broccoli and stock in prepared dish. Bake until vegetables begin to soften, 10 to 12 minutes. Remove from oven. Add spinach and zucchini.
- Place fish on top of vegetables. Drizzle with sauce. Bake until fish is cooked through and vegetables are tender, 15 to 20 minutes.
- While fish cooks, prepare couscous as directed on package. Top each plate with 1/4 cup

couscous, 1/4 of vegetables and 1 fillet. Sprinkle with pine nuts, dill and feta.
- Serve immediately.

57. Braised Sea Bass With Leeks And Mushrooms Recipe

Serving: 2 | Prep: | Cook: 1hours | Ready in:

Ingredients

- For the sea bass
- 55g/2oz butter
- ½ onion, peeled, chopped
- 6 baby chestnut mushrooms
- salt and freshly ground black pepper
- 200ml/7fl oz fish stock
- 1 sea bass fillet, skin removed
- 50ml/2fl oz double cream
- 1 tbsp chopped fresh chives
- For the leeks
- 25g/1oz butter
- 5 baby leeks, blanched for 6 minutes in boiling water, drained
- salt and freshly ground black pepper

Direction

- For the sea bass, melt the butter in a sauté pan over a medium heat. Add the chopped onion and sauté for 4-5 minutes, or until softened.
- Add the mushrooms to the pan and cook for another 2-3 minutes. Season, to taste, with salt and freshly ground black pepper.
- Pour in the stock, bring to the boil, then reduce the heat until the mixture is simmering. Place the sea bass into the mixture, cover the pan with a lid and poach for 6-8 minutes, or until the sea bass is cooked through and opaque. Remove the sea bass from the pan and set aside to rest on a serving plate.
- Pour the cream into the poaching liquid, return to the boil and cook for 3-4 minutes, or until the volume of the liquid has reduced. Season, to taste, with salt and freshly ground

black pepper, then stir in half of the chopped chives.

- Meanwhile, for the leeks, melt the butter in a frying pan over a medium heat. Add the blanched leeks and fry for 2-3 minutes. Season, to taste, with salt and freshly ground black pepper.
- To serve, pour the cream sauce over the fish, spoon the leeks alongside and sprinkle with the remaining chopped chives.

58. Braised Sea Bass With Moroccan Spiced Sauce Recipe

Serving: 4 | Prep: | Cook: 20mins | Ready in:

Ingredients

- 1/4 cup chopped coriander
- 1/4 cup chopped parsley
- 3 cloves garlic, chopped
- 2 tbsp olive oil
- 1/2 tsp crushed red pepper flakes or to taste
- 2 tsp ground cumin
- 2 tsp sweet paprika
- Pinch cinnamon
- 3 tbsp lemon juice
- 1 tsp grated lemon zest
- Salt and freshly ground pepper to taste
- Four 6 oz Chilean sea bass fillets, skin removed
- Moroccan spiced Sauce:
- 2 tbsp olive oil
- 1/2 cup chopped onion
- 2 cups chopped canned or fresh tomatoes

Direction

- In a food processor or by hand, combine coriander, parsley and garlic.
- Process until chunky.
- Add olive oil, red pepper flakes, cumin, paprika, cinnamon, lemon juice and zest.
- Season with salt and pepper.
- Process until all ingredients are combined.

- Spread half of spice mixture over fish fillets in a baking dish and marinate for 30 minutes.
- For sauce, heat olive oil in a large skillet on medium heat.
- Add onion and sauté 2 minutes or until onion is softened.
- Stir in remaining spice mixture and tomatoes.
- Simmer together for 10 minutes.
- Place fish on top of sauce, cover and simmer for 10 to 15 minutes or until fish is cooked and it begins to split on top.
- Place fish on serving plate and pour sauce around.

59. Brazilian Fish Stew Recipe Recipe

Serving: 0 | Prep: | Cook: 22mins | Ready in:

Ingredients

- 1 spring onion (white and green parts), chopped
- 4 shallot, chopped
- 1 small piece fresh ginger, peeled and finely chopped
- 4 large cloves garlic, minced
- 5 tablespoons peanut oil
- 2 tablespoons extra-virgin olive oil
- 4 tablespoons chopped cilantro
- 1 1/4 pounds sea bass, cut into 2-inch chunks
- 1/2 cup freshly chopped green bell pepper
- 1/3 cup freshly chopped yellow bell pepper
- 1 1/2 cups fish stock/chicken stock
- 1 cup coconut milk
- 2 tablespoons tomato paste
- 1 tablespoon lemon juice
- salt and freshly ground black pepper
- 1/3 cup canned or jarred hearts of palm, drained and diced
- 2 plum tomatoes, peeled, seeded, and diced

Direction

- In a bowl, mix together half of the spring onions, half of the shallots, half of the ginger, and half of the garlic. Add 2 tablespoons of the peanut oil, all of the olive oil, and half of the cilantro. Place the chunks of fish in a resealable plastic bag and add the marinade, pressing the bag to evenly coat the fish. Remove all of the air from the plastic bag and seal it. Place the bag in a shallow bowl, making sure the chunks of fish are completely covered by the marinade, and refrigerate for at least 3 hours.
- Take the fish out of the refrigerator 30 minutes before cooking. Preheat the oven to 350°F (175°C).
- Place the remaining 3 tablespoons of the peanut oil in a large sauté pan over medium heat. Add the remaining spring onions and shallots along with the green and yellow bell peppers, and cook until softened for about 3 minutes.
- Add the remaining ginger and garlic to the pan and cook, stirring to combine, for another minute or until it's hot. Add the fish stock and let it come to a full boil. Add the coconut milk and tomato paste and return to a boil. Immediately lower the heat to medium-low and simmer the sauce while you prepare the fish.
- In the meantime, place the fish and its marinade in a casserole dish. Pour the lemon juice on top and season lightly with salt and pepper. Bake until the fish is almost but not quite cooked through for about 10 to 12 minutes.
- Carefully transfer each chunk of fish to the pan with the gently simmering sauce. Add any juices in the dish from the fish and marinade. Cover the pan, reduce the heat to low, and cook just until the fish is soft and tender, 5 to 8 minutes.
- Uncover the pan, add the hearts of palm and tomatoes, and just let them get hot, which will take only a minute or two.
- Taste the stew, season it with salt and pepper, and sprinkle with the remaining fresh cilantro.

Serving: 2 | Prep: | Cook: 15mins | Ready in:

Ingredients

- 2 Large Bass fillets
- 10 large scallops, rinsed
- 1 Cup trimmed broccoli, frozen or fresh
- breadcrumbs, preferably plain
- 1 Jumbo egg
- 1 Tbspn whole milk
- 3 cloves garlic
- 1/3 Cup white wine
- juice from 1/2 lemon and about 1 Tbspn of the Zest
- 1 Tbspn dried dill
- 1 tspn onion powder (to bring out the garlic)
- Chopped parsley
- salt and pepper to taste
- oil and/or butter for frying and coating
- Optional: 1-2 Tbspns grated Parmesan to mix in with the breadcrumbs.

Direction

- Beat the egg and milk in a bowl until blended, then use it to coat the Bass fillets. If desired, mix the cheese with the breadcrumbs and coat the fish evenly. Put the breaded fish into the fridge for 30 minutes to an hour to let it set.
- When ready to sauté, put oil in a large fry pan with the garlic over medium heat and allow it to get fragrant, about 2 minutes. Push all the garlic to one side. (Preferably away from any hot spots)
- Let the pan get very hot before you put the scallops in, and once they're in, try not to move them around too much. You'll need a lot of oil for the breaded fish. One of the old-fashioned chefs I used to work with would always tell me, "Bread likes to swim". This goes especially if you're working with butter

only. You'll probably need about 1/2 cup's worth to keep it from sticking.

- Throw the broccoli in and mix well with the garlic. Let that sit for a while, stirring once in a while to keep it from burning while the fish cooks.
- Pour in the white wine, lemon juice, and then sprinkle your seasoning over the whole mess. (Might I suggest you save some for when you flip the fish over? Or you can just add more like I do)
- Once the initial side of your fish is browned to your liking, flip those suckers and season the other side. Be sure to keep an eye on your broccoli.
- The entire meal shouldn't take longer than 15 minutes to cook. If you fry fish too long, especially something as delicate as scallops, they will turn out rubbery.
- When both sides of the fish are browned, divide them evenly onto plates and garnish with a sprinkle of the lemon zest and more parsley.
- I know that any doctor will tell you the portion is too much and that the FDA only recommends you eat half or even a third as a single serving, but we're real people with real appetites here, aren't we? Pssht, seriously.

61. Butter Parmesan Striped Bass Recipe

Serving: 4 | Prep: | Cook: 20mins | Ready in:

Ingredients

- 1-2 lb striped bass filet-trimmed and cut into serving size portions
- kosher salt
- black pepper
- 4 Tbsp butter
- 2 Tbsp white wine, dry-not cooking wine
- 2 1/2 Tbsp fresh grated parmesan cheese
- 1 tsp lemon zest, grated

- 1/4 tsp paprika

Direction

- Sprinkle fish with salt and pepper on both sides and set aside.
- Place just the butter, in shallow baking dish, large enough to accommodate all the fish.
- Place the dish with just the butter in a 375-degree oven till the butter browns.
- Now take the seasoned fish and dip both sides of the fish in this browned butter and bake for 10 minutes, uncovered, on middle rack.
- Then remove from oven and sprinkle with lemon zest, wine, parmesan cheese and paprika. Then broil on top rack at 500 degrees for 2-3 minutes or till parmesan cheese starts to bubble and brown.
- To serve spoon butter/wine sauce over fish.

62. Chilean Sea Bass (from Asakuma Restaurant) Recipe

Serving: 4 | Prep: | Cook: 2hours15mins | Ready in:

Ingredients

- 1 cup orange juice
- 1 cup shoyu, regular, full strength
- ½ cup white sugar
- ½ cup mirin or sake
- Garlic and ginger to taste

Direction

- Combine all ingredients but the fish and heat until sugar dissolves.
- Marinate Chilean Sea Bass or Gindara Black Cod (also known as Butterfish in Hawai'i) for 2 hours.
- Broil skin side first then flip to other side; or poach in marinade sauce.

63. Chilean Sea Bass Recipe

Serving: 6 | Prep: | Cook: 20mins | Ready in:

Ingredients

- 6 8oz chilean sea bass Filets
- 1 can lump crab meat
- 3 tablespoons minced garlic
- 1 stick of butter or margarine
- 1 bunch green onions
- 1/2 cup Italian or garlic bread crumbs
- 1/2 cup cream sherry
- 1/2 cup chicken stock
- garlic salt
- Mrs. Dash garlic herb mix

Direction

- Preheat oven to 350 degrees.
- Chop up green onions including some of the shallots into fine pieces and place in mixing bowl.
- Open can of lump crab and drain, dump crab into mixing bowl.
- Pour bread crumbs into mixing bowl and set aside.
- In medium-sized pan, pour sherry and chicken stock into pan, add minced garlic and bring to boil for 5 minutes.
- With a filet knife, insert end of knife into end of filet and form a small pocket by pushing your finger into slit formed by knife.
- Take half of sherry chicken stock mixture into mixing bowl with crab, and bread crumbs; stir adding more bread crumbs until consistency is like thick cookie dough consistency.
- Take stuffing and insert it into filets pushing down with your finger. Don't fill too full or filets will split on top.
- Place filets in baking dish pouring remaining stock over filets.
- Add seasonings and take butter and cut 1/4 inch squares and place on top of filets.
- Bake for 20 minutes.
- Serve with Caribbean rice and brown sugar glazed carrots. Great combination of flavors!!

64. Chilean Sea Bass With Tomato And Grapefruit Sauce Recipe

Serving: 2 | Prep: | Cook: 70mins | Ready in:

Ingredients

- *Cook time includes the sixty minutes to marinade and about ten minutes to boil the bok choy.
- 2 four ounce fillets of Chilean sea bass
- 1 bunch bok choy
- 3 ounces green beans (boiled, shocked and cut into 2 inch lengths)
- 1 cup grapefruit juice
- 1/2 teaspoon tomato powder
- marinade
- 4 tablespoons soy sauce
- 2 ounces mirin
- 2 ounces sake

Direction

- Marinate Chilean sea bass in marinade for one hour.
- Heat grapefruit juice over medium heat. When juice is reduced to half, mix in the tomato powder.
- Grill Chilean sea bass.
- Boil bok choy and strain.
- Top Chilean sea bass with tomato and grapefruit sauce. Serve with green beans and bok choy.

65. Chilean Sea Bass Marinated In Sake Lees Gindara Kasuzuke Recipe

Serving: 6 | Prep: | Cook: 15mins | Ready in:

Ingredients

- 4 - 6 oz Chilean Sea-bass
- Marinade:
- 6 ounces (2/3 cup) sake lees – can be bought at Japanese or Oriental Grocery
- 1 ounce (2 tablespoons) mirin
- 8 ounces (1 cup) water
- 2 teaspoons light soy sauce
- 6 tablespoons sugar
- 2 teaspoons salt
- 2 teaspoons grated ginger

Direction

- Combine marinade ingredients well. Marinate fish, refrigerate at least 18 hours.
- Broil or bake fillets 13 to 15 minutes or until fish is opaque.

66. Chinese Steam Fish With Steam Rice Recipe

Serving: 2 | Prep: | Cook: 30mins | Ready in:

Ingredients

- bass fish 1pc
- chinese seasonde soy sauce   a little
- salt   a little
- green chinese onion   a little
- ginger   a little

Direction

- 1. Take out fish viscera and wash.
- 2. Put some salt, green Chinese onion, ginger (peeled) on fish.
- 3. Put in Chinese steam pot, steam 10 mins till fish is done.
- 4. Use another pan to cook some oil put on fish.
- 5. Put some Chinese seasoned soy sauce can eat.

67. Ginger Sea Bass Over Wilted Greens Recipe

Serving: 4 | Prep: | Cook: 10mins | Ready in:

Ingredients

- 6 cups fresh baby spinach leave
- 4 (5 oz) sea bass fillets
- 4 tsp peeled and minced fresh ginger
- 2 tsp minced garlic
- 1/2 cup dry marsala wine
- 8 tsp soy sauce
- 2 tsp sesame oil
- 1 lime, quartered
- 2 tbsp thinly sliced fresh basil leaves

Direction

- Cut 4 (12-inch square pieces) aluminum foil. Preheat oven to 400 degrees F.
- Working with 1 foil sheet at a time, place the foil sheets on the work surface. Place 1 1/2 cups of spinach in the center of each foil sheet.
- Top with a sea bass fillet. Sprinkle with 1 tsp of ginger and 1/2 tsp of garlic, then drizzle 2 tbsp of Marsala, 2 tsp of soy sauce, and 1/2 tsp of sesame oil over the fish and spinach.
- Gather the foil sheets over the fish. Fold in the foil edges and pinch tightly to seal. Place the foil packages on a heavy large baking sheet.
- Bake until the spinach wilts and the fish is just cooked through, about 10 minutes.
- Transfer the packages to wide shallow bowls. Cool 5 minutes. Open package and fold down to reveal fish, being careful of hot steam. Squeeze lime juice over the fish. Sprinkle basil over and serve.

68. Grilled Bass WIth Green Tomato And Watermelon Salsa Recipe

Serving: 6 | Prep: | Cook: 30mins | Ready in:

Ingredients

- 1-1/2 cups finely chopped green tomatoes
- 1-1/2 cups finely chopped red watermelon
- 2/3 cup minced red onion
- 1 fresh serrano pepper minced with seeds
- 1/4 cup chopped fresh cilantro
- 1 teaspoon fresh lime juice
- 3/4 teaspoon salt
- 6 center cut pieces striped bass fillet with skin
- 1-1/2 tablespoons olive oil

Direction

- Prepare gas or charcoal grill for cooking.
- Toss tomatoes, watermelon, onion, chili, cilantro, lime juice and salt.
- Pat fish dry then brush with oil and season with salt.
- Grill fish starting with skin sides down on lightly oiled rack turning over once 8 minutes.
- Serve fish topped with salsa.

69. Grilled Chilean Sea Bass Recipe

Serving: 4 | Prep: | Cook: 20mins | Ready in:

Ingredients

- Arbol chili Rub:
- 1-ounce coriander, dried and ground
- 1/2-ounce lemon pepper
- 1/4-ounce arbol chili, dried and ground
- 1/4-ounce allspice
- 1/4-ounce cinnamon
- 1/4-ounce salt
- 1/4-ounce achiote paste
- lemon mint Vinaigrette:
- 1 egg yolk*
- 1 teaspoon water
- 3 teaspoons sherry wine vinegar
- 1 tablespoon lemon juice, fresh
- 2/3 cup olive oil
- 2 teaspoons mint leaves
- 1 tablespoon onion, minced
- 2/3 teaspoon lemon pepper
- 1/4-ounce chives
- 4 (7-ounce) sea bass fillets
- salt

Direction

- For the Arbol Chili Rub: In a dry sauce pot, heat and stir coriander, lemon pepper, arbol chili, allspice, cinnamon, salt, and achiote paste until it just starts to smoke and flavors are released. Transfer to a blender or food processor and grind until it is powder. Remainder may be stored in an airtight container.
- For the Lemon Mint Vinaigrette: In a mixing bowl, whip egg yolk and water. Place in a blender, add 1/3 of the vinegar and lemon juice. On high speed, drizzle in approx. 2/3 of the olive oil. Add remainder of the vinegar and lemon juice and drizzle in the rest of the olive oil, add mint, onions, lemon pepper, and chives. Refrigerate immediately.
- Rub fillets with Arbol Chili Rub and salt and grill to 130 degrees (medium). Drizzle plate with Lemon Mint Vinaigrette and top with Habanero Salsa (recipe follows). Serve with rice of your choice.
- *RAW EGG WARNING
- Food Network Kitchens suggest caution in consuming raw and lightly-cooked eggs due to the slight risk of Salmonella or other food-borne illness. To reduce this risk, we recommend you use only fresh, properly-refrigerated, clean, grade A or AA eggs with intact shells, and avoid contact between the yolks or whites and the shell.
- HABANERO SALSA
- 1/2 habanero pepper, dried
- 1/3 ancho chili pepper, dried
- 1/3 papaya, chopped
- 1/3 mango, chopped
- 1/2 Roma tomato, diced
- 3 teaspoons Sherry wine vinegar
- 1 teaspoon cilantro, finely chopped
- 1 teaspoon mint, finely chopped
- 1 tablespoon onion, diced

- 1/2 teaspoon garlic, minced
- 1/3 teaspoon steak salt blend
- Soak the habaneros and anchos in hot water to soften. De-seed (use gloves) and remove stems before they are diced. Combine remaining ingredients in a mixing bowl. Transfer to a storage container and refrigerate. Yield: 4 servings

70. Grilled Sea Bass With Orange And Red Onion Sauce And Citrus Couscous Recipe

Serving: 6 | Prep: | Cook: 50mins | Ready in:

Ingredients

- orange and red onion Sauce:
- 1½ Tbsp olive oil
- 1 lb red onions, cut into ¼-inch slices
- 2 cups freshly squeezed orange juice
- 2 Tbsp flat-leaf parsley, finely chopped
- Dash of Tabasco sauce
- Pinch of ground coriander
- ¼ tsp salt
- Freshly ground black pepper to taste
- Citrus Couscous:
- 3 cups light chicken stock
- Grated zest of 1 orange
- Grated zest of 1 lemon
- Grated zest of 1 lime
- ¼ tsp Chinese chile paste
- 2 Tbsp extra virgin olive oil
- 1½ cups instant couscous
- ½ tsp salt
- ¼ tsp freshly ground black pepper
- Grilled Sea Bass:
- 6 (4- to 5-ounce) skinless, boneless sea bass fillets, about 1-inch thick
- 1 Tbsp olive oil
- ½ lemon
- salt and freshly ground black pepper
- Sprigs of chervil

Direction

- Heat olive oil in a large skillet over medium-low heat.
- Add red onions and sauté, stirring occasionally, for about 10 minutes, or until the onions are softened but not browned.
- Add orange juice and bring mixture to a boil. Simmer until the liquid is reduced by half, about 10 minutes.
- Remove from heat and stir in parsley, Tabasco, coriander, salt, and pepper. Set aside.
- In a medium saucepan, combine stock, citrus zests, chile paste, and olive oil.
- Bring the mixture just to a boil over medium heat, and then immediately stir in couscous.
- Remove from heat, cover pan, and let stand until the couscous is tender, about 10 minutes.
- When all of the liquid has been absorbed, fluff the couscous with a fork and add salt and pepper.
- Brush sea bass fillets on all sides with olive oil.
- Preheat a grill or broiler to medium-high.
- Season fillets with salt and pepper and grill them for about 3 minutes on each side, or until done through and opaque.
- During the last minute of cooking, squeeze a little lemon juice over each fillet.
- To plate, put a mound of couscous on each of 6 heated dinner plates and place a grilled fillet on top.
- Drizzle the onion sauce around the edge of the plates and garnish with a few sprigs of chervil.

71. Healthy Ish Breaded Basa Recipe

Serving: 4 | Prep: | Cook: 20mins | Ready in:

Ingredients

- 2 Basa Fillets
- 1 Whole egg, 1 egg white, beaten
- 3/4 Cup 4C whole wheat breadcrumbs

- 2 Tbsp Smart Balance or other non-hydrogenated margarine
- dill, garlic and onion powder, Smoked or regular paprika, pepper to taste
- lemon juice or wedges, for serving

Direction

- Put the desired amount of herbs and spices into your breadcrumbs and lay them out on a plate next to your bowl of beaten eggs. Cut each Basa fillet in half to make 4, then rinse and pat them dry with paper towels. Submerge them into the beaten eggs making sure they coat well. Immediately coat them with the breadcrumb mixture and coat evenly. If you'd like you may put the coated fish into the fridge for an hour or so to allow the breading to set, but it's not necessary. Melt the margarine into a pan and place the breaded fillets right in there. Add more spices at this stage if desired, especially if you have damaged taste buds like me. Allow the breading to turn golden-brown and then flip, but try not to flip them more than 2-3 times or you risk losing the breading. Once done, serve hot, squeeze lemon juice over it and enjoy.

72. Herbed Sea Bass Recipe

Serving: 2 | Prep: | Cook: 20mins | Ready in:

Ingredients

- 2 6oz sea bass fillets
- 1/4 cup butter
- 1/4 cup fresh chopped parsley,
- 2 tablespoons chopped dill weed,
- 1 tablespoon dried dill weed
- 2/3 cup finely chopped onions
- 1/4 cup chopped fresh chives
- 2 cloves of garlic chopped
- 1 tablespoon fresh lemon juice
- salt & pepper to taste

Direction

- Preheat oven to 360 degrees.
- In a casserole dish, add bass, butter, onions, parsley, dill weed, onions, chives, garlic, lemon juice, salt and pepper.
- Cook until fish is lightly browned and flaky (about 20 mins).
- Serve with sauce over fish.

73. Homemade Fish Sticks

Serving: 0 | Prep: | Cook: | Ready in:

Ingredients

- 1/2 cup dry bread crumbs
- 1/2 teaspoon salt
- 1/2 teaspoon paprika
- 1/2 teaspoon lemon-pepper seasoning
- 1/2 cup all-purpose flour
- 1 large egg, beaten
- 3/4 pound cod fillets, cut into 1-inch strips
- Butter-flavored cooking spray

Direction

- Preheat oven to 400°. In a shallow bowl, mix bread crumbs and seasonings. Place flour and egg in separate shallow bowls. Dip fish in flour to coat both sides; shake off excess. Dip in egg, then in crumb mixture, patting to help coating adhere.
- Place on a baking sheet coated with cooking spray; spritz with butter-flavored cooking spray. Bake 10-12 minutes or until fish just begins to flake easily with a fork, turning once.
- Nutrition Facts
- 1 serving: 278 calories, 4g fat (1g saturated fat), 129mg cholesterol, 718mg sodium, 25g carbohydrate (2g sugars, 1g fiber), 33g protein. Diabetic Exchanges: 4 lean meat, 1-1/2 starch.

74. Hot And Crunchy Bass Recipe

Serving: 4 | Prep: | Cook: 15mins | Ready in:

Ingredients

- Bear's SAUCE
- 1/2 clove garlic, smashed
- 1 tb lemon juice
- 1/4 c butter
- 1/8 ts pepper
- 1/2 ts salt
- 1 tb Finely minced parsley
- THE fish
- 1/4 c yellow cornmeal
- 1/4 c flour
- 4 1-lb. bass, dressed and skinned
- 4 tb butter
- salt and fresh pepper
- This recipe includes a very simple sauce that enhances sautéed, broiled or baked fish.
- It can be made in camp if you brought parsley and usually impresses any old "fried fish angler."

Direction

- Make the sauce first.
- In a bowl, set the butter out to soften.
- Then cream it with a fork and then a spoon until it is light and fluffy.
- Work in the salt and pepper.
- Mix the smashed garlic and the lemon juice, and then work this liquid into the butter.
- Takes a bit of time to do this.
- Mix in the parsley and serve in a gravy boat with a spoon.
- Pan-fry the bass remembering to brown the fish on both sides but not to overcook.
- Serve hot on hot plates and pass the sauce.

75. Incredible Stuffed Sea Bass Recipe

Serving: 6 | Prep: | Cook: 40mins | Ready in:

Ingredients

- 2 whole sea bass fillets with skin still intact totaling about 4 pounds
- 1/4 cup butter
- 1 small white onion chopped
- 3 stalks celery chopped
- 2 eggs beaten
- 1/2 teaspoon dried sage
- 1/2 teaspoon dry mustard
- 1/4 cup fresh parsley chopped
- 2 cups plain bread crumbs
- 1/2 teaspoon salt
- 1 teaspoon freshly ground black pepper

Direction

- Place butter in a skillet and melt then sauté onion and celery until tender.
- Meanwhile combine eggs, sage, mustard, parsley, bread crumbs, salt and pepper then mix well.
- Add onion and celery then mix well.
- Place one fillet skin side down on the bottom of a lightly greased baking dish.
- Spread stuffing mixture on the fillet and place remaining fillet on top skin side up.
- Bake at 350 for 40 minutes.

76. LOUP DE MERR AU FENOUIL STRIPED BASS WITH FENNEL Recipe

Serving: 8 | Prep: | Cook: 20mins | Ready in:

Ingredients

- 2 two pound striped bass
- flour
- vegetable oil

- Dried fennel branches
- 4 garlic cloves minced
- 1 tablespoon minced parsley
- toasted bread crumbs
- Coarsely minced hardboiled eggs
- Sauce:
- 1 glass of dry white wine
- 1/2 teaspoon salt
- 1 teaspoon freshly ground black pepper
- 1 teaspoon fennel seed
- 1 cup fish stock

Direction

- Clean and split fish.
- Coat lightly in flour and sauté in hot oil until golden brown on both sides.
- Place in 350 oven for 15 minutes.
- Remove fish from oven and arrange on bed of fennel branches in an oven dish.
- Cover with minced garlic, parsley, bread crumbs and hard boiled eggs.
- To make sauce combine all ingredients and simmer 15 minutes.
- Pour sauce over fish and return to oven for 10 minutes.

77. Lemon Poppyseed Fish Recipe

Serving: 4 | Prep: | Cook: 20mins | Ready in:

Ingredients

- 1 lb skinless striped bass, portioned into 4 fillets
- 1/2 tsp each Kosher salt and black pepper
- Zest of 1 large lemon
- 1/3 cup poppy seeds
- 1 egg white, beaten
- 1 tsp olive oil

Direction

- Place the fish fillets on a plate and season with salt and pepper.

- In a small dish stir together the lemon zest and poppy seeds.
- Brush the top side of the fillets with the egg white, then sprinkle with a generous amount of the poppy seed mixture.
- In a large non-stick skillet, heat the oil over medium heat.
- Add the fish, seed side down, and cook 2 minutes.
- Flip fillets carefully and cook for another 2 minutes.
- Serve over beds of spinach or lemon rice (or lemon-spinach rice!)

78. Lemon Seabass Fillets Recipe

Serving: 4 | Prep: | Cook: 20mins | Ready in:

Ingredients

- 4 seabass fillets
- 1 lemon, juice and zest
- 1 clove garlic, diced
- salt and pepper
- 1 tbsp olive oil

Direction

- Start by scoring the fish skin in a diagonal angle.
- Place the fish on a plate and season with salt, pepper, garlic and lemon juice&zest. Marinade for a few minutes.
- Remove garlic.
- Pour the olive oil on a hot frying pan and place the fillets skin side down. Cook undisturbed for 4 minutes until the skin becomes crisp and golden. Don't touch it, fuss over it, or in any way fiddle with it. Let it form a crust.
- Now turn the fish over, turn the heat to low and cook for 2 minutes. Your fish will be crispy and moist.
- Serve immediately.

79. Mediterranean Poached Bass Recipe

Serving: 4 | Prep: | Cook: 8mins |Ready in:

Ingredients

- 1 medium onion, chopped
- ½ red bell pepper, chopped
- 1 cubanelle pepper, seeded and diced
- 4 medium garlic cloves, minced
- 2 cups canned diced tomatoes
- ½ cup fish or vegetable broth
- 2 tbsp sliced green olives
- 2 tsp brined capers, drained
- 1 ½ pound sea bass, quartered

Direction

- Sauté onion and peppers 7 minutes in a large non-stick pan.
- Add garlic and cook 1 minute more.
- Stir tomatoes, broth, olives and capers into onion mixture and heat to simmer.
- Arrange fish in skillet. Cover and cook 8 to 10 minutes.
- To serve, remove fish to plates and spoon tomato and olive mixture over fish.

80. Mediterranean Sea Bass Recipe

Serving: 2 | Prep: | Cook: 30mins |Ready in:

Ingredients

- 2 sea bass fillets scaled keeping skin on
- 15g breadcrumbs
- 2 sundried tomatoes
- pinch oregano
- 3 black olives, pitted
- 8 fresh basil leaves
- pinch cracked black pepper
- 1/2 Tbsp olive oil

Direction

- (1) Preheat the oven to Gas mark 4 (180c).
- (2) Apart from the Sea Bass, put all the ingredients into a food processor & blend into a paste.
- (3) Spread the paste onto the skin side of the sea bass fillets.
- (4) Place the Sea Bass onto a baking tray skin side up & cook for 30 mins in preheated oven.
- (5) Serve with pan fried garlic new potatoes & salad.

81. Miso Glazed Sea Bass Recipe

Serving: 4 | Prep: | Cook: 10mins |Ready in:

Ingredients

- 1/3 cup sake
- 1/3 cup mirin (sweet Japanese rice wine)*
- 1/3 cup light yellow miso (fermented soybean paste)*
- 3 tablespoons (packed) brown sugar
- 2 tablespoons soy sauce
- 4 6-ounce sea bass fillets (each about 3/4 inch thick)
- 2 tablespoons chopped green onions
- 2 tablespoons chopped fresh basil

Direction

- Mix first 5 ingredients in shallow glass baking dish. Add fish and turn to coat. Cover and refrigerate at least 2 hours and up to 6 hours.
- Preheat broiler. Remove fish from marinade. Place fish on rimmed baking sheet. With broiler door slightly open, broil fish 6 inches from heat source until just opaque in center, about 6 minutes. Transfer to plates. Sprinkle with green onions and basil and serve.
- *Available at Japanese markets, specialty foods stores and in the Asian foods section of some supermarkets.

82. Mojo Bass Recipe

Serving: 4 | Prep: | Cook: 9mins | Ready in:

Ingredients

- 1 tablespoon fresh orange juice
- 1 tablespoon fresh lime juice
- 1 teaspoon ground coriander
- 1 teaspoon bottled minced garlic
- 1 teaspoon olive oil
- 1/2 teaspoon ground cumin
- 4 (6-ounce) striped bass fillets (about 1 inch thick)
- cooking spray
- 2 tablespoons chopped fresh mint

Direction

- Preheat broiler.
- Combine first 6 ingredients, stirring with a whisk.
- Arrange fish, skin side down, on a foil-lined baking sheet coated with cooking spray. Brush half of orange juice mixture over fish; broil 4 minutes. Brush with remaining orange juice mixture; broil 4 minutes or until fish flakes easily when tested with a fork. Sprinkle with mint.

83. Orange Saffron Grilled Striped Bass Recipe

Serving: 6 | Prep: | Cook: 5mins | Ready in:

Ingredients

- 1/2 C butter
- 3T frozen orange juice concentrate, thawed
- 1/2 tsp white wine vinegar
- Generous pinch of saffron trhead
- sea salt
- 6 striped bass (or trout) whole dressed
- 1 large naval orange, juiced
- 1 large orange sliced thin
- veggie oil spray

Direction

- Do ahead;
- In a small bowl, combine butter, OJ concentrate, wine vinegar and saffron until blended.
- Season with salt & pepper, cover & chill 23 hours.
- Cut diagonal slits on each side of fish at 1" intervals.
- Arrange fish in a baking dish and fill each cavity with sliced orange.
- Sprinkle inside and out with orange juice.
- Cover at room temp for 1 hour.
- Spray the fish and the grill with non-stick spray.
- Grill on medium-high heat basting constantly with orange mixture.
- Grill about 5 minutes or until opaque in the center.
- Serve right away.

84. Pan Fried Sea Bass With A Lemon And Wine Sauce Recipe

Serving: 2 | Prep: | Cook: 30mins | Ready in:

Ingredients

- Sunflower Oil - sufficient only to cook the fish
- 2 x 180g/6oz Fillets Sea Bass - deboned but skin on
- Salt and freshly ground black pepper
- LEMON AND WINE SAUCE
- 100ml/6tbsp Dry White Wine
- 45ml/3tbsp Lemon Juice
- Fresh Lemon Zest - to taste
- 30g/1oz butter

Direction

- FISH
- Warm 2 serving plates;
- Season the fish on both sides with salt and pepper;
- Put a large frying pan on a medium heat;
- Pour sufficient oil to cook the fish into the pan and add the fish, skin side down;
- Press down with a fish slice to help the skin crisp up;
- Cook for some 4 minutes or so, jiggling the pan every now and then, and turning for the last 20 to 30 seconds or so to finish it off - you want to cook it about 90% of the way through on the skin side;
- Place on top of whatever veggies you are serving with the dish e.g. Broccoli/Leeks.
- SAUCE
- Remove the pan from the heat, add the wine, butter, lemon juice and Zest to taste, stirring continuously to mix together well with the pan juice;
- Return the pan to a low medium heat and cook briefly until sauce heated through and thickens a Little to consistency required;
- Pour into serving bowl and drizzle a little on the plate around the veggie/fish and serve the remainder with the dish.

85. Pan Seared Sea Bass With Blood Orange Butter Sauce Recipe

Serving: 2 | Prep: | Cook: 15mins | Ready in:

Ingredients

- For sauce:
- 1 tablespoon unsalted butter
- 1 large shallot, minced
- juice from 1 small lemon
- 1/2 cup freshly squeezed blood orange juice
- 1/2 a turkish bay leaf
- 6 Tablespoons unslated butter, cut into Tablespoon-sized bits

- kosher salt and freshly cracked black and white pepper, to taste
- ~
- For Fish:
- olive oil
- (2) 6 oz. portions of Chilean sea bass
- kosher salt and black pepper
- ~
- For the asparagus:
- 1/2 pound asparagus, trimmed
- drizzle of olive oil
- kosher salt and freshly ground black pepper

Direction

- For asparagus:
- Preheat the oven to 400 degrees F. Snap or cut the dry stem ends off each asparagus and place on a heavy baking sheet. Drizzle with olive oil, sprinkle with salt and pepper, and toss. Roast until the asparagus is tender, about 8-12 minutes (depends on how thick they are). Cool slightly and serve warm or at room temperature.
- For sauce:
- Melt 1 Tbsp. butter in a small saucepan over medium heat. Add shallots and cook until tender and just beginning to color (do not brown them), about 3 minutes. Add the lemon and orange juice and bay leaf and simmer on low until reduced by about half (about 5 minutes). Stirring constantly, add butter one tablespoon at a time, incorporating each piece fully before adding the next. Add salt and pepper, to taste.
- For fish:
- In a medium sauté pan, heat a couple tablespoons of olive oil over medium-high heat. Season sea bass with salt and pepper, then place in pan and sear on both sides, turning only once. Cooking time will vary depending on the thickness of your fish, but fish is done when it flakes easily in the center with a fork.
- To plate:

- Place asparagus all facing the same direction on serving plate. Top with fish and spoon butter sauce over the fish.

86. Pan Seared Sea Bass With Peach Salsa Recipe

Serving: 4 | Prep: | Cook: 15mins | Ready in:

Ingredients

- 4-6 ounce sea bass fillets
- olive oil to coat fish
- 1 large peach, chopped
- 1 large avocado, chopped
- 1/2 small red onion, diced
- 1/2 cup red bell pepper, diced
- 2 teaspoons peeled and grated fresh ginger
- 2 tablespoons fresh chopped cilantro
- 2 tablespoons olive oil
- 1 tablespoon maple syrup
- 1/2 teaspoon ground cumin
- 3 tablespoons lime juice
- 1/4 teaspoon freshly ground pepper

Direction

- For the Salsa:
- In a medium-sized bowl, combine the peach, avocado, onion, pepper, ginger and cilantro.
- In a small bowl, whisk together 2 tablespoons olive oil, maple syrup, lime juice, cumin and pepper.
- Pour the liquid mixture over the peach mixture and stir well. Refrigerate for 1 hour.
- For Fish:
- Heat pan on stove top.
- Coat fish with olive oil, and gently place in heated pan.
- Cook 5-6 minutes each side or until fish is flakey with a fork.
- Note* you can also cook fish on the grill.
- When fish is done, spoon some of the salsa over the top and serve.

- Enjoy

87. Pan Seared Tilapia Or Bass With Chile Lime Butter Recipe

Serving: 6 | Prep: | Cook: 15mins | Ready in:

Ingredients

- For chile lime butter:
- 1/2 stick (1/4 cup) unsalted butter, softened
- 1 tablespoon finely chopped shallot
- 1 teaspoon finely grated fresh lime zest
- 2 teaspoons fresh lime juice
- 1 teaspoon minced fresh Thai or serrano chile (preferably red), including seeds
- 1/2 teaspoon salt
- ****
- For fish:
- 6 (5- to 6-oz) pieces skinless tilapia fillet or farm-raised striped bass fillets with skin
- 1/2 teaspoon salt
- 2 tablespoons vegetable oil

Direction

- Make chile lime butter:
- Stir together butter, shallot, zest, lime juice, chile, and salt in a bowl.
- ****
- Prepare fish:
- If using striped bass, score skin in 3 or 4 places with a thin sharp knife to prevent fish from curling (do not cut through flesh). Pat fish dry and sprinkle with salt. Heat 1 tablespoon oil in a 12-inch nonstick skillet over moderately high heat until just smoking, then sauté 3 pieces of fish, turning over once with a spatula, until golden and just cooked through, 4 to 5 minutes, and transfer to a plate. Sauté remaining fish in remaining tablespoon oil in same manner.
- Serve each piece of fish with a dollop of chile lime butter.

- **NOTE:** Chile lime butter can be made 1 day ahead and chilled, covered. Bring to room temperature before using.
- Enjoy.

88. Pistachio Crusted Chilean Sea Bass Recipe

Serving: 2 | Prep: | Cook: 20mins | Ready in:

Ingredients

- 2- 6 oz Fillets of Chilean sea bass
- 1/2 C Unsalted Chopped pistachios
- 3 Tbsp olive oil
- juice of 1 lime
- salt & pepper to taste
- **You can find unshelled pistachios in your local grocery store
- *** Chop nuts in mini food prep (processor)

Direction

- Pre heat oven to 350 degrees F.
- Place pistachios in shallow dish.
- Place fish in second shallow dish.
- Squeeze juice of lime onto fish.
- Drizzle with 1 Tbsp of olive oil.
- Season with salt & fresh ground pepper.
- Be sure to roll fish around in order to coat both sides, let stand for about 20 minutes.
- Press fish into ground pistachios on one side.
- Heat olive oil in oven-proof skillet until very hot but not smoking.
- Place fish in skillet, nut side down to sear, about a minute or two.
- Turn fish over and bake in oven for about 15 - 20 minutes or until done.

89. Roasted Bass With Miso Glaze On Jasmine Rice Recipe

Serving: 4 | Prep: | Cook: 30mins | Ready in:

Ingredients

- 1/4 cup white miso
- 1/2 cup mirin
- 2 tablespoons sugar
- 1 tablespoon soy sauce
- 1 teaspoon minced garlic
- 1 teaspoon minced ginger
- 1 tablespoon sesame oil
- 4 (3-ounce) bass fillets
- 1 cup jasmine rice
- 1 1/4 cups water

Direction

- In a small bowl, combine the miso, mirin, sugar, soy sauce, garlic, and ginger. Slowly stir in the sesame oil to make the miso glaze. Marinate the bass in the miso glaze for 5 to 6 hours, refrigerated.
- In a pot, combine rice and water and cook in rice cooker until done. Reserve and keep warm.
- Arrange the fish fillets on a roasting pan. Generously coat with the miso glaze, and discard the rest of the glaze. Bake in a preheated 500 degree F oven for about 10 minutes or until medium done.
- Spoon about 1/2 cup of the jasmine rice on plate, place a fillet on top and drizzle miso glaze from roasting pan over the bass.

90. Roasted Sea Bass With Fennel Oranges And Olives Recipe

Serving: 6 | Prep: | Cook: 25mins | Ready in:

Ingredients

- 6 tablespoons extra virgin olive oil plus more for serving
- 2 fennel bulbs sliced paper thin
- 6 garlic cloves thinly sliced
- 3/4 cup dry white wine
- 1/2 cup fresh orange juice
- 6 pieces orange peel
- 1/4 teaspoon salt
- 1 teaspoon freshly ground black pepper
- 6 sea bass fillets
- 2 oranges peeled and cut into 1/8" slices
- 1 cup mixed pitted green and black olives
- 6 bay leaves

Direction

- Preheat oven to 400.
- In a large oval roasting pan over medium high heat warm 3 tablespoons of the olive oil.
- Add fennel and garlic then cook stirring occasionally for 5 minutes.
- Add wine and boil for 1 minute.
- Add orange juice and peel and simmer for 2 minutes.
- Season with salt and pepper.
- Remove from heat.
- Season fish with salt and pepper and place on the fennel mixture.
- Drizzle fish with remaining 3 tablespoons oil.
- Place oranges, olives and bay leaves on and around the fish.
- Roast for 25 minutes.
- Remove bay leaves and discard.
- Spoon some of the liquid over the fish and drizzle with oil.
- Serve immediately.

91. STRIPED BASS WITH CORN RELISH Recipe

Serving: 4 | Prep: | Cook: 35mins | Ready in:

Ingredients

- 2T EVOO
- 4 STRIPED BASS FILLETS, SKIN ON
- COURSE salt
- 1 SM onion
- 2 garlic cloves, MINCED
- 1/2 jalapeno OR serrano pepper, REMV SEEDS, SLICE THIN
- 1/2 C dry white wine
- 2 EARS corn, HUSKS & SILK REMV'D, KERNELS SCRAPED OFF
- 6 OZ cherry tomatoes, QUARTERED
- 1/2 C CHOPPED basil
- 1/4 C SHOPPED cilantro

Direction

- 1. In a large skillet, heat oil over medium-high. Season fish with salt and pepper, and sear, skin side down, for 4 minutes. With a wide metal spatula, turn fish over and cook 1 minute. Do not cook through. Remove from the pan; set aside.
- 2. Add onion to the pan, reduce heat to medium, and cook, stirring occasionally, until onion is tender and the edges begin to brown, about 4 minutes. Add garlic and cook 1 minute.
- 3. Add jalapeno, wine, 1/4 cup water, corn, tomatoes, and fish, skin side up. Cover and cook 4 minutes, or until the fish is just cooked through; transfer, skin side up, to four wide shallow bowls. Stir basil and cilantro into vegetable mixture and spoon around fish.

92. Sake Marinated Sea Bass With Coconut Curry Sauce Recipe

Serving: 6 | Prep: | Cook: 15mins | Ready in:

Ingredients

- 1/2 cup mirin (sweet Japanese rice wine)
- 1/4 cup sake
- 1/4 cup tamari or regular soy sauce

- 2 tablespoons yellow miso (fermented soy bean paste)
- 2 tablespoons rice vinegar
- 1 tablespoon chopped peeled fresh ginger
- 1 tablespoon brown sugar
- 6 6-ounce sea bass fillets
- 1 tablespoon vegetable oil
- Steamed white rice
- Chopped fresh cilantro
- coconut-Curry Sauce:
- 1/2 cup mirin*
- 1/4 cup chopped fresh lemongrass**
- 1 tablespoon chopped peeled fresh ginger
- 1/4 cup dry white wine
- 2 cups whipping cream
- 3/4 cup canned unsweetened coconut milk*
- 2 teaspoons Thai green or red curry paste*
- *Available at Asian markets and in the Asian foods section of some supermarkets.
- **fresh lemongrass can be found in the produce section (not Asian foods section) of some supermarkets.
- Place mirin, lemongrass and ginger in heavy medium saucepan. Boil until reduced to 1/4 cup, about 6 minutes. Add wine and boil until reduced to 1/4 cup, about 6 minutes. Add cream and coconut milk; bring to boil. Reduce heat to medium. Simmer sauce until slightly thickened, stirring occasionally, about 12 minutes. Stir in curry paste. season sauce to taste with salt and pepper. (Can be prepared 1 day ahead. Cover and refrigerate. Rewarm over medium heat before serving.)

Direction

- Purée first 7 ingredients in blender.
- Place fillets in single layer in glass baking dish. Pour marinade over. Cover; refrigerate 2 hours, turning fish occasionally.
- Preheat oven to 400°F.
- Remove fillets from marinade; pat dry with paper towels.
- Sprinkle both sides of fillets with salt and pepper.

- Heat oil in large ovenproof nonstick skillet over medium-high heat. Add fillets and sear until golden brown, about 2 minutes.
- Turn fillets over; transfer skillet to oven. Bake fillets until just opaque in center, about 8 minutes.
- Place some steamed rice in center of each of 6 plates. Top with fillets.
- Spoon some Coconut-Curry Sauce around rice on each plate. Garnish with chopped fresh cilantro and serve.

93. Sake Steamed Sea Bass With Ginger And Green Onions Recipe

Serving: 4 | Prep: | Cook: 15mins | Ready in:

Ingredients

- 1 cup uncooked medium-grain rice
- 3/4 cup sake
- 3/4 cup bottled clam juice
- 1 tablespoon minced peeled ginger
- 4 5-ounce sea bass fillets
- 2 large green onions, chopped
- 4 teaspoons soy sauce
- 1 teaspoon oriental sesame oil
- 3 tablespoons chopped fresh cilantro
- 2 teaspoons sesame seeds, toasted (in dry skillet over medium heat for 3-5 minutes)

Direction

- Cook rice according to package directions.
- Meanwhile, combine sake and next 3 ingredients in large skillet deep enough to hold steamer rack. Bring liquid to boil. Reduce heat; simmer 5 minutes.
- Arrange fish on rack; sprinkle with salt and pepper. Place rack in skillet. Top fish with onions; drizzle with soy sauce and sesame oil. Cover skillet; steam fish until opaque in center, about 5 minutes.

- Remove steamer rack.
- Mix cilantro into juices in skillet. Spoon rice onto plates.
- Top with fish, juices from skillet, and sesame seeds.
- Nutritional Info: Per serving: calories, 367; total fat, 5 g; saturated fat, 1 g; cholesterol, 62 mg; fiber, 1 g

94. Salmon Sea Bass And Bay Scallop Ceviche Recipe

Serving: 6 | Prep: | Cook: 180mins | Ready in:

Ingredients

- 1/2 pint grape tomatoes
- 1 medium purple onion, chopped
- 1 bunch fresh cilantro (leaves only)
- 1 heaping tbls vegetable and herb powder mix
- 1 tbls garlic powder
- 1/8 tsp ground cayenne pepper (or a little more)
- 1 tsp evaporated Celtic sea salt
- juice of 2 lemons
- juice of 15 limes
- 2 tbls raw soy sauce called nama shoyu
- 1 lb sushi-grade salmon, cubed
- 1 lb sushi-grade Chilean sea bass, cubed
- 1 lb sushi-grade bay scallops, cubed

Direction

- In a large bowl, combine the tomatoes, onion, herbs and spices, lemon and lime juices, and soy sauce.
- Gently fold in the cubed salmon, sea bass and scallops.
- Let marinate in the refrigerator for 3 hours before serving.

95. Salt Crusted Sea Bass Recipe

Serving: 4 | Prep: | Cook: 20mins | Ready in:

Ingredients

- 1 seabass about 2 lbs
- extra virgin olive oil
- 4 lbs coarse sea salt
- 2 inch rosemary sprig, leafs removed
- A few slices of fresh garlic (optional)
- 6 black peppercorns or to taste
- 6 pink peppercorns or to taste

Direction

- Clean and scale the fish. For presentation, leave the fish whole.
- Place the rosemary and peppercorns inside the fish along with the garlic if using.
- Brush the whole fish with extra virgin olive oil. In an oven-proof fish pan, set a thick layer of coarse sea salt.
- Lay the fish on the salt and completely cover it with the rest of the salt, pressing gently.
- Bake at 350F for 15/20 min.
- When ready, bring the pan to the table, and break the salt shell in front of your guest. Remove the fish from the pan and take off the skin. Lift the fillets of bass from each side and serve.

96. Sauted Sea Bass Recipe

Serving: 2 | Prep: | Cook: 6mins | Ready in:

Ingredients

- sea bass, halibut, or cod
- vegetable Supreme
- olive oil
- butter
- Brussels sprouts, asparagus or other vegetable or salad.
- French's fried onions

Direction

- Cut skin from fish steaks.
- Pour a little olive on steaks and rub in.
- Sprinkle seasonings on both sides.
- Melt butter in pan.
- Allow the butter to brown a little on medium high heat.
- Cook each side about 3 minutes.
- Cut Brussels sprouts in half and boil.
- When sprouts are done, on plate, sprinkle with Vegetable Supreme and add Fried Onions.

97. Sea Bass In Pesto Sauce Recipe

Serving: 4 | Prep: | Cook: 15mins | Ready in:

Ingredients

- 1 pound sea bass fillet
- 1/2 teaspoon salt
- juice of 1/2 lemon plus 2 tablespoons divided use
- 6 tablespoons cooking oil
- 1 teaspoon cumin seeds
- 1 bunch green onions including tops chopped
- 1 bunch watercress chopped
- 1/2 bunch cilantro chopped
- 1/2 bunch mint chopped
- 4 serrano chilies chopped
- 8 large cloves garlic chopped
- 1 tablespoon dry fenugreek leaves
- 1/2 teaspoon cayenne pepper
- 1/2 cup water

Direction

- Cut fish into 4 equal strips then wash and pat dry with sprinkle with salt and juice of half lemon.
- Set aside then heat oil in large skillet over medium heat.
- Add cumin seeds and sauté until fragrant about 1 minute.

- Add green onions, watercress, cilantro, mint, green chilies and garlic.
- Stir for a few minutes then add fenugreek and cayenne then season to taste with salt.
- Transfer mixture to blender then add remaining 2 tablespoons lemon juice and water and puree.
- Return pureed mixture to skillet then add fish pieces and coat evenly with mixture.
- Cover and simmer on low heat 10 minutes then serve with steamed basmati rice.

98. Sea Bass Recipe

Serving: 0 | Prep: | Cook: 20mins | Ready in:

Ingredients

- 2 MEDIUM sea bass (400-500 GM)
- 3 spring onion
- 1 CUP OF dry white wine
- 1 small potato
- 2-3 cherry tomatoes
- salt & pepper TO TASTE
- 2 TBSP OF olive oil
- AND SOME olive oil PARSELY FOR GARNISHING

Direction

- In a skillet, pour 2 tbsp of olive oil. Slice one small potato in a chips and add it to olive, fry it till it makes a lovely golden crust. Then add roughly chopped spring onion and the whole cherry tomatoes; sauté for 1-2 mins; add 1 cup of dry white wine and simmer for 2-3 mins.
- Clean and wash the fish and add it whole to the vegetables. Sprinkle salt and pepper according to taste and cover the pan for at least 3-5 mins till the fish is well steam cooked under a medium flame.
- Garnish with fresh olive oil and parsley.
- Ready to eat!!!
- Bon Appétit :)

- Variations: - I added some mushrooms which turned out good...try it!

99. Sea Bass Steamed In Cabbage Leaves With Caviar Recipe

Serving: 4 | Prep: | Cook: 30mins | Ready in:

Ingredients

- 1 cup chardonnay
- 1 cup clam juice
- 1 cup heavy cream
- 1 tomato, peeled,* seeded and chopped
- 7 to 8 savoy cabbage leaves (use the large outer ones)
- 1 pound sea bass fillet
- salt and pepper, to taste
- 4 teaspoons caviar, preferable osetra
- Italian parsley leaves, for garnish, (optional)

Direction

- Cook the wine in a saucepan until reduced to 1/4 cup. Add the clam juice and reduce by 1/2. Stir in the cream and tomatoes, cook over high heat for 5 minutes. Process with a hand-held immersion blender, or put into a blender and blend until smooth. Taste and adjust seasonings. Keep warm (I keep mine in a thermos).
- Blanch the cabbage leaves in a large saucepan of salted water. When soft, immediately put in a bowl of ice water to stop the cooking process. Pat the leaves dry, then using a paring knife, trim the center vein to a uniform thickness. Place outside down on a work surface. (The center vein should be on the outside so you can easily fold it.)
- Cut the fish into equal pieces and season well with salt and pepper. Place a piece of fish in the center of each cabbage leaf, (you may have to use two, slightly overlapped). Fold into packages to enclose the fish.

- Line a steamer with the remaining cabbage leaves; place the fish packages, seam side down, on top. Steam for 15 minutes, or until the fish springs back when touched.
- Ladle some of the warm sauce onto each warmed plate. Place a cabbage package in the center and place a dollop of caviar on top. Garnish with parsley, if desired.

100.   Sea Bass With Fennel Recipe

Serving: 4 | Prep: | Cook: 20mins | Ready in:

Ingredients

- Ingredients:
- Large pinch of dried fennel
- 2 and 1/4 lbs sea bass, spines trimmed, scaled and cleaned
- extra virgin olive oil, for brushing
- 2 fl oz brandy
- salt and pepper
- Fresh fennel slices, to serve

Direction

- Directions:
- Preheat the oven to 350
- Sprinkle the dried fennel inside the cavity of the fish.
- Make several diagonal slashes on each side of the fish, brush it with olive oil and place on a baking sheet.
- Bake, turning and brushing with more olive oil occasionally, for about 20 minutes.
- Season with salt and pepper.
- Make a bed of fresh fennel slices on a serving dish and place the sea bass on top.
- Gently warm the brandy in a ladle, then pour it over the fish and ignite.
- Serve when the flames have died down.

101. Sea Bass With Ratatouille Jus And Roasted Lemon Asparagus Recipe

Serving: 4 | Prep: | Cook: 75mins | Ready in:

Ingredients

- 1½ lb sea bass fillet, about 1 inch thick, cut into 4pieces
- olive oil
- basil
- salt and pepper
- Ratatouille Jus:
- 1 large onion, thinly sliced
- 2 red peppers, cored and thinly sliced
- 2 garlic cloves, smashed
- 2 small zucchini, cut in half and thinly sliced
- 2 small yellow squash, cut in half and thinly sliced
- olive oil
- red wine vinegar
- Tabasco .
- salt and pepper
- roasted lemon Asparagus:
- 2 Tbsp fresh lemon juice
- 1 Tbsp extra-virgin olive oil
- 1 tsp finely grated lemon zest
- 12 asparagus spears, peeled and trimmed
- salt and pepper

Direction

- For the Ratatouille Jus
- Add olive oil to a sauté pan over medium heat. Add all the sliced vegetables and garlic.
- Cook for 3-5 minutes – do not brown. Add salt and pepper.
- At this point, I generally pull out about 3 slices of zucchini, 3 slices of yellow squash, and 4 slices of red pepper. I will keep these vegetables cool until I am ready to plate the fish. Then I finely dice the reserved vegetables and use them as a garnish just before serving. This is entirely up to you, but it does make a much better presentation, and adds a bit of crunch.

- Reduce heat and cook remaining vegetables slowly for 1 hour. Add a touch of water if necessary (though I've never felt the need to add any water).
- Place cooked vegetables in a blender with a touch of water at the bottom of blender.
- Blend, adjust seasoning, and allow to cool.
- Once the mixture has cooled, add a touch vinegar and Tabasco and check seasoning again. The sauce should have a nice consistency, not too thick and not runny.
- For the Roasted Asparagus
- Preheat oven to 450° F.
- Mix lemon juice, oil, and lemon zest in a small bowl.
- Place asparagus in a larger bowl and pour in sauce. Sprinkle with salt and pepper and toss.
- Place asparagus on a baking sheet.
- Roast asparagus until crisp-tender, turning occasionally, about 8 to 12 minutes.
- To Serve:
- Brush fish with olive oil and season with salt and pepper.
- Heat 2 Tbsp olive oil in a skillet, add fish fillets carefully, and sauté 3-4 minutes on each side, flipping very gently after the first 3-4 minutes (being careful not to break up the fillets).
- Squeeze lemon juice over fish.
- Pour a small amount of ratatouille jus on the plate to form a circle, lay one fish fillet on top of the jus, and arrange asparagus. If you like, spoon a bit more ratatouille jus over the fish before arranging the asparagus.
- Garnish with basil leaves and (if you've reserved any of the vegetables) a bit of the finely diced squash, zucchini, and red pepper.

102. Sea Bass With Rock Salt Crust Recipe

Serving: 4 | Prep: | Cook: 45mins | Ready in:

Ingredients

- 2kg coarse sea salt
- rosemary, chopped
- thyme, chopped
- 2 lemons, zest removed and set aside.
- 2 egg whites
- 1 large sea bass, approx 1kg, gutted

Direction

- 1. Preheat the oven to 200C/gas 6.
- 2. Pour the sea salt into a large bowl and add the rosemary, thyme and lemon zest.
- 3. Whisk together the egg whites with equal quantities of cold water to make a foam. Add enough of the egg foam to the salt to lightly coat it.
- 4. Cut the lemons into thick slices and put inside the cavity of the sea bass.
- 5. Take a deep roasting tin and put a decent layer of the salt on the bottom.
- Put the sea bass on top of the layer and pour the rest of the salt on top of it.
- Make sure all the fish is covered by patting it all over.
- 6. Cook in the oven for 45 minutes.
- 7. Take the fish out of the oven and use a knife to lift away the salt crust.
- Serve with a niçoise salad.

103. Sea Bass With Sweet Mushroom Sauce Recipe

Serving: 4 | Prep: | Cook: 45mins | Ready in:

Ingredients

- 1/4 cup chopped portobello mushroom caps
- 2 tbs chopped red bell pepper
- 2 tbs diced fresh pineapple
- 1 clove minced garlic
- 1/4 cup dice onion
- 1 tsp olive oil
- 2 tsp white port wine
- 1 tsp lemon juice

- 1/4 cu claim juice
- 1 tsp cornstarch
- 2 tsp heavy cream
- 1/2 cup milk
- 1/2 tsp butter
- 1/2 tsp salt
- 2 tsp chopped fresh cilantro
- 2 tsp chopped fresh dill
- 4 4-oz sea bass fillets

Direction

- Preheat oven to 400 degrees.
- Wrap mushrooms, pepper, pineapple, and garlic in foil. Cook in oven for 30 min. or until vegetables are golden brown. Allow to cool.
- In a medium sauté pan, sauté onion in olive oil until translucent. Add wine and cook briefly. Add lemon juice and clam juice. Simmer 5 min.
- In a small bowl or cup, mix cornstarch with 1 tsp water to make a thin paste. Set aside.
- Combine cream, milk, butter, and salt in a medium saucepan. Bring to a boil and whisk in cornstarch mixture with a wire whip. Simmer to 1 to 2 minutes or until thickened. Cool slightly.
- Transfer cream mixture to a blender and add onion mixture and roasted vegetables. Puree until smooth. Remove from blender and stir in chopped fresh herbs.
- Preheat grill or broiler and cook fish 3 to 5 minutes on each side until cook through. Serve fish with sauce.

104. Sea Bass In Paper Orata Al Cartoccio Recipe

Serving: 4 | Prep: | Cook: 90mins | Ready in:

Ingredients

- seafood Stock:
- 2 Medium green bell peppers - diced
- 1 Medium orange Bell pepper - diced

- 5 small cloves of garlic - minced
- 3 small shallots (purple onion)
- virgin olive oil (drizzle bottom of cookie sheet)
- sea bass in Paper:
- A sea bass, weighing at least 3 pounds (1 1/2 k)
- 1/4 cup (50 g) unsalted butter
- 1/4 pound (100 g) fresh shrimp
- 1/2 pound (200 g) fresh clams, scrubbed and purged
- 1/2 pound (200 g) fresh mussels, scrubbed and purged
- olive oil
- A bunch of parsley, minced
- 5 cloves garlic
- brandy
- 8 plum tomatoes
- salt and pepper to taste

Direction

- Seafood Stock:
- Preheat oven to 375 degrees
- Drizzle bottom of cookie sheet with Olive Oil.
- Roast for one hour.
- Thirty minutes into the roasting, give it a good shake to keep the veggies from sticking to the bottom of the pa
- After roasting, puree all the veggies.
- Finally, get a large pan - medium high heat, combined the veggies and 1 can of vegetable broth. Stir until it is well combined - less than five minutes.
- Place in a jar and refrigerate until you are ready to bake the Seabass in Paper.
- Note: You can make this a few days ahead.
- Sea Bass in Paper:
- ... if you are short on time or fresh shellfish are unavailable, you can use canned ones instead; make the sauce with the juices, and place the shellfish on the fish before you put it in the oven. The above quantities will serve 4.
- Clean and scale the fish. Wash it and pat it dry. Season the cavity with salt, pepper, and a few drops of olive oil. Mince two cloves of garlic, mix it with 2 tablespoons of the minced parsley, fill the cavity with the mixture, and

skewer it shut with toothpicks. Sprinkle the fish with the brandy and let it rest for about 15 minutes.
- Meanwhile, blanch and peel the tomatoes, seed them, and cut them into thin strips. Heat 1/4 cup of olive oil and flavor it by browning the remaining cloves of garlic, peeled and crushed, in it for a few minutes. Remove the garlic, add the tomatoes, salt and pepper to taste, and a heaping tablespoon of parsley. Simmer the sauce for about ten minutes, then stir in the clams, mussels, and shrimp, and cover it.
- Preheat the oven to 400 F (200 C).
- Grease a large sheet of oven proof paper with half the butter, lay the fish on it, and pour the shellfish sauce over it. Dot the fish with the remaining butter, crimp the paper so as to seal the fish, then to this, add the seafood stock.
- Finally, bake the fish for about 15 minutes per pound.
- Open it at the table.
- (If you don't have an oven proof bag, merely place it in a Pyrex oblong dish and seal tightly with aluminum foil.)

---

105.   Sea Bass With Celeriac Recipe

Serving: 4 | Prep: | Cook: 30mins | Ready in:

Ingredients

- 1 medium-sized celeriac (celery root), about 3/4 lb.
- 1 cup Swanson's ,(contains no hydrolyzed proteins) chicken broth
- 2 TBSP lemon juice
- 1 small onion, chopped
- 4 sea bass fillets
- sauce:
- 2 TBSP apricot oil
- 2 TBSP brown rice flour
- 1 cup reserved cooking liquid

- 1/4 cup dry white wine
- 3/4 TSPN fresh thyme
- 1 cup small shrimp (optional)
- salt to taste

Direction

- Peel and grate celeriac, a processor makes this part easy.
- Combine with chicken stock, lemon juice, and onion.
- Mix thoroughly.
- Spoon into one large ovenproof casserole.
- Top with sea bass fillets and season with a little more lemon juice.
- Cover casserole tightly and bake at 400 degrees for about 25 minutes, or until fish is flakey with a fork.
- Hold top of casserole and drain cooking liquid into a pan, there should be about a cup of liquid.
- Heat oil in a saucepan, and stir in flour.
- Stir in fish liquid, wine and thyme.
- Keep stirring until sauce thickens.
- This is when you add shrimp if you would like, and salt to taste.
- Spoon sauce over fish, and serve with brown rice and sliced fresh tomatoes.
- Enjoy,

106. Sea Bass With Fresh Tarragon Sauce Recipe

Serving: 24 | Prep: | Cook: 10mins | Ready in:

Ingredients

- 1 T olive oil
- 1 bay leaves
- 2 garlic cloves
- 4 shallots, chopped (or substitute a small mild onion)
- 1 whole Anaheim or other mildly spicy pepper , seeded, membrane removed, and chopped
- 1/2 jicama, julienned

- 2 T fresh tarragon leaves
- 1 T crushed tomatoes
- 1-T white wine
- 1-T water
- 1/2 t dried tarragon
- 2 sea bass fillets
- butter, for sautéing
- ½ cup diced crimini or local wild mushrooms
- salt

Direction

- Heat the olive oil in a large sauté pan over medium heat. Add the bay leaves, garlic, and Anaheim pepper and sauté for 2 minutes. Add the jicama and tarragon and continue to sauté for about a minute. Add the crushed tomato, white wine, and water, stir, and remove from the heat.
- Poach the sea bass fillets in water with the dried tarragon in a large sauté pan; cook until a knife slides in easily and fish is opaque throughout.
- Meanwhile, heat the butter in a small sauté pan. Add the mushrooms, shallots and salt, to taste. Sauté until the mushrooms are cooked through.
- Serve the Sea Bass topped with the sauce, and the sauce topped with the mushrooms-and-shallots.

107. Sea Bass In Salt Crust Recipe

Serving: 4 | Prep: | Cook: 40mins | Ready in:

Ingredients

- 1 sea bass, about 2.2 lb cleaned and scaled
- 1 sprig each of fresh fennel, rosemary, and thyme
- Mixed peppercorns
- 4.5 lb coarse sea salt

Direction

- Preheat the oven to 475°F. Fill the cavity of the fish with the sprigs of fresh fennel, rosemary, and thyme, and grind over some of the mixed peppercorns.
- Spread half the salt on a shallow cookie sheet (ideally oval) and lay the sea bass on it. Cover the fish all over with a 1/2 inch layer of salt, pressing it down firmly. Moisten the salt lightly by spraying with water from an atomizer. Bake the fish for 30-40 minutes, until the salt crust is just beginning to color.
- Bring the sea bass to the table in its salt crust. Use a sharp knife to break open the crust and cut into four portions.
- Serve.

108. Smoked Sea Bass Rillettes Recipe

Serving: 1 | Prep: | Cook: 7mins | Ready in:

Ingredients

- sea bass belly.
- White truffle oil.
- Sumac.
- liquid smoke.
- onion Jus.
- Fleur de Sel.
- Chopped chives.
- Mixed Micro Greens.
- lemon juice.
- Home Made Brioche.
- Clarified foie butter.

Direction

- Roast Sea Bass belly in 400 degree oven for 20-30 minutes or until golden brown.
- Remove bones from Sea Bass belly.
- Flake with hands and place in a Kitchen Aid mixing bowel.
- Beat with paddle attachment and add liquid smoke, fleur de Sel, chopped chives and onion jus to taste. (To make onion jus, simply

simmer caramelized onions with sugar, white wine, butter and kosher salt for 45 minutes).
- Beat with paddle attachment until ingredients become well incorporated and the Sea Bass separates into individual, stringy fibres.
- Pack Sea Bass mixture into 3 oz. ramekins and top with warm clarified foie butter. (To make clarified foie butter, simply clarify butter over a double boiler with your foie gras scraps in it; skim the scum that rises to the top and then strain through a chinois).
- Chill in a refrigerator for 1-3 weeks.
- When ready to serve, throw into a 500 degree oven for 15 seconds, (to loosen fat cap), and turn out onto a rectangular serving plate.
- Add sliced brioche, sumac, truffle oil, fleur de sel, and micro greens dressed with lemon juice to order.

109. Steamed Fish With Ginger

Serving: 6 | Prep: | Cook: 20mins | Ready in:

Ingredients

- 1 pound halibut fillet
- 1 teaspoon coarse sea salt or kosher salt
- 1 tablespoon minced fresh ginger
- 3 tablespoons thinly sliced green onion
- 1 tablespoon dark soy sauce
- 1 tablespoon light soy sauce
- 1 tablespoon peanut oil
- 2 teaspoons toasted sesame oil
- ¼ cup lightly packed fresh cilantro sprigs

Direction

- Pat halibut dry with paper towels. Rub both sides of fillet with salt. Scatter the ginger over the top of the fish and place onto a heatproof ceramic dish.
- Place into a bamboo steamer set over several inches of gently boiling water, and cover. Gently steam for 10 to 12 minutes.

- Pour accumulated water out of the dish and sprinkle the fillet with green onion. Drizzle both soy sauces over the surface of the fish.
- Heat peanut and sesame oils in a small skillet over medium-high heat until they begin to smoke. When the oil is hot, carefully pour on top of the halibut fillet. The very hot oil will cause the green onions and water on top of the fish to pop and spatter all over; be careful. Garnish with cilantro sprigs and serve immediately.
- Nutrition Facts
- Per Serving:
- 360.6 calories; protein 48.1g 96% DV; carbohydrates 2g 1% DV; fat 16.8g 26% DV; cholesterol 72.6mg 24% DV; sodium 1908mg 76% DV.

110.   Steamed Seabass With Green Sauce (Chutney) Recipe

Serving: 2 | Prep: | Cook: 15mins |Ready in:

Ingredients

- 2 medium size sea bass
- kosher salt to taste
- For the green sauce or chutney
- a bunch of fresh corriander leaves or cliantro leaves
- few strigs of spare mint leaves
- 4-5 green chillies
- 1/2 freshly squeezed lemon
- cummin powder
- 4-5 cloves of garlic
- salt to taste
- 1/2 teaspoon of sugar
- 1 small sized of onion
- Some olive oil

Direction

- Wash and clean well the fish, cutting all the fins and clean the stomach. Rub kosher salt on the fish and keep it aside.

- Grind all the above mentioned ingredients for the green sauce. Don't worry about the chili as when it will be steamed it won't be spicy or hot at all. Grind it into fine thick paste not watery.
- Now rub this sauce on the fish generously all around and fill some sauce in the stomach area and let it marinate at least for 5mins or more till you fix your steaming cooker.
- Today I had some fresh cabbage leaves so I just took some large leaves laid on the steam plate which was already covered with some aluminum foil and then I laid the fish on it. Just to preserve the juice of it but it's totally optional; if you don't have cabbage leaves, you can just put some aluminum foil paper and then put the fish on the top of it.
- Steam it for 6-7 mins. Don't open it directly; let it settle down for 5- 6mins then add some olive oil on the top of it. You can discard the bones before serving; it will be easier to remove bones from cooked fish.
- Serve it as a side dish or main dish whatever you prefer; good amount steam veggies can go along or just freshly made potato chips.
- Enjoy!!!!!
- Tip: Fish is one of the healthiest foods ever known ... but as little it's cooked it's best for the health.... steamed fish is most healthy.
- Try it! Hope you like....
- Ps: - If u like my recipes, please rate it as it inspires me to write more. Thank you very much.... :-)

111.   Striped Bass In Walnut Sauce Recipe

Serving: 6 | Prep: | Cook: 20mins |Ready in:

Ingredients

- 3 ounces ground walnuts
- 8 cloves garlic peeled
- 1/2 cup flat leaf parsley chopped

- 1/2 teaspoon sweet Spanish paprika
- 2-1/4 cups fish stock
- 1/2 teaspoon salt
- 1/2 teaspoon freshly ground black pepper
- 1/4 cup olive oil
- 6 striped bass filets
- 6 walnuts coarsely chopped for garnish

Direction

- Process walnuts, garlic, parsley, paprika, fish stock, salt and pepper in blender until smooth.
- Heat oil in a large skillet and sauté fish for two minutes on each side then add sauce.
- Cover and cook over low heat for 20 minutes.
- Put fish on a serving platter and pour sauce over top.
- Garnish with coarsely chopped walnuts and serve immediately.

112.   Striped Bass With Green Curry Sauce Recipe

Serving: 4 | Prep: | Cook: 25mins | Ready in:

Ingredients

- 1/2 cup packed fresh cilantro leaves
- 2 scallions cut into large pieces
- 2 tablespoons fresh lime juice
- 3 tablespoons flaked coconut
- 1 large jalapeno pepper sliced
- 1-1/2 teaspoons ground cumin
- 1 teaspoon salt
- 1 teaspoon freshly ground black pepper
- 1 cup long grain rice
- 1 teaspoon turmeric
- 4 striped bass fillets with skin on and any visible bones removed

Direction

- In a food processor or blender, combine the cilantro, scallions, lime juice, coconut,

jalapeño, cumin, 1/2 teaspoon of the salt and black pepper.
- Add 1/4 cup water and process until the green curry paste is smooth and well combined.
- In a medium saucepan, combine rice, 2 tablespoons of the green curry paste, 2-1/2 cups water, turmeric and the remaining 1/4 teaspoon salt.
- Bring to a boil then reduce to a simmer.
- Cover and cook 17 minutes.
- Preheat grill to a medium heat then hen spread remaining green curry paste on the skinless side of the fish.
- Spray the rack with nonstick cooking spray.
- Grill fish skin side down for 5 minutes.
- Serve immediately.

113.   Striped Bass With Toasted Shallot Vinaigrette And Spinach Recipe

Serving: 4 | Prep: | Cook: 20mins | Ready in:

Ingredients

- 1/2 cup plus 3 tablespoons extra-virgin olive oil
- 3 shallots, sliced into rings
- 1 tablespoon capers chopped
- 1 tablespoon red wine vinegar
- kosher salt and pepper
- 4 6-ounce pieces striped bass or halibut
- 2 bunches spinach (about 1 pound), trimmed

Direction

- In a saucepan, over medium-low heat, combine 1/2 cup of the oil and the shallots. Simmer until the shallots are light golden brown, about 12 minutes.
- Transfer to a bowl and stir in the capers, vinegar, 1/4 teaspoon salt, and 1/4 teaspoon pepper; set aside.

- Heat 1 tablespoon of the oil in a large skillet over medium-high heat.
- Season the fish with 1/4 teaspoon salt and 1/4 teaspoon pepper and cook until opaque, about 4 minutes per side. Divide among plates.
- Wipe out the skillet and heat the remaining oil over medium heat. Add the spinach, 1/2 teaspoon salt, and 1/4 teaspoon pepper. Cook, stirring, until wilted, 2 to 3 minutes.
- Serve with the striped bass, drizzle the vinaigrette over the top.
- Try serving with some garlicky mashed potatoes, with a sprinkling of crunchy bonito flakes on top.
- Enjoy!! These are for you! Just hit 'enter' after every step.

---

114. Tonys Fried Sea Bass With Leeks And Creamy Coconut Grits Recipe

Serving: 4 | Prep: | Cook: 15mins | Ready in:

Ingredients

- For Fried Fish:
- 4 Chilean sea bass fillets (center cut, no skin)
- 2 cups Sweet rice flour
- 1 tbsp white pepper
- 1 tbsp kosher salt
- chili oil(to taste)
- canola oil for frying
- ~~~~~~~~~~~~~~~~~~~~~~~~~~~~~~~~~~~ ~~~~~~~~~~~~~~~~~~~
- Sauce:
- 1 large leek, cleaned and thinly sliced (white & light green part only)
- 7 garlic cloves, peeled and minced
- 2 tbsp fish sauce
- 1Tbsp lime juice
- ½ cup sugar
- water
- ~~~~~~~~~~~~~~~~~~~~~~~~~~~~~~~~~~~ ~~~~~~~~~~~~~~~~~~~

- coconut Grits:
- 4 fresh shitake mushrooms, fine dice
- Quick grits (4 servings worth)
- ½ cup coconut milk
- ~~~~~~~~~~~~~~~~~~~~~~~~~~~~~~~~~ ~~~~~~~~~~~~~~~~~~~
- Garnish:
- Saifun noodle threads, fried
- nori (dried sea weed sheet), julienned

Direction

- Season sea bass fillets with white pepper and salt, dredge in rice flour.
- In a non-stick skillet, bring canola oil and chili oil up to temp for shallow frying. After flipping the fillets, spoon oil over the fillets while frying the other side. Pan-fry fillets for approx. 4 mins per side depending on thickness. Using a thermometer, the center should be 130 degrees.
- For the sauce, sprinkle garlic with salt. Strain the garlic and salt in a sauce pan thru a strainer using about 3 cups warm water. Discard minced garlic. Add sugar, fish sauce, and lime juice. Bring to a boil, reduce heat to medium and cook for 20 mins so sauce will thicken slightly (sauce should be delicate, and not too thick). Add leeks to the sauce and cook for about the last 10 minutes until tender.
- In a small pot, add water and bring to boil, add quick grits, and shitake mushrooms, stirring occasionally. Once grits start to thicken after 4 minutes, add coconut milk (cream) stir for about a minute or two more. The grits will thicken up more after removed from heat.
- In a shallow serving bowl, add a dollop of coconut grits, put fish on top, spoon some of the leeks on top of the fish, ladle some of the sauce around the bowl, garnish with saifun noodle and nori.

115. Sea Bass Cuban Style Recipe

Serving: 2 | Prep: | Cook: 15mins | Ready in:

Ingredients

- 2 tablespoons extra virgin olive oil
- 1 1/2 cups thinly sliced white onions
- 2 tablespoons minced garlic
- 4 cups seeded, chopped plum tomatoes
- 1 1/2 cups dry white wine
- 2/3 cup sliced stuffed green olives
- 1/4 cup drained capers
- 1/8 teaspoon red pepper flakes
- 4 (6 ounce) fillets sea bass
- 2 tablespoons butter
- 1/4 cup chopped fresh cilantro

Direction

- Heat oil in a large skillet over medium heat. Sauté onions until soft. Stir in garlic, and sauté about 1 minute. Add tomatoes, and cook until they begin to soften. Stir in wine, olives, capers, and red pepper flakes. Heat to a simmer.
- Place sea bass into sauce. Cover, and gently simmer for 10 to 12 minutes, or until fish flakes easily with a fork. Transfer fish to a serving plate, and keep warm.
- Increase the heat, and add butter to sauce. Simmer until the sauce thickens. Stir in cilantro. Serve sauce over fish.

Chapter 3: Mahi Mahi Recipes

***

116. Baja Mahi Mahi Recipe

Serving: 2 | Prep: | Cook: 15mins | Ready in:

Ingredients

- 2 Mahi Mahi filets
- 1 Avacado
- cilantro
- 1-2 limes
- 2 roma tomatos
- 4oz tequila
- salt
- pepper
- oil
- herb butter

Direction

- For salsa, chop avocado, tomato and cilantro coarsely, combine and toss with lime juice, salt and pepper to taste then sit in fridge.
- Preheat oven to 350.
- Heat 3 tablespoons olive oil in oven-safe pan until the oil is almost smoking.
- Pat mahi filets dry.
- Coat both sides with herb butter (or use herb-infused olive oil).
- Place filets in pan; sear filets on each side until caramelized, about 1-2 minutes.
- Once sides are caramelized, place pan in oven for 4 minutes.
- Remove from oven, plate fish, deglaze pan with tequila, a teaspoon of herb butter, and a squeeze of lime juice.
- Top with salsa and serve.

117. Baked Mahi Mahi Recipe

Serving: 2 | Prep: | Cook: 25mins | Ready in:

Ingredients

- 2 6-ounce Mahi-Mahi fillets
- 1/4 cup Dale's seasoning

- 1/4 cup scallion, sliced
- 1/4 cup tomato, chopped
- 2 cloves garlic, minced
- 2 lemon wedges, optional

Direction

- Preheat oven to 375 degrees Fahrenheit.
- Place Mahi-Mahi fillets in a glass baking dish. Pour Dale's Seasoning over Mahi-Mahi fillets and place in refrigerator for 10 minutes.
- Rinse and dry scallion and tomato. Slice Scallion into thin slices. Chop tomato and mince garlic.
- Remove Mahi-Mahi fillets from the fridge and top with Scallion, Tomato and Garlic.
- Place in preheated oven and bake for 20-25 minutes.
- Fillets are done when the meat easily pulls away with a fork.
- Remove from baking dish, transfer to serving plate and serve immediately.
- Squeeze fresh lemon juice over each fillet, if desired.

---

118.   Brazilian Fish Stew

Serving: 0 | Prep: | Cook: | Ready in:

Ingredients

- 2 cups water
- 1 cup uncooked white rice
- 1 tablespoon olive oil
- 1 yellow onion, thinly sliced
- 1 teaspoon salt, plus more to taste
- 2 tablespoons tomato paste
- 4 cloves minced garlic
- 2 teaspoons paprika
- 1 teaspoon ground cumin
- cayenne pepper to taste
- 1 (14 ounce) can full-fat coconut milk
- 1 teaspoon soy sauce
- 1 red or yellow bell pepper, halved and thinly sliced

- 2 eaches jalapeno peppers, seeded and thinly sliced
- ¼ cup chopped green onion
- 1 ½ pounds sea bass fillets, cut into chunks
- 1 pinch salt
- ¼ cup chopped cilantro leaves
- 2 tablespoons freshly squeezed lime juice

Direction

- Bring water and rice to a boil in a saucepan. Reduce heat to medium-low, cover, and simmer until rice is tender and liquid has been absorbed, 20 to 25 minutes.
- Heat olive oil in a skillet over medium heat. Add onions and 1 teaspoon salt. Cook and stir just until onions start to get soft, 3 or 4 minutes. Add tomato paste, garlic, paprika, cumin, and cayenne pepper. Continue cooking about 3 minutes. Pour in coconut milk and add soy sauce. When mixture starts to bubble, let it simmer about 5 minutes.
- Increase heat to medium-high. Stir in bell peppers, jalapeno peppers, and green onions. Let mixture come back to a simmer. Transfer fish to skillet; stir. Cover and cook over medium-high heat until fish starts to flake, about 5 minutes. Remove from heat. Add salt, cilantro, and lime juice; stir carefully to avoid breaking up the fish. Serve with rice.
- Nutrition Facts
- Per Serving:
- 399 calories; protein 25.6g 51% DV; carbohydrates 32.6g 11% DV; fat 19g 29% DV; cholesterol 46.9mg 16% DV; sodium 599.8mg 24% DV.

---

119.   Cajun Mahi Mahi And Beurre Blanc Recipe

Serving: 6 | Prep: | Cook: 30mins | Ready in:

Ingredients

- 6 mahi mahi fillets(8oz each) can sub sword or monkfish, if desired
- about 1/4 cup Creole or cajun seasoning blend(your favorite purchased, or make your own. There are several great options, but basically, it should include kosher or sea salt, fresh ground pepper, cayenne, garlic, onion, paprika with our without some citrus zest and herbs)
- olive oil
- For the Beurre Blanc
- 1/2 cup white wine
- 1 lemon
- 1 lime
- about 1/4 cup heavy cream
- 2 sticks cold butter, cut each stick into 16 pieces
- 1t hot sauce

Direction

- For Beurre Blanc
- In medium, heavy sauce pan, heat wine and juice from the lemon over medium high heat until about 1-2T of liquid remains.
- Add cream and maintain a high simmer to reduce by about half.
- Reduce heat and add butter, one piece at a time, whisking well between each until melted. Immediately add next piece and continue until all butter is incorporated.
- Remove from heat and add the juice from the lime and the hot sauce and whisk once more. Set aside and keep warm, if possible (if not, it's okay, just heat it briefly prior to plating).
- For Fish
- Heat a little olive oil in a large heavy skillet or on a griddle, etc. (you can also just grill or broil this, if desired).
- Drizzle cleaned, dry fish with a little olive oil.
- Sprinkle first side of each piece with the Cajun seasoning.
- Cook, seasoning side down for about 3 minutes, sprinkle up side with a little more of the seasoning, then flip and cook another 2 minutes. You only wanna cook until the fish flakes easily. Do not overcook.

- Serve with the beurre blanc and extra lemon wedges, if desired.
- (This sauce is ridiculously delicious over any veggie you may happen to serve (hello, asparagus), too!).

120.   Cioppino Recipe

Serving: 4 | Prep: | Cook: 60mins | Ready in:

Ingredients

- 1 large yellow onion, finely chopped
- 6 cloves garlic, minced
- 3 tbsp. olive oil
- 1 jalapeno pepper, whole
- 1 can whole peeled tomatoes (preferably San Marzano) in juice
- 4 sprigs fresh thyme (or 1 tsp. dried)
- 2 sprigs fresh rosemary (or 1 tsp. dried & chopped)
- 4 sprigs fresh oregano (or 1 tsp. dried)
- 2 bay leaves
- Kosher or Grey salt, to taste
- fresh ground black pepper, to taste
- 1 tsp. cayenne pepper
- 2 tsp. Old Bay or Chesapeake seafood seasoning (or more to taste)
- 1 jar clam juice
- 4 c. seafood stock or fish buillion
- 1 c. dry white wine
- 2 thick firm white fish fillets, such as cod, pollock, halibut, tilapia, mahi mahi or flounder, cut into 2 inch cubes
- 12 littleneck clams, scrubbed and rinsed
- 12 mussels, beards removed, scrubbed and rinsed
- 1 lb. sea scallops, cut in halves or 1 lb. bay scallops (optional)
- 1 lb. shrimp, deveined and peeled (you can leave tails on)
- 3 squid tubes (calamari) cut into rings or 1 bag frozen calamari (rings and baby squid), thawed

- 1 lb. alaskan crab, king crab or Dungeness crab clusters, broken into smaller pieces

Direction

- In a large stock pot, sauté the onion and garlic in olive oil over medium heat until fragrant.
- Add a pinch of salt to "sweat "the onion further and add the jalapeno pepper, whole and all of the other herbs and spices.
- Sauté for 1 minute more and add the tomatoes, crushing with your hands over the pot while adding, reserve juice from tomatoes.
- Gently simmer over medium heat for about 5 minutes or until tomatoes have broken up and cooked down.
- Add clam juice, reserved tomato juice and stock, bring to a boil.
- Reduce heat, cover and simmer for 30 minutes.
- Remove cover, add wine and simmer for an additional 10 minutes.
- Add fish cubes, sea scallops if used (do not add bay scallops for another 5 minutes to avoid overcooking), clams and mussels, cook for 5 minutes
- Add crab pieces, shrimp, squid and bay scallops if used and simmer, stirring frequently another 10 minutes or until clams and mussels have opened, fish is opaque and flaky and shrimp have turned pink.
- Discard any unopened clams or mussels.
- Serve in large bowls with crusty bread, crab mallets or lobster crackers & lots of napkins - enjoy!

121.   Coconut Mahi Mahi With Passion Fruit Sauce Recipe

Serving: 4 | Prep: | Cook: 20mins |Ready in:

Ingredients

- 1 cup unsweetened coconut, shredded
- 3/4 cup flour
- 1/2 cup milk
- 2 eggs
- 1 teaspoon salt plus more for the fish
- 4 6-ounce mahi mahi fillets, about 1/2-inch thick
- Freshly ground black pepper
- 2 tablespoons EVOO
- 2 tablespoons unsalted butter
- *
- For passion fruit Sauce
- 1/2 cup dry white wine
- 2 shallots, peeled and minced
- 2 teaspoons fresh lime juice
- 1/4 cup passion fruit purée
- 4 tablespoons unsalted butter

Direction

- * PASSION FRUIT SAUCE
- Bring the wine, shallots, lime juice and passion fruit purée to a boil in a small, heavy saucepan and let it cook down until it's reduced to 1/3 cup, about 5 minutes.
- Remove the pan from the heat, and whisk in the butter until it's melted and the sauce is slightly thickened.
- * FISH
- Put the coconut, flour, milk and eggs in separate, shallow dishes.
- Beat the eggs well with 1 teaspoon salt, (This breaks up the whites and makes for a more even coating.)
- Sprinkle the fillets with salt and pepper.
- Dip filets one at a time in the milk, the flour, the egg mixture and then the coconut, coating them well on both sides.
- Place the fillets on a wire rack, and refrigerate for at least 10 minutes to help the coating adhere.(Fish can be coated, covered and refrigerated for up to 3 or 4 hours before cooking.)
- Heat the oil and butter in a 12-inch skillet over medium-high heat.
- Sauté the fillets, turning once, until the coconut is golden brown and the fish is opaque throughout, about 8 minutes.
- Transfer the fish to dinner plates, drizzle with passion fruit sauce, and serve immediately.

122. Coriander Crusted Mahi Mahi Recipe

Serving: 2 | Prep: | Cook: 20mins | Ready in:

Ingredients

- 6 ounce mahi mahi filet
- 1 teaspoon salt
- 1 teaspoon pepper
- 1 teaspoon coriander
- 6 tiny bay shrimp
- 3 ounces plain risotto
- 12 ounces chicken stock
- 1 tablespoon butter
- 1 tablespoon parmesan cheese
- 1 teaspoon chives
- 1 teaspoon salt
- 1 teaspoon pepper

Direction

- Season mahi-mahi with salt and pepper and coat one side with coriander.
- Sauté until coriander is lightly toasted then place in the oven.
- Sauté shrimp then add in the rice along with the chicken stock.
- Cook slowly, stirring constantly.
- When rice is cooked, stir in butter, parmesan, salt and pepper.
- Serve mahi-mahi over rice.

123. Fish Fillet Florentine Recipe

Serving: 4 | Prep: | Cook: 30mins | Ready in:

Ingredients

- 1 1/4 lbs mild white fish (tilapia, swai, halibut, mahi mahi)
- 6 oz bagged, already washed baby spinach
- 8 oz sliced button mushrooms
- 2 large or 3 medium shallots
- salt and pepper to taste
- 2 Tbsp butter
- Topping:
- 3/4 plain bread crumbs
- 1/4 cup grated paremsan or romano cheese
- 4 Tbsp butter

Direction

- Preheat the oven to 350 F.
- Melt the 2 Tbsp butter in a large skillet and sauté the shallots over low to medium heat. When they are limp, add the mushrooms and stir to coat. Add the spinach and cover for 2-3 minutes to wilt. Add salt and pepper to taste.
- Stir gently to make sure the spinach is wilted uniformly and flavors are mixed. (Don't overcook, it will be cooking more in the oven.)
- Pour sautéed vegetables into the bottom of a small to medium casserole dish.
- Lay the fish in an even layer over the vegetables.
- Prepare the topping by melting the 4 Tbsp of butter and mixing in the grated cheese and bread crumbs.
- Sprinkle the topping evenly over the top of the fish.
- Bake for 30 minutes or until the fish is firm and flaky.

124. Fish Tacos Recipe

Serving: 6 | Prep: | Cook: 45mins | Ready in:

Ingredients

- 1 1/4 pound mahi-mahi fillet, cut into 12 pieces
- 1 medium red onion
- 7 tablespoons fresh lime juice, divided

- 1/2 cup cider vinegar
- 1/4 cup sugar
- 1/4 cup chopped cilantro
- 1 tablespoon olive oil
- 2/3 cup mayonnaise
- 2/3 cup crema or sour cream
- 12 medium sized corn tortillas
- 6-8 radishes
- 1 or 2 firm-ripe avocados
- 1/2 small head, thinly sliced green cabbage
- 2 limes

Direction

- Very thinly slice onion crosswise into rings with slicer. Set slicer aside. Heat vinegar, sugar, and 1/2 teaspoon salt in a small heavy nonreactive saucepan until sugar has dissolved. Remove from heat and stir in onion, then let stand until ready to use (about 25 minutes).
- Meanwhile, stir 1/4 cup lime juice together with cilantro, oil, and 1/2 teaspoon salt. Add fish and toss to coat, then marinate at room temperature 15 minutes.
- Whisk together mayonnaise, crema, 1/2 teaspoon salt, and remaining 3 tablespoons lime juice to make sauce.
- Preheat a gas grill with burners on high, covered, 10 minutes, then reduce heat to medium-high.
- Thread each piece of fish onto a skewer (discard marinade). Wrap exposed part of each skewer in heavy-duty foil to protect it from charring.
- Wrap tortillas in 2 foil packages and warm on grill, turning once, about 3 minutes total.
- Oil grill rack, then grill fish, covered, turning once, until opaque and just cooked through (for mahi-mahi), about 6 minutes total, about 4 minutes.
- Very thinly slice radishes with slicer. Halve, pit, and peel avocados, then cut into 1/2-inch-thick slices. Drain onions.
- Serve fish with tortillas, crema sauce, onions, and remaining toppings.

---

125. Fish Tacos With Tequila Lime Aioli, Red Cabbage Slaw And Avocado Salsa Recipe

Serving: 0 | Prep: | Cook: 2hours |Ready in:

Ingredients

- 1 package taco-sized corn tortillas (8 inch)
- 1 lb Mahi Mahi (1 lb makes about 8 tacos total)
- For the fish Marinade
- 1 tablespoon tequila
- 1 teaspoon ground cumin
- 1 teaspoon salt
- 1 teaspoon black pepper
- juice of 1 lime
- For the avocado Salsa
- 4 roma tomatoes, diced, some (or all if you like) of the seeds removed
- 2 tablespoons chopped cilantro leaves (or parsley - I do half parsley half cilantro as cilantro has a strong taste not everyone loves)
- 1 avocado, slightly mashed up - you still want some chunks to remain
- 1/2 red onion, minced
- 1 teaspoon minced garlic
- 1 jalapeno, seeded and minced
- 1-2 lime(s), juiced
- 1 tsp honey
- 2 tablespoons canola oil
- salt and pepper
- For the tequila lime Aioli
- 3 tablespoons premium tequila
- 1 lime, juiced
- 8 ounces sour cream
- 2 teaspoons minced garlic
- 1/2 teaspoon ground cumin
- 2 tablespoons minced cilantro leaves
- salt and pepper
- red cabbage Slaw
- 1/4 cup rice vinegar
- 1 tablespoon sugar
- 2 tablespoons canola oil
- 1/4 head red cabbage, finely shredded

- 1 large carrot, cut into fine julienne
- 1/4 cup chopped cilantro (or parsley) leaves
- salt and pepper

Direction

- First, work on the aioli. This needs to chill for at least an hour. Mix all the ingredients, stirring well, cover and put in the refrigerator.
- Next, make the marinade. Combine all the ingredients, toss the fish (cut into individual-sized pieces) to coat, cover and put in the refrigerator. Let marinate at least 15 minutes.
- The next step is the red cabbage slaw. Combine all the ingredients, cover and put in the refrigerator. It doesn't really have to chill, but letting the flavors meld a bit is worth it. I shred the carrot and cabbage in the food processor to save time/sanity.
- Finally, work on the avocado salsa. It's best to leave this until last to ensure that the avocado doesn't get too mushy or brown. The lime juice will help it keep its color. They key here is to make sure you don't make the avocado too smooth - some chunks are what make it more salsa-like and less of a guacamole. Cover and put in the refrigerator.
- Get your marinated fish. Heat a couple tablespoons of oil in a frying pan. Place the fish in the pan. Cook on all sides for about 3-4 minutes per side. Once the fish starts to flake, you know you're done.
- In a small frying pan, heat about 1-2 tsp. oil. Lightly fry a tortilla on both sides until it's pliable, just a couple of minutes. Let cool slightly (but not too much or it will become stiff again, and will rip when you make the taco). Now build a taco. First fish, then salsa, slaw and top with aioli. The aioli has some kick - use less if you don't want it to be as spicy.
- This takes about two hours since the aioli needs at least an hour in the refrigerator, plus making all the various components takes longer than you might think. Once you get to the fish cooking part it only takes a few minutes before it's time to eat. If you were

serving this to guests, you could do most of the prep work ahead of time, then start cooking the fish when you're ready to eat.
- If you choose, you can deep fry the fish. Personally, I think this takes away from the flavors of the fish and the marinade, and replaces them with breading. If you do want to fry them, a panko-based breading is ideal.

---

126. Fish With Blood Orange Avocado Amp Red Onion Salsa Recipe

Serving: 2 | Prep: | Cook: 10mins | Ready in:

Ingredients

- 1 blood orange (or regular orange)
- 1/2 cup 1/3-inch cubes avocado
- 1/3 cup chopped red onion
- 2 teaspoons minced red jalapeño
- 2 teaspoons fresh lime juice
- 2 teaspoons olive oil
- 2 6-ounce mahi-mahi fillets

Direction

- Using small sharp knife, cut peel and white pith from orange. Working over small bowl, cut between membranes to release segments. Add avocado, onion, jalapeño, and lime juice to oranges in bowl; stir gently to blend. Season salsa to taste with salt.
- Heat oil in heavy medium skillet over medium-high heat. Sprinkle fish with salt and pepper. Add fish to skillet and sauté until brown and cooked through, about 5 minutes per side.
- Place 1 fillet on each of 2 plates. Spoon salsa atop fish and serve.

127. Garlic And Herb Crusted Mahi Mahi With Salsa Recipe

Serving: 4 | Prep: | Cook: 20mins | Ready in:

Ingredients

- 1 cup seeded and diced Japanese cucumber
- 1/2 cup seeded and diced red tomato
- 3 yellow pear tomatoes cut in half
- 2 tablespoons finely minced ginger
- 1/4 cup finely minced onion
- 2 tablespoons soy sauce
- 2 tablespoons spicy sesame oil
- 1/2 teaspoon salt
- 1 teaspoon freshly ground black pepper
- garlic herb Crust:
- 1/4 cup coarsely chopped garlic
- 1 teaspoon chopped fresh parsley
- 1 tablespoon chopped fresh basil
- 1 teaspoon chopped fresh tarragon
- 4 anchovy fillets
- 4 shallots roughly chopped
- 1 teaspoon virgin olive oil
- 4 mahi mahi fillets
- 1 teaspoon canola oil

Direction

- Combine all salsa ingredients in mixing bowl and stir until well combined then chill.
- Place all crust ingredients in a food processor or blender and puree.
- Coat one side of each fillet with crust and allow to sit 15 minutes.
- Heat canola in non-stick sauté pan and sear crusted fillets over high heat for 1 minute per side.
- Place fish crust side up on 4 serving plates and spoon salsa over and around each serving.

128. Ginger Glazed Mahi Mahi Recipe

Serving: 4 | Prep: | Cook: 7mins | Ready in:

Ingredients

- 3 tablespoons honey
- 3 tablespoons soy sauce
- 3 tablespoons balsamic vinegar
- 1 teaspoon grated fresh ginger root
- 1 clove garlic, crushed or to taste
- 2 teaspoons olive oil
- 4 (6 ounce) mahi mahi fillets (I use basa or flake here)
- salt and pepper to taste
- 1 tablespoon vegetable oil

Direction

- In a shallow glass dish, stir together the honey, soy sauce, balsamic vinegar, ginger, garlic and olive oil. Season fish fillets with salt and pepper, and place them into the dish. If the fillets have skin on them, place them skin side down. Cover, and refrigerate for 20 minutes to marinate.
- Heat vegetable oil in a large skillet over medium-high heat. Remove fish from the dish, and reserve marinade. Fry fish for 4 to 6 minutes on each side, turning only once, until fish flakes easily with a fork. Remove fillets to a serving platter and keep warm.
- Pour reserved marinade into the skillet, and heat over medium heat until the mixture reduces to a glaze consistently. Spoon glaze over fish, and serve immediately.
- I don't always make it with the reserve glaze but just barbecued in the marinade is beautiful.

129. Grilled Fish Tacos Recipe

Serving: 6 | Prep: | Cook: 8mins | Ready in:

Ingredients

- 2 pounds fresh grouper, snapper, mahi-mahi or haddock fillets
- 8-12 flour tortillas, soft
- 1 head shredded lettuce
- marinade
- 2 tablespoons olive oil
- 2 tablespoons garlic, minced
- 1 teaspoon cumin
- 1 teaspoon chili powder
- 2 tablespoons lime juice

Direction

- Combine fish fillets with marinade mixture and refrigerate for 1 hour. Grill fillets on a hot grill. Chop cooked fillets into bite-sized pieces. Fill tortilla with shredded lettuce, fish pieces, and Mango/Avocado Salsa.
- Mango/Avocado Salsa
- 2 mangos, diced medium
- 1 avocado, diced medium
- 1/4 cup red onion, diced
- 1 tablespoon jalapeno pepper, minced
- 2 tablespoons cilantro, chopped
- 1 tablespoon lime juice
- 1 tablespoon olive oil
- Salt and pepper to taste
- Preparation
- Combine all ingredients; mix well and refrigerate until ready to use.

130.　　Grilled Fish WMelon Avacado Salsa Recipe

Serving: 4 | Prep: | Cook: 10mins | Ready in:

Ingredients

- 1 Ripe Avacado - Diced
- 1 C honeydew melon - Diced
- 1/2 C red onion - Diced
- 1/2 C Fresh cilantro - chopped
- 3 T fresh lime juice

- 4 thick fish filets such as Mahi Mahi, halibut, Swordfish
- 1 T olive oil
- 5 T Jamaican Jerk seasoning

Direction

- Prepare BBQ - med high heat - brush the grill with some oil so the fish won't stick.
- Toss first 5 ingredients, season with salt and pepper to taste.
- Place Jamaican seasoning in a shallow plate. Brush fish with olive oil and press into the seasoning on both sides.
- Grill fish until just opaque in center - about 4 min. per side.
- Serve immediately with Salsa.

131.　　Grilled Mahi Mahi Fillets With Asparagus Orange And Sesame Recipe

Serving: 4 | Prep: | Cook: 20mins | Ready in:

Ingredients

- 4 portions, 6 to 8 ounces each, mahi mahi fillets
- salt and pepper
- 2 limes, juiced
- 3 tablespoons dark tamari soy sauce
- 2 inches fresh ginger root, grated, about 1½ tablespoons
- 1 tablespoon vegetable or canola oil
- 20 blades fresh chives, chopped or 3 scallions, thinly sliced, for garnish
- Asparagus:
- 1 to 1¼ pounds thin asparagus spears
- 2 navel oranges
- 1-inch fresh ginger root
- 2 tablespoons toasted sesame seeds

Direction

- Preheat grill pan to over medium high to high heat. Season mahi-mahi fillets with salt and pepper. Combine the lime juice, dark soy, ginger and a little vegetable or canola oil in a shallow dish. Turn the mahi-mahi in the citrus soy marinade and let it sit for 10 minutes. Grill on a hot grill pan for 6 minutes per side for a 1-inch fillet or until fish is firm and opaque.
- Take 1 spear of asparagus and hold it at each and. Bend the asparagus until it snaps and breaks. Use this spear as your guide on where to trim the ends of your bundle of spears. Using a peeler, make thin long strips of orange zest from both oranges. Cut the ends off the zested oranges and stand them up right on a cutting board. Remove the pith in strips using sharp knife and cutting down from the top of the orange. Discard the pith. When the oranges are both peeled and trimmed, turn them on their sides and slice into ¼-inch rounds, cross sectioning the whole. Set the orange disks aside.
- In a skillet with a cover, bring 1-inch water to a boil with the zest of the oranges and grated fresh gingerroot. Allow the orange zest and ginger to simmer for at least 1 minute then add salt and asparagus spears. Simmer the spears 3 to 5 minutes until just tender. Drain the asparagus. Discard the orange zest and ginger. Assemble a few spears on each dinner plate, layering them back and forth, crisscrossing the spears over orange slices. Sprinkle sesame seeds over asparagus and oranges and top with 1 portion of grilled mahi-mahi. Garnish assembled fish and asparagus with chopped or thinly sliced chives.

132. Grilled Mahi Mahi Recipe

Serving: 4 | Prep: | Cook: 10mins | Ready in:

Ingredients

- 4 Skinless mahi mahi fillets aprox 2 pounds

- 2 tsp kosher salt
- 1/2 cup diced red onion
- 1/4 cup fresh squeezed lime juice
- 1/4 cup fresh squeezed orange juice
- 1 jalapeno minced
- 1/4 cup brown suger packed
- 1/4 cup tequila
- 1 Tbs olive oil
- 1/4 cup fresh chopped cilantro

Direction

- Rub the fillets with kosher salt.
- In a non-reactive, combine the onion, cilantro, lime juice, orange juice, jalapeno, sugar and tequila.
- Mix to dissolve sugar, and add the fillets to the bowl.
- Marinade in refrigerator for 2 hours, turning fillets once after an hour.
- Remove fillets from marinade, lightly coat with olive oil.
- Heat grill to high and place the fillets over direct heat until they are just cooked through but are still moist, approx. 4-5 mins per side.
- While fish is cooking, transfer the marinade to a sauce pan and heat until it is reduced to about 3/4 cup.
- Remove fillets to serving plate and divide sauce equally over them.

133. Grilled Mahi Mahi With Vegetable Slaw Recipe

Serving: 6 | Prep: | Cook: 15mins | Ready in:

Ingredients

- 6 (6 oz.) mahi mahi fish fillets, 1/2" thick
- 3 Tbsp. chopped fresh cilantro
- 2 Tbsp. chopped fresh parsley
- 1/3 cup lemon juice
- 1/4 cup olive oil
- 1 Tbsp. honey

- 4 cloves garlic, minced
- 1/2 tsp. salt
- 1/8 tsp. white pepper
- 2 cups shredded coleslaw mix
- 1 cup shredded cucumber

Direction

- Rinse fish and pat dry with paper towels. For dressing, in a small bowl combine cilantro, lemon peel and juice, oil, honey, garlic, and salt. Mix well. Pour half of dressing over cabbage and cucumber in medium bowl and toss to coat. Cover and refrigerate until ready to serve.
- Place fish fillets into glass baking pan and pour remaining dressing over; turn fish to coat. Cover and refrigerate for 30 minutes.
- Lightly grease indoor electric grill and preheat. Drain fish, discarding marinade. Place fish on the grill rack, tucking under any thin edges. If using a covered grill, close lid.
- Grill until fish flakes easily when tested with a fork, about 2 to 3 minutes per 1/2-inch thickness of fish on a two sided grill. On uncovered grill, cook for 4 to 6 minutes per 1/2-inch thickness of fish, turning once halfway through grilling. Serve the fish with coleslaw mixture.

---

134. Grilled Mahi Mahi With A Chunky Cucumber Cilantro Sauce Recipe

Serving: 4 | Prep: | Cook: 12mins | Ready in:

Ingredients

- !/2 medium cucumber
- 1/4 cup chopped green onions
- 1/4 cup chopped cilantro
- 2 1/2 Tbs olive oil
- 1/8 -1/4 cup chopped red onion
- 2 large garlic cloves chopped very fine (doesn't break up well in food pro.)

- 1 jalapeno (more or less to your taste)
- 1 Tbs balsamic vinegar
- juice of 1 lime
- 4 8 oz fillets mahi mahi
- 1 1/2 tsp cumin
- 1 1/2 tsp. garlic powder
- S&P

Direction

- Pat fish with cumin and garlic powder and S&P.
- Grill about 5-6 minutes on each side.
- While waiting on fish combine cucumber, both onions, cilantro, garlic, jalapeno, balsamic, lime, olive oil and some S&P to taste in food processor. Blend until chunky. If you really prefer it thinner then go ahead and process longer. You may need to add a little more olive oil to get your right consistency. Place a fillet on a plate and top with a generous helping of sauce!

---

135. Grilled Mahi With Mango Papaya Salsa Served Over Curried Couscous Recipe

Serving: 4 | Prep: | Cook: 37mins | Ready in:

Ingredients

- Mahi Mahi:
- 1 lime, juiced
- 4 (8-ounce, 1 1/2-inch thick) portions mahi mahi steak
- A drizzle extra-virgin olive oil
- salt and pepper
- Salsa:
- 1 ripe mango, peeled and diced
- 1 ripe papaya, peeled and diced
- 1/2 ripe pineapple, peeled and diced
- 1/2 red onion, diced
- 1 clove of garlic minced
- 1 Small red bell pepper, seeded and diced

- 1 jalapeno or serrano, seeded and finely chopped
- 1 Inch fresh ginger root, grated or minced
- 1/4 Seedless (European or English) cucumber, peeled and chopped
- 2 tablespoons of chopped cilantro
- 1 lime, juiced
- Couscous:
- 2 cups chicken broth or water
- 2 teaspoons (1 palmful) curry powder or 1 rounded teaspoon mild curry paste
- 1/2 teaspoon coarse salt
- 1 tablespoon extra-virgin olive oil
- 1 Handful raisins or craisins
- 1 cup couscous
- 2 scallions, sliced on an angle
- 1 carrot, shredded or grated
- 1 Navel orange, peeled and chopped
- 2 ounces sliced almonds (available on baking aisle)

Direction

- Preheat grill pan or indoor electric grill to high heat. Squeeze juice of 1 lime over fish. Drizzle steaks with a little oil and rub oil into fish to coat. Season steaks with salt and pepper. Cook steaks 5 minutes on each side on hot grill.
- To assemble salsa, combine all ingredients for salsa in a small bowl.
- To make couscous, bring broth or water to a boil with curry powder, salt, oil, and raisins. Place couscous in a bowl. Add boiling liquid to bowl and cover. Let couscous stand 10 minutes. Fluff couscous with a fork and combine with scallions, carrot, orange pieces, and almonds.
- Top fish with salsa and serve with generous portions of curry couscous.
- Have some gourmet chips on hand for snacking with leftover salsa.
- Yield: 4 servings

136. Grilled Mahi Mahi Ceviche Style Recipe

Serving: 4 | Prep: | Cook: 8mins | Ready in:

Ingredients

- 4 skinless mahi-mahi filets, approximately 2 pounds
- 2 tsp kosher salt
- 1/2 diced red onion
- 1/4 cup freshly squeezed lime juice
- 1/4 cup of orange juice
- 1 tbs minced jalapeno
- 1/4 cup dark brown sugar, packed
- 1/4 cup tequila
- 1 tbs olive oil
- 1/4 cup freshly chopped cilantro leaves

Direction

- Rub the fillets with kosher salt and set aside in a non-reactive bowl
- Combine onion, lime juice, orange juice, jalapeno, sugar, cilantro leaves and tequila, I just put it all in the blender.
- Put filets and mixture into zip lock bag marinade for 2 hours in refrigerator.
- Remove the fillets from the marinade and set it aside.
- Transfer remaining marinade to a saucepan and heat until it is reduced to about 3/4 cup. You may want to start this while fish is reaching room temperature.
- Pat the fillets dry with paper towels and lightly coat with the olive oil.
- Heat grill to med-high and place the fillets over direct heat until they are just cooked through-opaque at the center but still moist, approximately 3-4 mins per side.
- Serve with marinade sauce and extra cilantro on top.
- ENJOY

137.   Grilled Teriyaki Mahi Mahi With Mango Salsa Recipe

Serving: 4 | Prep: | Cook: 10mins | Ready in:

Ingredients

- salsa recipe
- 1/4 cup finely chopped red onion
- 1 tablespoon vegetable oil
- 1 tablespoon fresh lime juice
- 1 tablespoon finely chopped fresh mint
- 1 teaspoon minced jalapeno pepper, with seeds
- 1/4 teaspoon kosher salt
- marinade recipe
- 1/4 cup soy sauce (La Choy is wheat free)
- 1/4 cup sweet sake
- 1 tablespoon vegetable oil
- 1 tablespoon light brown sugar
- 1 teaspoon grated fresh ginger
- 1 teaspoon minced garlic
- 4 mahi mahi fillets, about 6 oz. each and 1 inch thick
- vegetable oil

Direction

- For the salsa: Peel the mango and cut into 1/4 inch diced pieces.
- Put mango pieces in a small bowl with the remaining salsa ingredients; stir to combine.
- Cover bowl with saran wrap and refrigerate until ready to serve.
- For the marinade: In a small bowl, whisk together the soy sauce, sweet sake, vegetable oil, light brown sugar, fresh ginger, and minced garlic; set aside.
- Place the mahi-mahi fillets in a large zip-lock plastic bag.
- Pour marinade into bag; press the air out of the bag and seal tightly.
- Turn/shake the bag to coat fillets with marinade.
- Refrigerate for 20-30 minutes.
- Take fillets out of bag and throw away marinade.
- Brush or spray both sides of fillets with vegetable oil.
- Grill over high heat until fish is opaque throughout, 8 to 10 minutes, turning once halfway through grilling time.
- Serve warm with salsa.

138.   Macadamia Crusted Mahi Mahi Recipe

Serving: 6 | Prep: | Cook: 20mins | Ready in:

Ingredients

- 1/2 pound roasted and salted macadamia nuts
- 1-1/2 cups flour divided
- 1 egg
- 3/4 cup whole milk
- 6 mahi mahi fillets
- 2 tablespoons butter
- 1/2 cup white wine
- 8 ounces crushed pineapple drained and juice reserved
- 1/2 cup whipping cream
- 1 cup cold butter cut into chunks

Direction

- In food processor combine nuts and 3/4 cup flour.
- Process until nuts are chopped medium to fine.
- Make egg wash by beating together egg and milk.
- Dust fillets with remaining flour then dip into egg wash then in the nut mixture.
- Preheat oven to 350.
- Sauté fillets in butter top side first until golden.
- Turn fillets and sauté another 2 minutes to brown other side.
- Transfer to baking pan and finish cooking in preheated oven 15 minutes.
- In medium pan combine wine, juice from canned pineapple and cream.

74

- Cook over low heat until mixture thickens to coat back of spoon stirring constantly.
- This should take about 10 minutes.
- Whisk in cold butter and stir until melted.
- Add reserved pineapple and heat through.
- Divide pineapple sauce among 6 plates.
- Put 1 fillet over sauce on each plate.

139. Macadamia Nut Crusted Mahi Mahi Recipe

Serving: 4 | Prep: | Cook: 10mins | Ready in:

Ingredients

- 4 (4 - 6 ounce) Mahi Mahi or halibut filets, skin removed
- 2 tablespoons coconut milk (or my second favorite coating holder, mayonnaise, but I served this with coconut jasmine rice, so I already had it opened)
- salt and pepper
- 1/2 cup macadamia nuts, toasted and chopped fairly fine by hand or in a food processor
- 1/4 cup panko
- 2 tablespoons macadamia nut oil (or olive oil, or olive oil and butter mix)

Direction

- Spread (spoon?) the coconut milk (or mayo if using that) on one side of the fish. Season with salt and pepper.
- Mix together the panko and chopped macadamia nuts. Dredge the coated side of the fish in the nut/panko mixture.
- In a skillet or sauté pan, heat the oil over medium high heat, add the fish, crusted side down; sauté until browned, turn and cook the other side. About 3 - 4 minutes each side depending on how thick the fish is. The fish should just be opaque and separate easily.

140. Macadamia Nut Mahi Mahi Recipe

Serving: 4 | Prep: | Cook: 30mins | Ready in:

Ingredients

- 1/2 cup macadamia nuts, chopped
- 1 1/2 cup panko
- 4 mahi-mahi fillets, 6 oz each
- salt and white pepper to taste
- togarashi spice, or pinches of crushed red pepper
- 1 cup flour
- 2 eggs, beaten
- 1/4 cup vegetable oil
- Tropical chutney
- 1 small fresh pineapple, chopped
- 1 medium fresh papaya, chopped
- 1 TBS fresh ginger, minced
- 6 TBS granulated sugar
- 1 TBS Sambal (Asian chili sauce)

Direction

- Mix macadamia nuts and Panko, set aside. Season fillets with salt, white pepper and togarashi spice. Dredge in flour, dip in eggs and dredge in breading. Heat a heavy cast iron skillet over a medium high grill. Add oil and when it comes to a shimmer (385-400 degrees) add breaded Mahi, and cook for two to three minutes on each side.
- Chutney
- In a medium saucepan, combine all ingredients except chili paste. Cook on low heat for one hour until mixture has a syrupy consistency. Fold in the chili paste and serve.

141. Mahi Mahi Fishcakes Recipe

Serving: 0 | Prep: | Cook: 30mins | Ready in:

Ingredients

- Leftover Mahi Mahi (or other white fish) – chop in processer just till finely broken up
- Remaining praline sauce – warm just to mix together easily
- Grainy mustard
- Egg
- Minced jalapeno
- S&P
- A few Ritz crackers – for binding, plus coating, finely crushed.

Direction

- Mix all together, form into patties and chill for a couple of hours before frying or baking. I like to make at least one mini-fish cake and cook it right away to see if seasoning/heat/flavors are just right before making all the patties.

---

142.   Mahi Mahi Satay Recipe

Serving: 2 | Prep: | Cook: 15mins | Ready in:

Ingredients

- 1 teaspoon canola oil
- 1 tablespoon rice vinegar
- 1 garlic clove bruised
- 1/2 teaspoon salt
- 1/2 teaspoon freshly ground black pepper
- 3/4 pound mahi mahi
- 2 wooden or metal skewers
- Peanut sauce:
- 2 tablespoons crunchy peanut butter
- 2 tablespoons soy sauce
- 1 tablespoon rice vinegar
- 2 tablespoons granulated sugar
- 6 drops hot pepper sauce
- 1 teaspoon cornstarch
- 1 tablespoon water

Direction

- Preheat grill or broiler then mix oil, rice vinegar and garlic then season with salt and pepper.
- Slice mahi-mahi into strips 1/2" thick and 4" long.
- Marinate 10 minutes turning after 5 minutes to coat all sides then thread fish strips onto skewers.
- Place on grill grates directly over heat then grill 2 minutes per side.
- To make sauce mix peanut butter, soy sauce and vinegar in saucepan until smooth consistency.
- Add sugar and pepper sauce.
- Separately mix cornstarch and water then blend into peanut mixture.
- Cook over medium heat until thick about 2 minutes.
- Serve skewers with some sauce on a plate and serve remaining sauce on the side for dipping.

---

143.   Mahi Mahi Tacos With Ginger Lime Dressing Recipe

Serving: 6 | Prep: | Cook: 10mins | Ready in:

Ingredients

- 1 tablespoon olive oil
- salt and pepper to taste
- 6 (3 ounce) fillets mahi mahi fillets
- 1/3 cup sour cream
- 1 tablespoon lime juice
- 1 teaspoon minced fresh ginger root
- 1/4 teaspoon ground cumin
- 1 dash cayenne pepper
- 1 large mango - peeled, seeded and diced
- 1 cup diced fresh pineapple
- 1 avocado - peeled, pitted and diced
- 1 jalapeno pepper, minced
- 6 (6 inch) flour tortillas, warmed
- 1 cup chopped fresh cilantro

Direction

- Heat the olive oil in a large skillet over medium-high heat.
- Season the mahi-mahi with salt and pepper.
- Cook the fillets in the hot oil until the fish is golden brown on each side, and no longer translucent in the center, about 3 minutes per side.
- Meanwhile, whisk together the sour cream, lime juice, ginger, cumin, cayenne pepper, salt and pepper to taste; set aside.
- Gently combine the mango, pineapple, avocado, and jalapeno in a bowl.
- To assemble, place a cooked mahi-mahi fillet into the center of a warmed tortilla.
- Place a scoop of the mango salsa onto the fish, then drizzle with the sour cream sauce, and finish with a generous pinch of chopped cilantro.

144. Mahi Mahi With Mango Lime Butter Sauce Recipe

Serving: 4 | Prep: | Cook: 30mins |Ready in:

Ingredients

- 3 tbsp unsalted butter
- 1 tsp cornstarch
- 1/8 tsp red pepper flakes
- 1 ea Ripe mango, peeled and diced
- 2 tbsp Granulated sugar
- 1/4 cup dry sherry (or mango nectar for alcohol-free version)
- 2 tbsp Fresh lime juice (1 Lime)
- 1 tsp Finely Grated Fresh lime zest **optional**
- ********
- 4 ea mahi mahi fillets
- 2-3 tbsp unsalted butter, melted

Direction

- Melt butter in small saucepan over medium low heat; blend in cornstarch and red pepper. Add mango, sugar, and sherry (or mango nectar) and bring just to a boil.

- Reduce heat and simmer 5 minutes or until fruit is soft and the sauce has thickened.
- Stir in lime juice and zest and cook an additional 1 or 2 minutes.
- Rinse the fish and pat dry. Brush fish with melted butter.
- Place fish skin side down over medium heat or under a broiler for about 5 minutes.
- Turn and baste the top with more melted butter; cook an additional 5 minutes or until fish flakes easily with a fork.
- Transfer fish fillets to a plate and spoon warm sauce over fish and serve.

145. Mahi Mahi With Cucumber Tomato Salse Recipe

Serving: 2 | Prep: | Cook: 20mins |Ready in:

Ingredients

- 1 lb Mahi Mahi filets
- 1 heaping tsp McCormick's garlic and extra virgin olive oil
- extra extra virgin olive oil
- soy sauce
- kosher salt
- Salsa:
- 1/2 c tomato, chopped
- 1/2 c cucumber, peeled, seeded, and chopped
- 1/2 c sweet onion, chopped
- 1/2 c red bell pepper, chopped
- 1 tb lime juice
- 4 tb fresh cilantro, chopped
- 1 - 2 tsp red pepper flakes
- salt and pepper to taste
- cooked white rice

Direction

- Thaw the mahi-mahi, if frozen, in cold water. When thawed, place in a deep bowl. In a small dish, mix the garlic and oil and a couple of extra dashes of extra virgin olive oil. Add about a Tbsp or soy sauce. Blend and then pour over the mahi-mahi. Sprinkle the fish with kosher salt, cover, and place in refrigerator.

- Begin cooking the rice. Usually, 1 part rice to 2 parts water with a tsp salt for each multiple.
- Prepare the Salsa.
- Chop the tomato, cucumber, onion and red bell peppers. Place in a medium-sized bowl. Add the lime juice, cilantro and pepper flakes. Season to taste with salt and pepper.
- Start the grill.
- When the coals are hot, cover the grill with non-stick aluminum foil. Poke holes in the foil to allow smoke to penetrate through to the fish. Place the mahi-mahi on the foil and cook covered until the fish turns white and flakes.
- Remove and place each filet over a bed of cooked rice. Smother with Salsa. Enjoy.
- A serving variation is to serve over a bed of chopped lettuce, or a bed of lettuce over rice. No matter what variant you choose, this is a delicious, easy and quick way to end a day.
- Goes well with dark beer.

---

146. Mahi Mahi With A Bit Of Attitude Recipe

Serving: 4 | Prep: | Cook: 20mins | Ready in:

Ingredients

- •1 1/2 pounds mahi-mahi
- •2 tablespoons olive oil
- •1 medium onion, chopped
- •4 cloves garlic, minced
- •5 button mushrooms, sliced
- •1/4 cup white cooking wine
- •1 tablespoon fresh lemon juice
- •1 teaspoon cornstarch
- •salt and pepper to taste
- •2 tablespoons water

Direction

- In a large skillet, heat olive oil and cook onions, mushrooms and garlic over medium heat until onions are transparent.
- Cut the mahi-mahi into 3 inch long filets.
- Place the mahi-mahi fillets over the onions, mushrooms and garlic.
- Salt and Pepper the first side of the filets to taste.
- Add white cooking wine and lemon juice.
- Cover and cook 4 to 5 minutes.
- Turn the filets over and salt and pepper the second side to taste.
- Cook 4 to 5 minutes or until fish flakes easily.
- Remove only the fish to a heated plate and keep warm until sauce is ready.
- In the same skillet with all the onions, mushrooms, garlic and cooking wine, raise heat to medium/high.
- Bring to a boil.
- Dissolve cornstarch in the 2 tablespoons of water stir into skillet.
- Stir the sauce continuously until sauce thickens to desired consistency.
- Pour sauce over mahi-mahi fillets. Serve immediately.

---

147. Mediterranean Mahi Mahi A La Nancy Recipe

Serving: 3 | Prep: | Cook: 15mins | Ready in:

Ingredients

- 1/2 small onion, chopped fine
- 3 cloves crushed garlic
- 4 large mushrooms, sliced
- 1/2 bell pepper, chopped
- 1 small jar pimiento peppers, chopped
- 1/4 cup kalamata olives, seeded and sliced
- 1/2 cup chopped tomatoes (use fresh, canned, or sun dried)
- 2 tablespoons olive oil
- salt to taste
- pepper to taste

- Fresh or dried oregano to taste
- 12 ounces mahi mahi fillets
- 1/2 cup heavy whipping cream
- 1/2 cup mixed grated parmesan and asiago cheese
- 1 cup uncooked jasmine rice
- 1 1/2 cups water

Direction

- Bring the water to a boil in a sauce pan. When the water boils, add the rice, reduce heat to low, cover and cook for 15 minutes.
- Heat the oil in a large skillet over medium heat while you chop the onions.
- Add onions.
- Crush the garlic and slice the mushrooms while the onions cook.
- Add the garlic and mushrooms. Stir and toss.
- Slice the bell pepper and add to the pan. Toss and stir.
- Add salt, pepper, and oregano. Taste, and adjust seasoning.
- Either push the vegetables to the side of the pan, or in another skillet heat a dab of olive oil over medium heat and add the mahi-mahi fillets.
- While the mahi-mahi is cooking, slice the Kalamata olives and chop the tomatoes.
- Cook mahi-mahi about 5 minutes on each side.
- When you turn the fish, add the pimientos, Kalamata olives and tomatoes.
- While the fish is cooking, heat the cream in a small sauce pan over medium-low heat.
- When the cream is heated, add the cheese and whisk often until the cheese melts.
- I serve the fish topped with vegetables topped with sauce, with the rice on the side.
- You could also add artichoke hearts and/or asparagus.
- Serve with a sparkling chardonnay.

148.   Munchy Crunchy Mahi Mahi With Sauteed Squash Onion N G G Garlic Recipe

Serving: 2 | Prep: | Cook: 20mins | Ready in:

Ingredients

- 2 fresh or fresh-frozen mahi-mahi filets
- washed and patted dry
- 2 scrambled eggs with salt and pepper added
- 1 cup flour
- after the popcorn is popped remove kernal (it is worth the short time it takes to make such a crunchy 'breading'
- 1 cup breadcrumbs combined with one cup 'blenderized' popped popcorn
- dash chili powder
- ------
- 2 yellow squash , washed ,peeled and julliened
- 2 zuchinni, washed, peeled and julliened
- 1 white onion peeled , halved and sliced into strips
- 4 cloves slivered garlic
- place in bowl together with a small amount of kosher salt , ground pepper and chili powder

Direction

- Heat oil in 2 separate pans - one on low, the other, medium high.
- Prepare filets:
- Egg
- Flour
- Egg
- Breadcrumb/popcorn mixture
- ---
- Fry fish in hotter pan until crispy golden brown.
- While sautéing vegetables quickly in other skillet, remove fish to a paper towel and quickly drain.
- Serve immediately with your favorite fish sauce or as is.
- Plate with sautéed vegetables.

149. Panko/asiago Crusted Mahi W/crimini&squash Risotto Recipe

Serving: 2 | Prep: | Cook: 1hours30mins | Ready in:

Ingredients

- This is my "dinner tonite" meal--panko/grated Asiago Encrusted (locally caught) Mahi-Mahi over Crimini mushroom/Local Organic yellow squash Risotto, served with a crusty baguette, and paired with Bella Sera 2008 Pinot Grigio.
- I attached a couple of photos, and will try to explain the steps for preparing the meal, instead of the parts separately, since I feel that the most challenging part of cooking is getting everything to the table at the right moment and at the perfect timing for each dish. I can tell you that it is not easy, and I admire the professional chefs (as well as all the support staff) who have to do this on a grand scale many times each night!
- List of all Ingredients:
- (2) Four to six ounce FRESH Mahi Mahi filets (Try to source it from sustainable practice sources, which is not as difficult as it sounds--no matter where you are, modern shipping methods will make it possible to receive good quality product; online sources of meat proteins are extremely numerous)
- **kosher or sea salt, fresh cracked black pepper, and a bit of tarragon "to taste"
- (1/4) cup all purpose flour for dusting the filets
- (1/2) cup panko bread Crumbs
- (1/2) cup freshly-grated Dry asiago cheese
- (1) egg
- (1/4) cup milk
- (1) large or (2) medium summer squash--try your local organic farms or even your neighbor for the best-tasting varieties!
- (6 oz.) sliced crimini mushrooms--even these can be sourced locally in a lot of locations, or search the web for small producers....fungus is the ultimate organic food LOL
- (1) cup arborio or other short-grain rice
- (1-1/2) cups chicken stock
- (1/2) cup good-quality white wine (I used the same wine that I drank with dinner!)
- (2) TBSP extra virgin olive oil (I like cold-pressed)
- (1) Tsp (or 2 cloves) Chopped or minced garlic
- (1/4 to 1/2) cup freshly Grated Dry asiago cheese--amount depends on consistency of risotto desired
- salt, black pepper, tarragon (fresh or dried), all will be used "to taste"
- Optional, for garnish--deep fried Sweet basil leaves (this makes a very nice presentation, as you can see in the photo, and is delightfully edible, as well!)

Direction

- I prep the mushrooms and squash--slice the mushrooms and cube the squash...then sauté them on the stovetop in one tablespoon EVOO and one Tablespoon unsalted butter. Be sure to season with salt, pepper and tarragon to taste (tarragon is strong--be sure to taste along the way) . Set aside and start the rice....
- I prepare the Risotto rice in the classical way until it is 3/4 of the way done and then add the mushrooms and squash, stir, remove it from the heat and let it rest a bit before you add the last 1/2 cup of stock (while you are fixing the fish).
- Prepare the crusting mixtures in 3 different bowls--first one has AP flour, a pinch of salt and pepper; the second has the egg and milk with a pinch of salt and a few turns of the pepper mill (whisk until pale yellow and uniform consistency); in the third bowl, blend the panko crumbs and asiago cheese well and add a pinch of salt and a few turns of the pepper mill.
- Heat 2 TBSP EVOO on medium to medium-high heat (depending on your stove--they vary widely in what is just the right temp. Too hot

and you have burned crust and raw fish; too low and you have soggy, pale crust and bad texture on the fish--and a tendency to overcook and it gets dry--yuck), add the tarragon to the flesh of the fish, a pinch of salt and a few turns of the pepper mill to each side of each filet, and then dredge the filets in the flour, just enough to dust them--shaking off the excess, then dip them in the egg/milk bath, and transfer to the panko/asiago mixture and press the crumbs firmly onto the surfaces of the fish. Place the filets in the well-heated sauté pan, and sauté until the breading is golden-brown, and the fish is cooked through, but still tender--this takes approximately 3-4 minutes on each side for a 1" thick filet.

- While the fish is cooking, return the risotto to the heat, (this is where the extra set of hands is helpful!) add the last 1/2 cup of stock, and cook, stirring constantly, until the consistency is just starting to turn creamy and the grains are tender, but still "al dente", then add the cheese, stir until the desired creaminess, and plate.
- If you have been keeping an eye on the filets, they should also be ready to plate as soon as you get the risotto on the plate. Place the risotto in the middle of the plate and place the filet on top. Garnish with the fried basil.
- If you have someone to help you in the kitchen, this goes MUCH more smoothly, and the stress level is lower. LOL! It is just the last minute when two things need to be done at once...stirring constantly the risotto, and making sure the filets are sautéing nicely and not over-cooking.

---

150.   Savory Shrimp Scallop Kabobs Recipe

Serving: 4 | Prep: | Cook: 15mins | Ready in:

Ingredients

- 1/2 pound scallops (or) halibut or Mahi Mahi
- 3/4 pound shrimp(tails on)
- 30 chunks cantaloupe
- 30 chunks honeydew melon
- 30 medium-size mushroom caps
- 1/4 cup lemon juice
- 4 Tbsp butter, melted (do not substitute)
- BRIE BASTE
- 1/4 cup brie cheese
- 1/4 cup Half&Half (do not substitute)
- In small saucepan, melt brie cheese and gradually whisk in Half&Half

Direction

- Alternate seafood, melon and mushrooms on 6 (8-inch) skewers.
- Combine lemon juice and better.
- Broil kabobs 10 minutes, turning and brushing with lemon & butter mixture until seafood is opaque.
- Drizzle BRIE BASTE over kabobs and broil for 1 to 2 minutes (or) until golden brown.

---

151.   Seared Mahi Mahi W Rainbow Medley Recipe

Serving: 2 | Prep: | Cook: | Ready in:

Ingredients

- Ingredients: Serves 2 people
- •2 mahi-mahi fillets (about .5 oz each)
- •1/4 bell peppers (red and green), diced into cubes
- •1/4 fresh mango, diced into small cubes
- •1/2 tsp lemon and pepper seasoning
- •1/2 bunch asparagus
- •1 lime wedges
- •2 tbsp olive oil

Direction

- Directions:
- 1. Season fillets with seasoning and let sit at room temperature until ready to cook.

- 2. Cut fibrous, hard ends of asparagus and give them a good wash. Usually sand and grit can be found if not wash thoroughly.
- 3. On medium-high heat with 1 tbsp olive oil, sauté the asparagus about 10 minutes or until browned. Set aside on serving plate.
- 4. In a non-stick frying pan, add 1 tbsp olive oil and sear mahi-mahi fillets. Cook on medium or medium-high for about 10 minutes on each side. Try to flip only once, which will prevent flaking.
- 5. Meanwhile, prepare the rainbow medley by dicing the vegetables and mango into small cubes. Mix together in a mixing bowl and sprinkle one piece of lemon wedge.
- 6. Place components accordingly on a serving plate and serve hot.

152. Seared Mahi Mahi W Risotto And Mango Sauce Recipe

Serving: 4 | Prep: | Cook: 50mins |Ready in:

Ingredients

- Ingredients:
- 1 mango
- 1 teaspoon rice wine vinegar
- 1 tablespoon fresh cilantro leaves
- 1 clove garlic, quartered
- 1 teaspoon chopped fresh ginger
- 1-ounce bottled water
- 1/4 cup canola oil
- 1 1/2 teaspoons stone-ground mustard
- 1 lime
- salt and pepper (to taste)
- 1 tablespoon olive oil
- 1 tablespoon chopped shallots
- 1 cup arborio rice
- 1/2 cup white wine
- 3 cups chicken stock
- 2 tablespoons unsalted butter
- 4 (6-ounce) mahi-mahi fillets
- 1/4 cup olive oil
- Freshly ground black pepper
- 2 or 3 scallions, chopped, for garnish

Direction

- Peel the mango, cut into slices, and drop into the feed tube of a running blender to puree. Add the rice wine vinegar, cilantro, garlic, ginger, water, oil, mustard, and lime juice. Season with salt and pepper, to taste, and set aside.
- Bring chicken stock to a simmer. In a separate large saucepan on an adjacent burner, heat the olive oil and add the shallots and the rice. Lightly sauté: you actually are toasting the rice. Cook until the rice becomes translucent and the shallots become soft, stirring constantly. Add the white wine to deglaze the pan. Begin slowly adding the warm stock, 1 ladle-full at a time, to the rice pan, stirring as you go. This will bring out the starch in the rice and make the mixture creamy. As the mixture absorbs the broth, ladle more into the pot.
- When the first ladle of stock has been absorbed into the rice. When all of the stock has been ladled into the rice pot, slowly simmer until the rice is soft and creamy. Stir the butter into the risotto for more flavor and creaminess. Set aside, keeping warm until needed.
- Heat a sauté pan for the fish. Rub fish fillets with oil, salt and pepper. Place in pan, skin side facing up. Turn the fish over after 3 to 4 minutes. Cook for another 3 to 4 minutes or until done. Do not overcook the fish. It is done when the flesh springs back. Remove the fish to a utility platter. Place a mound of risotto on each plate. Top with mahi-mahi. Drizzle some mango sauce around the plate and top with chopped scallions.

153. Sesame Crusted Mahi Mahi 2 Recipe

Serving: 4 | Prep: | Cook: 20mins | Ready in:

Ingredients

- 1 tbsp sesame seeds
- 3/4 pounds mahi mahi fillets, thawed if frozen
- 1 tsp toasted sesame oil
- 1/4 tsp garlic pepper
- 1 1/2 tsp fresh gingerroot, peeled and grated

Direction

- Preheat oven to 400 degrees. Coat a shallow baking dish with non-stick cooking spray. Place sesame seeds in small skillet and place over medium heat. Cook, stirring occasionally, 2 to 4 minutes or just until golden and toasted. Remove from heat, cool slightly.
- Pat fish dry with paper towels. Drizzle or brush sesame oil on fillets, sprinkle evenly with garlic pepper, ginger and sesame seeds, pressing to coat. Place fillets, in baking dish. Bake 10 to 15 minutes until fish flakes easily with a fork.

154. Sesame Crusted Mahi Mahi I Recipe

Serving: 4 | Prep: | Cook: 15mins | Ready in:

Ingredients

- 4 (8oz) mahi mahi fillets, thawed if frozen
- 2 tsp sesame oil
- 4 tbsp white sesame seeds
- 1 tbsp vegetable oil

Direction

- Pat dry if fillets are wet with a paper towel. Rub each fillet with sesame oil and sprinkle with sesame seeds on non-skin side. Gently press seeds in with your fingers.

- In a large non-stick skillet, heat vegetable oil over medium heat. Add fillets, seeded side down. Cook for 4 minutes. Gently flip fillets and cook 3 to 5 minutes more, or until fish flakes with a fork.
- Serve with your favorite side.

155. Spicy Poached Mahi Mahi Recipe

Serving: 4 | Prep: | Cook: 20mins | Ready in:

Ingredients

- 1 16-24 oz jar of favorite salsa or picante, any heat
- 1 pound of Mahi Mahi filets or favorite fish filets

Direction

- Before using fish in recipe, please clean or rinse fish, then pat dry with paper towels. Then place on a plate and store in refrigerator until ready, covered.
- In a 2-4-inch deep skillet, heat salsa or picante sauce to a boil. Then turn down on low to a simmer, place cleaned mahi-mahi on top of sauce. Spoon sauce over fish, lightly.
- Cover with lid and poach for 10 to15 minutes, or until fish is white and flaky.
- Serve hot with your favorite side.
- Enjoy
- *****NOTE: If a salsa or picante sauce is not your thing, you can use 1 large can of Italian stewed tomatoes.

156. Sweetly Succulent Mahi Mahi Recipe

Serving: 4 | Prep: | Cook: 12mins | Ready in:

Ingredients

- 3 tablespoons brown sugar
- 4 tbsp water
- 3 tablespoons soy sauce
- 1 tablespoon balsamic vinegar
- 2 teaspoons grated fresh ginger root
- 2 cloves garlic, crushed
- 1 teaspoon olive oil
- 24oz raw mahi mahi fillets, cut in 4
- salt and pepper to taste

Direction

- In a shallow glass dish, stir together the sugar, water, soy sauce, balsamic vinegar, ginger, garlic and olive oil.
- Season fish fillets lightly with salt and pepper, and place them into the dish.
- Cover, and refrigerate for 20 minutes to marinate.
- Preheat broiler.
- Remove fish from the dish, and reserve marinade.
- Place fish on a baking tray and broil 4 to 6 minutes on each side, turning only once, until fish flakes easily with a fork. Remove fillets to a serving platter and keep warm.
- Pour reserved marinade into the skillet, and reduce until the mixture reduces to a glaze.
- Spoon glaze over fish, and serve immediately.

---

157. Tomato Basil Mahi Mahi Recipe

Serving: 2 | Prep: | Cook: 15mins | Ready in:

Ingredients

- 2-8 oz mahi mahi fillets
- 2 1/2 cups strawberry tomatoes, cut in half and deseeded
- 1/2 cup fresh basil leaves, chopped
- 1/3 cup red shallots, sliced
- 1/4 cup onion, diced

- 1/4 cup garlic, chopped (approx. 5 cloves)
- 2/3 cup chicken stock
- 2 Tbsp tomato paste
- 2 Tbsp fish sauce (or substitute soy sauce)
- 1 Tbsp vinegar or lemon juice
- 1 Tbsp sugar

Direction

- Coat pan with cooking oil and pan fry mahi-mahi fillets until golden brown, and set aside.
- To prepare sauce, sauté garlic, onion and shallots in pan until translucent, add tomatoes, tomato paste, fish sauce, lemon juice, and sugar. Stir in chicken stock and simmer until sauce thickens. Remove from heat and add basil.
- To serve, top mahi-mahi fillets with generous helping of tomato basil sauce.
- You can substitute any mild white flesh fish instead of mahi-mahi if you can't get it in your area.

---

158. Tuna Steaks With Roasted Red Pepper Sauce Recipe

Serving: 4 | Prep: | Cook: 15mins | Ready in:

Ingredients

- 2 Yellowfin tuna steaks, about 1 1/2 pounds (or swordfish or mahi mahi)
- 2 teaspoons olive oil
- Freshly grated pepper, to taste
- 1 cup roasted red bell pepper (jarred)
- 1/4 cup chopped green onion
- 1 tablespoon tomato paste
- 1 garlic clove, chopped
- 1/4 to 1/2 teaspoon red pepper flakes

Direction

- Brush tuna steaks with olive oil and sprinkle with pepper

- For every inch (in thickness) of tuna steak, broil or grill for 10 minutes, turning once to cook evenly
- Puree rest of ingredients in a blender or food processor
- Serve sauce over cooked tuna, garnish with parsley sprigs

159. Wasabi Infused Mahi Mahi Sandwiches With Napa Slaw Recipe

Serving: 4 | Prep: | Cook: 10mins | Ready in:

Ingredients

- 1/4 cup finely minced shallots
- 2 tablespoons finely minced garlic
- 2 tablespoons finely minced ginger
- 2 teaspoons wasabi paste
- 1/2 cup seasoned rice vinegar
- 2 tablespoons tamari
- 2 tablespoons light brown sugar
- 1/4 cup toasted sesame oil, divided
- 4 (6-ounce) mahi mahi fillets
- 8 slices ciabatta or 4 rolls, split
- 2 tablespoons tahini
- 1 1/2 cups very finely shredded napa cabbage
- 1 cup very finely shredded red cabbage
- 1/2 cup grated carrot
- 1/4 cup chopped green onions
- mayonnaise

Direction

- Whisk together first 7 ingredients in a bowl; whisk in 2 tablespoons sesame oil. Reserve 1/2 cup marinade, and set aside. Place fillets in a zip-top plastic bag; pour remaining marinade over fillets. Seal bag; chill 1 hour.
- Remove fish and discard marinade. Grill fish, skin side up, over medium-high heat (350° to 400°) for 3 to 4 minutes. Turn fish, and grill 3 to 4 minutes or until fish flakes easily with a

fork. Remove and discard skin. Cover and keep warm. Grill bread slices 3 minutes or until toasted. Set aside.
- Stir together remaining 2 tablespoons sesame oil and tahini. Stir sesame oil mixture into reserved 1/2 cup marinade.
- Combine Napa cabbage and next 3 ingredients in a bowl. Pour marinade mixture over slaw; toss gently to combine.
- Lightly spread one side of each bread slice with mayonnaise. Place fish over 4 pieces of bread; top with slaw and remaining 4 pieces of bread.

160. Yellow Curry Thai Stylie Recipe

Serving: 8 | Prep: | Cook: 60mins | Ready in:

Ingredients

- For the Paste:
- 1 onion (i do one-half red and one-half white)
- 4+ cloves garlic (depending on personal taste)
- 1-2 chile peppers
- 2-3 jalapenos
- 3/4-1 tablespoon fresh grated ginger
- 2 teaspoons turmeric
- 1 2/3 teaspoon cumin
- 1 teaspoon coriander
- 2/3 teaspoon cayenne pepper
- 1/4 teaspoon cinnamon
- 1/5 teaspoon nutmeg
- 1/5 teaspoon allspice
- 1/4+ teaspoon black pepper
- 1/5 teaspoon white pepper
- olive oil
- For the Curry:
- 3 cans coconut milk (i personally dislike the lite version, but rock it if you feel it)
- 2 bay leaves
- 1 sweet potato or regular potato, cut into 1/2 inch squares
- 3 carrots, sliced into circles

- 1 zucchini, cut into squares
- 1 squash, cut into squares
- 1-2 red bell peppers, cut into 1 inch pieces
- green beans, cut into 1/2 or 1/3
- cabbage, sliced into 3 inches by 1/2 inch
- 1/2 package cherry tomatoes, cut in halves
- 8 oz fresh mushrooms, sliced
- (you can also add broccoli, cauliflower, peas, get creative with it!)
- **also, IF YOU'RE NOT A VEGETARIAN add 12oz+ meat such a chicken, salmon, tuna steaks, mahi mahi, etc-the fish oils work Wonders with the flavor of the curry**if you are, you can easily add tofu at the end, if so desired
- you can also add a tablespoon of fish oil if you're feelin frisky~~
- Serve With:
- couscous, rice, or acini de pepe pasta
- lime slices
- Greek yogurt or fat free cream cheese
- parsley, green onion, cilantro

Direction

- First, cut the onion, garlic, chilies into very small pieces. Grate the ginger.
- It works best if you prepare all the vegetables before starting to cook. Cut each as specified above.
- Next, add olive oil to a wok type pan or a medium-large cooking pot. Put on med-high heat and add onions, garlic, chilies. Allow to get sautéed and mildly mushy. Next, add ginger and all spices and constantly mix together until paste-like. Keep stirring ingredients until consistent through-out.
- Next, add cans of coconut milk slowly. Add bay leaves now. Also add ingredients that will take the longest to soften, including sweet potato, carrot, and any meat that you are using. Allow coconut milk to begin boiling, the immediately turn it down to med-lo/med heat. Give the vegetable a good while to semi-soften. Check their status every so often, and also give the pot a good mix.

- This is a good time to taste test the curry flavor. I usually do eyeball method as to how much of each spice I use. That being said, the amounts listed above are GUESSES. So MAKE Sure to taste test and add more spices accordingly. I end up dashing things in throughout the whole process. If it's too spicy, I recommended adding more turmeric to cut down the bite.
- Then it is time to add the rest of the vegetables, including: zucchini, mushrooms, squash, red bell peppers, green beans, and cabbage. You have the option of adding the tomatoes now (if you like cooked tomatoes; otherwise, wait until right before you take the pot off the stove-top to add the tomatoes). Stir together and allow ingredients to cook. Keeping the lid on the pot is up to you, it tends to cook the ingredients faster.
- While it's cooking, make a side of rice, couscous, or acini de pepe pasta.
- Yay! It's done! I recommend pouring a generous amount of curry over the side you choose (stated above) and adding a fresh squeeze of lime juice and parsley/onion/cilantro garnish. If it's too spicy, cut the curry with some yogurt or fat free cream cheese. Both are delicious with the recipe.

---

161. Sweet Ginger Mahi Mahi Recipe

Serving: 2 | Prep: | Cook: 10mins | Ready in:

Ingredients

- 2 8 oz mahi mahi fillets
- 3 tbsp honey (or maple syrup)
- 3 tbsp soy sauce
- 3 tbsp balsamic vinegar
- 1 tsp grated fresh ginger root
- 1 clove garlic, crushed
- 4 tsp olive oil

Direction

- Combine all ingredients except fish in a large freezer bag
- Add fish; turn to coat and refrigerate for 20 min
- Heat grill to Medium heat and brush lightly with olive oil
- Remove fillets from marinade (reserve liquid) and grill for 10-12 min, turning once-until fish flakes with a fork.
- Pour reserved marinade into a small skillet and heat over medium flame until mixture reduces to a thick glaze, 2-3 minutes
- Spoon glaze over fish and serve immediately
- Delicious!

Chapter 4: Haddock Recipes

***

162.	Baked Fish With Pasta Recipe

Serving: 4 | Prep: | Cook: 20mins | Ready in:

Ingredients

- * 2 tablespoons extra-virgin olive oil, twice-around-the-pan
- * 1 small onion, finely chopped, about 1/3 cup
- * 2 cloves garlic, chopped
- * 1/2 cup dry white wine
- * 1 (15-ounce) can stewed tomatoes
- * 3 tablespoons chopped flat-leaf parsley
- * 2 pounds cod or haddock, rinsed and dried
- * salt and pepper
- * 2 tablespoons butter

- * 1/2 pound angel hair, cooked just shy of al dente, about 4 or 5 minutes

Direction

- Preheat oven to 375 degrees F.
- To a small skillet preheated over medium heat, add extra-virgin olive oil, onion and garlic. Cook onions 5 minutes, until translucent. Add wine to the pan and reduce for 30 seconds. Add tomatoes and break up the sliced stewed tomatoes with a wooden spoon as they heat through. When the sauce comes to a boil (2 or 3 minutes) remove it from the heat and stir in the parsley. Season the fish with salt and pepper. Pour a few spoonfuls of sauce into the bottom of a shallow baking dish. Add fish to the dish in a single layer. Add remaining sauce and bake 15 to 17 minutes until fish is firm and opaque.
- Remove fish to serving plate or dinner plates. Spoon a few bits of tomato and sauce over the fish. To the remaining sauce in the baking dish add 2 tablespoons butter cut into small pieces. Add hot pasta to butter and sauce and turn pasta in dish to coat evenly and to allow pasta to absorb juices. Pile pasta alongside fish and serve. If you are entertaining, try bundling portions of pasta around a large, 2-pronged meat fork, by twisting the fork in the pasta allowing it to curl up the fork. Shimmy the twisted pasta off the fork on to a plate you will create pasta "nests." This simple "twist" adds a lot to the plate presentation.

163.	Baked Haddock Almondine Recipe

Serving: 2 | Prep: | Cook: 20mins | Ready in:

Ingredients

- 1 cup coarsely ground dry bread crumbs
- 1/4 cup toasted sliced almonds
- 3 tablespoons butter melted

- 1 teaspoon kosher salt
- 2 skinless haddock fillets
- 1/4 cup all-purpose flour
- 2/3 cup mayonnaise
- 1-1/2 cups water

Direction

- Preheat oven to 350.
- In a small bowl combine crumbs, almonds, butter and salt.
- Mix well.
- If necessary, add extra butter to hold crumbs together.
- Coat fish with flour, shaking off excess.
- Place fillets in a baking pan large enough to hold them in a single layer.
- Spread mayonnaise over the entire surface of fish.
- Cover evenly with crumb mixture lightly pressing into the fish.
- Carefully pour water around the fish.
- Bake for 20 minutes.

164.   Baked Haddock And Seafood Recipe

Serving: 6 | Prep: | Cook: 40mins | Ready in:

Ingredients

- 1 lb haddock fillets, cut into 6 pieces
- 4 oz bay (small) scallops
- 12 jumbo shrimp, peeled and deveined
- ½ cup white wine
- 2 tbsp lemon juice
- ¼ cup butter, melted
- 1 cup crushed Ritz crackers
- 2 tsp garlic powder
- ½ tsp black pepper
- Zest of ½ lemon

Direction

- Preheat the oven to 375F, line a roasting pan with parchment.
- Lay fish fillets in a single layer on the bottom of the dish, then top with scallops and shrimp.
- Pour the white wine and lemon juice overtop of the seafood.
- In a bowl, toss butter, cracker crumbs, garlic powder, black pepper and lemon zest.
- Sprinkle over the seafood.
- Bake 15 minutes, then turn the broiler to HI and broil 2 minutes, until browned.

165.   Baked Haddock Recipe

Serving: 4 | Prep: | Cook: | Ready in:

Ingredients

- 1- 1 1/2 pounds haddock
- 1/2 cups panko crumbs
- 3 cloves of garlic, micro planed or finely minced
- Slat and pepper to taste
- 1/8 tsp dried thyme
- 1/4 cup olive oil, approx.
- Salt and pepper to taste.
- 1/4 cup Parm. cheese or 2 Tbs Nutritional yeast and 2 tbs almond meal, pulsed in a food processor.
- Lemon wedges for serving

Direction

- Preheat oven to 450°.
- Dry fish with paper towel.
- Mix the garlic and bread crumbs, add the oil and mix well. This should look fairly coarse.
- Place the fish on a parchment-lined baking sheet and add salt and pepper.
- Press the crumb mixture into the fish.
- Bake for 14 mins per 1 inch thickness of fish.

166. Baked Haddock With Garlic Butter Crumble Topping Recipe

Serving: 8 | Prep: | Cook: 45mins | Ready in:

Ingredients

- 4 haddock fillets
- 2 cups Half & Half
- 1 1/2 Tbs.garlic powder
- 3 shallots
- 1 package ritz cracker
- 1 cup parmesan cheese
- salt & pepper to taste
- sweet paprika
- Chopped parsley
- 6 Tbs. butter
- 2 Tbs. flour

Direction

- Lay out fillets and pat dry.
- Season with salt & pepper to taste.
- Preheat oven to 350.
- Butter a large casserole dish and lay in fish.
- Cream Sauce:
- In a small pot, melt 2 tbsp butter.
- Add diced shallots, cook until clear.
- Add flour, stir.
- Add half & half, stir until thickened.
- Remove pot from heat, add parmesan and stir.
- Garlic crumble topping:
- Melt 4 tbsp butter in microwave.
- Crush Ritz crackers and put in bowl.
- Pour melted butter and garlic powder, mix well.
- Pour cream sauce over fish and sprinkle crumb mix over fish.
- Sprinkle Sweet paprika over fish.
- Bake for 35 mins.
- Sprinkle parsley over fish and serve...Enjoy!!!

167. Baked Haddock With Lime And Tomato Sauce Recipe

Serving: 4 | Prep: | Cook: 25mins | Ready in:

Ingredients

- 4 haddock fillets skinned and boned
- Sauce:
- 3 tablespoons vegetable oil
- 2 medium red onions finely chopped
- 1-1/2 teaspoons ground coriander
- 1/2 teaspoon cayenne
- 1 red bell pepper diced
- 1 green bell pepper diced
- 4 tomatoes peeled seeded and diced
- 6 tablespoons lime juice
- 1/2 teaspoon salt
- 1 teaspoon freshly ground black pepper
- 2 tablespoons chopped fresh cilantro

Direction

- Preheat oven to 375 degrees.
- Rinse fillets and pat dry.
- In large saucepan heat oil over medium high heat.
- Add onions and cook until tender about 10 minutes.
- Stir in coriander and cayenne then cook 2 minutes.
- Add diced red and green peppers and tomatoes.
- Reduce heat to low and cook uncovered for 10 minutes.
- Remove saucepan from heat and stir in lime juice then season with salt and pepper.
- Arrange fillets in a buttered shallow baking dish then cover with sauce.
- Bake uncovered for 25 minutes then sprinkle with cilantro and serve.

168.   Baked Haddock With Parmesan And Herb Stuffing Recipe

Serving: 4 | Prep: | Cook: 40mins | Ready in:

Ingredients

- 1 1/2 lbs haddock or cod fillets
- salt and pepper
- 3 slices white bread
- 1/3 Cup grated parmesan cheese
- 1 tsp crushed garlic
- 1 Tbsp chopped parsley
- 1 Tbsp fresh herbs, such as dill and chives, chopped
- 5 Tbsp butter, melted
- 1/3 Cup heavy cream

Direction

- Cut fish fillets into serving size pieces.
- Butter a 2-quart baking dish and pre-heat oven to 350 degrees
- Arrange fish fillets in baking dish and sprinkle with salt and pepper evenly.
- In a food processor, pulse the bread with Parmesan, garlic, parsley, and fresh herbs.
- Toss crumbs with the melted butter and sprinkle over the fish. Drizzle cream all over.
- Bake for 25-30 minutes, or until fish flakes easily with a fork.
- MOST IMPORTANT STEP: enjoy :)

169.   Baked Haddock With Tomatoes, Spinach And Mushrooms Recipe

Serving: 4 | Prep: | Cook: 35mins | Ready in:

Ingredients

- About 1 1/4 pounds haddock
- 2 tsp olive oil or butter
- 1 cup chopped spinach (packed)
- 1 tsp thyme
- salt & pepper
- 1 large tomato or abut 3/4 cup chopped
- 1 clove garlic
- 1 cup quartered mushrooms
- 1/3 cup white wine
- 1/4 cup parmesan cheese, grated
- 2 tbs chopped parsley
- lemon slices

Direction

- Cut haddock into four serving pieces.
- Grease baking dish with olive oil or butter. Place fish in baking dish and sprinkle with salt, pepper and thyme.
- Combine spinach, tomatoes and garlic; sprinkle evenly over fish.
- Arrange mushrooms around haddock. Pour wine over all.
- Sprinkle with parmesan.
- Bake for 20-30 minutes, or until fish is opaque and flakes easily with a fork.
- Garnish with parsley and lemon slices before serving.

170.   Baked Haddock With Sour Cream Recipe

Serving: 4 | Prep: | Cook: 35mins | Ready in:

Ingredients

- 1 lb. haddock
- 1 c. Dairy sour cream
- 1 tsp. lemon juice
- 1 tsp. salt
- 1 tsp. dried dill weed
- 2 Tbs. real maple syrup
- 1/4 c. bread Crumbs

Direction

- Preheat oven to 425 degrees.

- Arrange the fish in a greased baking pan (I use a 13x9 glass cake pan).
- Mix together the sour cream, lemon juice, salt, dill, maple syrup, and bread crumbs.
- Spread the sour cream mixture over the fish.
- Bake at 425 degrees for about 35 minutes, or until the fish flakes.

171.   Baked Stuffed Haddock Recipe

Serving: 15 | Prep: | Cook: 30mins | Ready in:

Ingredients

- 15 haddock filets
- 1 pound lump crabmeat
- 1/2 cup chopped celery
- 1/2 cup chopped white onion
- 2-1/2 tablespoons chopped parsley
- 1 tablespoon Old Bay Seasoning
- 2 cups regular bread crumbs
- 2 whole eggs
- 1/2 cup mayonnaise
- 2 tablespoons worcestershire sauce
- 1 tablespoon Dijon mustard
- 2 tablespoons chopped shallots
- 1 pinch flour
- 1/2 cup dry white wine
- 1/2 pound soft butter

Direction

- Mix crabmeat, celery, onion, parsley, old bay, bread crumbs, eggs, mayonnaise, Worcestershire and mustard together.
- Portion into 2 ounces and roll up in the haddock filets.
- Place in buttered casserole dish.
- Drizzle with white wine.
- Bake at 400 for 15 minutes.
- Sauté the shallots then add the flour and win and reduce by half.
- Gradually add butter whisking constantly.

- Strain and pour over haddock after it is baked.

172.   Chilled Poached Haddock With Cucumber Relish Recipe

Serving: 4 | Prep: | Cook: 65mins | Ready in:

Ingredients

- relish
- 2 cucumbers, peeled, seeded and finely diced
- 2 T red onion, finely diced
- 2 T mint, finely chopped
- ½ jalapeno pepper, seeded and finely diced
- 1 C finely diced watermelon
- 1 T sugar
- 2 T fresh lime juice
- 1 ½ tsp rice wine vinegar
- ¼ tsp salt
- haddock
- 1 C water
- ½ C white wine
- 1 small onion, sliced thin
- 12 sprigs parsley, divided
- ¼ tsp salt
- 1 ½ lbs fresh haddock fillets
- lemon wedges for garnish

Direction

- Relish
- Combine all ingredients in a glass or ceramic bowl, mix well and chill
- Haddock
- In a large saucepan with a tight fitting lid. Place water, wine, onion, 4 sprigs of parsley and salt
- Bring to a boil over high heat, then lower heat to medium and simmer
- Add fish fillets, skin side up
- Poach 5 minutes, uncovered
- Remove pan from heat, cover and let sit another 5 minutes

- Check to see if fish is cooked, if not replace lid and let sit another 5 minutes
- When fish is done, remove lid
- When fish is cool enough to handle, slip a sharp knife under skin and remove
- Carefully remove fish to a serving platter and cool 20 minutes at room temp
- Cover loosely with plastic wrap and refrigerate at least an hour
- When ready to serve, arrange remaining parsley sprigs around fish, along with lemon wedges
- Serve haddock chilled with cucumber relish on the side

173. Cod Or Haddock Baked In Cream Recipe

Serving: 4 | Prep: | Cook: 25mins | Ready in:

Ingredients

- 1 lb cod fish fillets or haddock fillets (1/2 to 3/4 in thick, fresh or frozen, thawed if frozem)
- 1/2 cup whipping cream
- 3 tablespoons grated parmesan cheese (divided)
- 2 tablespoons dry white wine
- 1 garlic clove, minced
- 1/4 teaspoon salt
- 1 dash pepper (or more to taste)

Direction

- Preheat oven to 350 degrees.
- Cut fish into four serving size portions.
- Rinse and pat dry with paper towels.
- Place fish in an 11" x 7" baking pan.
- In a mixing bowl, stir together whipping cream, 2 tbsp. Parmesan cheese, wine, garlic, salt and pepper. Pour over fish.
- Bake uncovered for 20-25 minutes or until fish flakes easily with a fork.
- Take fish out of sauce and place on a serving platter.

- Stir sauce to blend and pour over fish.
- Top with 1 tbsp. Parmesan cheese.

174. Delmonico Haddock Recipe

Serving: 4 | Prep: | Cook: 50mins | Ready in:

Ingredients

- 1-1/2 tsp salt,divided
- 1 c milk
- 1/2 c grated cheddar cheese
- 1/8 tso pepper
- 1/8 tsp paprika
- 2 lbs. haddock fillets
- 1/4 c minced onion
- 2 TB butter
- 2 TB flour
- 1 tsp dry mustard

Direction

- Sauté onion in butter till golden. Add flour, mustard, 1/2 tsp salt and milk. Cook till thickened, stirring constantly. Remove from heat and stir in cheese.
- Place fish in buttered casserole. Season with remaining salt and pepper. Pour cheese sauce over fish. Sprinkle with paprika and a little additional cheese if desired. Sprinkle with a little chopped parsley when done.
- Bake at 350° for 30 mins...

175. Dill Haddock Recipe

Serving: 6 | Prep: | Cook: 12mins | Ready in:

Ingredients

- 6 fresh skinless haddock fillets
- 6 slices lemon
- 2 tablespoons snipped fresh dill

- 1 teaspoon freshly ground black pepper
- 1 teaspoon seasoned salt

Direction

- Rinse fish and pat dry then season with salt, pepper and dill.
- Place in a foil pouch then place slices of lemon on top of each fillet and seal bag.
- Place on grill for 6 minutes per side then remove to serving platter and serve immediately.

176.   Easy Crunchy Batter Fried Fish Recipe

Serving: 4 | Prep: | Cook: 20mins | Ready in:

Ingredients

- 1 cup flour
- 1/2 cup cornstarch
- 1 tsp salt
- 1 tsp Old Bay seasoning- or similar seafood seasoning
- 2 tsp baking powder
- 1 tsp sugar
- 1 cup water
- 1 tsp oil
- oil to fry
- 2 Lbs fresh haddock, cut up in manageable pieces to home deep fry

Direction

- Combine the dry ingredients in a bowl.
- Combine the liquid ingredients.
- Before mixing both together in a batter, dip fish in some of the reserved dry mixture just to lightly coat each side.
- Place coated fish on a plate.
- Then make batter by mixing both wet and dry mixtures well.
- Dip fish in batter to coat well.

- Carefully drop pieces into hot deep oil, fry just a few pieces at a time not crowding fish when frying.
- Turn each side once until golden brown.
- Place pieces on absorbent toweling paper to drain.
- Serve immediately.
- We love this with tartar sauce, lemon wedges and fresh homemade coleslaw.
- Note: Make sure your oil is hot enough (350F) either using an electric deep fryer or a heavy duty pot to heat the oil when you do any frying.

177.   Easy Healthy Baked Haddock Or Cod Recipe

Serving: 4 | Prep: | Cook: 20mins | Ready in:

Ingredients

- 4   4 ounce fillets
- 1/2 c lime juice
- 1 Tbl dried minced onion
- 1   16 ounce can diced tomatoes, undrained
- 1 T dried parsley

Direction

- Preheat oven to 400 F.
- Spray a shallow baking dish.
- Combine juice, onion, tomatoes and parsley.
- Pour mixture over fish.
- Bake 15 to 20 minutes depending on thickness of fish.
- 4 servings, 149 calories, 3 gr fat, 1 gr fiber

178.   Easy, Perfect Baked Haddock Recipe

Serving: 4 | Prep: | Cook: 25mins | Ready in:

Ingredients

- 4 haddock fillets,cleaned,rinsed and pat dry
- 1/2 stick butter ,melted
- 3/4 roll Ritz crackers,crushed
- dash of black pepper or lemon pepper
- 1 TB(1/3 squeezed)lemon juice to taste
- 1/2 tsp dried or fresh parsley

Direction

- Preheat oven to 350.
- Melt butter in small glass bowl, add Ritz cracker crumbs and combine gently. Spray shallow baking pan with spray, put few cracker crumbs in bottom of pan. Lay haddock in pan, cover with remaining cracker crumbs, squeeze lemon and sprinkle parsley over fish.
- Bake 350° for 10-20 mins, watching closely, as fillets vary in size, don't overcook! Mine took 12 mins, I put under broiler for a min or two to crisp up a little more. Remove when fish is white and flakes easily.

179. Fancy Fish Sticks Recipe

Serving: 4 | Prep: | Cook: 30mins | Ready in:

Ingredients

- • 1 1/2 cup (360g) pumpkin seeds
- • 1 tsp (5g) cumin seeds
- • 1 tsp (5g) cayenne pepper
- • Kosher salt and freshly cracked black pepper
- • 2 egg whites
- • 1 kg fresh haddock fillets
- • 1/4 cup (65ml) vegetable oil

Direction

- 1. Preheat oven to 350°F.
- 2. Toss pumpkin seeds with the cumin, cayenne, salt and pepper, spread out on a baking sheet and toast for 5-10 minutes until golden brown.

- 3. Cool and pulse in a food processor until fine.
- 4. Season the haddock fillets with salt and pepper.
- 5. In a mixing bowl, whisk egg whites until frothy, dip the fillets into the whites and then coat in the pumpkin seed crust.
- 6. In a non-stick frying pan, heat the vegetable oil over medium heat and sear for 2-3 minutes each side, until golden brown.
- 7. Finish in the oven for 5-7 minutes until cooked through.
- 8. Pair with Molson Canadian 67 or other light beers. The lightness of the Molson Canadian 67 nicely balances the nuttiness from the pumpkin seeds and the spice from the cayenne and cumin.

180. Fast And Easy Haddock Au Gratin Recipe

Serving: 6 | Prep: | Cook: 15mins | Ready in:

Ingredients

- 1 1/2 to 2 pound haddock fillets or other firm white fish
- 1 can cream of cream of celery soup (I used reduced sodium)
- 1/2 cup milk
- 2 Tbsp. sherry
- 1/2 cup shredded mild cheddar cheese
- 1 1/2 cups bread crumbs tossed with 3 tablespoons melted butter
- 1 Tbsp. fresh parsley

Direction

- Arrange haddock in a shallow buttered baking dish. Combine soup with milk in a saucepan over medium low heat and heat through. Add sherry and stir to combine. Pour soup mixture over the fish. Sprinkle with shredded cheese. Combine parsley and buttered bread crumbs.

Bake for 10 to 15 minutes, or until golden on top and fish is flaky and cooked through.

---

181. Fish Stew Recipe

Serving: 2 | Prep: | Cook: 20mins | Ready in:

Ingredients

- 1 lb. of fish fillets cut into pieces. i use haddock or cod but use any other fish. if frozen thaw it first and rinse under cold water.
- 2 tbsp. olive oil
- 5 cloves of garlic, whole..
- 1 onion chopped
- 1 can 19 oz. tomatoes, cut up
- 2 tbsp. chopped parsley
- 1/2 tsp.or to your taste of hot pepper flakes
- 1/2 cup of apple juice
- 1/2 tsp. thyme
- salt an pepper, lemon juice

Direction

- Fry the onions, pepper flakes and garlic in oil for a few mins.
- Put in the tomatoes, thyme, salt and pepper.
- Bring to boil, cover, turn heat down and simmer for about 5 mins.
- Stir in parsley, apple juice, 1 tsp. lemon juice and the fish.
- Cover and simmer for about 6-7 mins.

---

182. Grilled Haddock Steaks With Yogurt Curry Sauce Recipe

Serving: 4 | Prep: | Cook: 10mins | Ready in:

Ingredients

- 1/2 teaspoon salt
- 1 teaspoon freshly ground black pepper
- 6 haddock steaks
- 1 large lemon juiced
- 1 garlic clove minced
- Sauce:
- 6 tablespoons fresh lemon juice
- 1-1/2 teaspoons curry powder
- 1/2 teaspoon ground cumin
- 1 teaspoon crushed coriander seeds
- 1/4 teaspoon salt
- 1/2 teaspoon freshly ground black pepper
- 1 teaspoon grated fresh ginger
- 2 cups plain nonfat yogurt

Direction

- Salt and pepper the fish steaks on both sides.
- Combine lemon juice, olive oil, garlic and more salt and pepper.
- Pour into 1 or 2 flat baking dishes large enough to accommodate all of the fish and add the steaks. Marinade for 2 hours in the refrigerator turning steaks over halfway through.
- Combine all sauce ingredients then taste and adjust seasonings.
- Preheat grill and brush fish on both sides with the marinade and grill for 3 minutes on each side.

---

183. Grilled Haddock W Potato Cruch Recipe

Serving: 2 | Prep: | Cook: | Ready in:

Ingredients

- 2 large potatoes halved
- 1 cup frozen vegetables
- 2 tbsp butter
- 2 smoked haddock fillets
- 2 tbsp melted butter with lemon seasoning
- ½ small bunch chives, chopped (or parsley flakes as substitution)

Direction

- Cook the potatoes until tender, then add the frozen vegetables for the last 2 minutes of cooking. Gently crush with half the butter.
- Heat the rest of the butter in a pan and cook the haddock for 3 or 4 minutes on each side. Meanwhile, melt the butter in microwave and add lemon seasoning. Stir in the chives or parsley flakes.
- Put the potato on 2 plates, top with the haddock and the chive butter.

184. HADDOCK WITH TOMATO AND ONION SALSA Recipe

Serving: 4 | Prep: | Cook: 6mins | Ready in:

Ingredients

- 1 red onion halved and thinly sliced
- 4 tomatoes, halved with cores removed
- 1 tsp crushed chili flakes
- 1 tsp grated fresh ginger
- 1 tsp sugar
- 1 tbsp tomato paste
- 1 tbsp balsamic vinegar
- 3 tbsp olive oil'divided
- 4 haddock fillets

Direction

- Separate onion slices into shreds and put into a bowl.
- Thinly slice tomatoes and add to onions.
- Sprinkle with chili flakes, ginger and sugar.
- Stir in tomato paste and vinegar.
- Stir in 2 tbsp of olive oil.
- Set aside.
- Preheat broiler to high, lightly grease broiler pan.
- Put on Haddock, skin side up, and brush with remaining oil.
- Cook 3 minutes.

- Turn fish and cook 3 minutes more or until cooked through.
- Divide salsa among 4 plates.
- Lay haddock on top.
- Serve.

185. Haddock Filets With Havarti And Mushrooms Recipe

Serving: 4 | Prep: | Cook: 20mins | Ready in:

Ingredients

- 1 tablespoon butter
- 4 large scallions sliced
- 1 pound mushrooms sliced
- 1-1/2 pounds haddock filets
- 1/4 cup dry white wine
- 2 tablespoons lemon juice
- 1/2 teaspoon dried marjoram
- 1 teaspoon freshly ground black pepper
- 4 slices havarti cheese cut into 1/2" strips
- 2 tablespoon unseasoned bread crumbs

Direction

- Preheat oven to 400 then grease a shallow baking dish with butter.
- Evenly scatter the scallions and mushrooms over bottom of dish.
- Place filets on top in a single layer.
- Mix wine and lemon juice together and pour over fish.
- Sprinkle with marjoram and black pepper then evenly distribute cheese strips over top.
- Crumple a large piece of waxed paper and wet it.
- Shake off excess water and place loosely over fish and bake 7 minutes.
- Remove fish from oven and take off waxed paper.
- Sprinkle fish with bread crumbs then bake 9 minutes.

- Remove fish from oven and heat broiler and broil just long enough to brown top of filets.

186. Haddock Filets In Wine Sauce Recipe

Serving: 6 | Prep: | Cook: 25mins | Ready in:

Ingredients

- 1 1/2 pounds skinless haddock filets, cut into serving pieces
- 1 green onion, thinly sliced
- 1/2 cup fresh mushrooms, thinly sliced (I use more)
- 2 large ripe tomatoes, seeded and coarsely chopped
- 1 cup white wine
- 1 teaspoon curry powder
- 1 cup light cream
- 1 teaspoon salt, or to taste
- 1/4 teaspoon ground white pepper
- 1/2 cup dry breadcrumbs
- 1/2 cup sharp cheddar cheese, shredded
- 2 tablespoons butter, melted
- lemon wedges

Direction

- Arrange fish filets in a greased 13x9 inch baking dish.
- Sprinkle fish with green onion, mushrooms and tomato.
- Combine wine and curry powder. Pour over filets.
- Bake at 325 degrees for 15 to 20 minutes or until fish filets flake easily.
- Remove from oven and carefully lift out fish filets and set aside.
- In saucepan, heat cream. Add pan juices to saucepan. Add salt and pepper. Heat just to a boil.
- Return filets to baking pan.
- Pour cream mixture over.

- Combine crumbs and cheese. Sprinkle over filets.
- Drizzle with melted butter.
- Broil until crumbs and cheese are golden brown.
- Serve with lemon wedges.

187. Haddock Filets With Mushrooms Recipe

Serving: 2 | Prep: | Cook: 20mins | Ready in:

Ingredients

- olive oil spray
- 3/4 pound haddock fillets
- 1 teaspoon olive oil
- 4 ounces sliced mushrooms
- 1 tablespoon chopped fresh thyme
- 1/2 teaspoon salt
- 1 teaspoon freshly ground black pepper
- 1/4 cup white wine

Direction

- Preheat the oven to 450.
- Line baking tray with foil and spray with olive oil spray.
- Place tray in the oven while oven preheats.
- Rinse fish and pat dry.
- Remove tray from oven and place fish on it.
- Brush fillets with olive oil then spoon mushrooms over top.
- Sprinkle with thyme, salt and pepper.
- Pour wine over fish and cover tray with foil then bake 10 minutes.
- Place fish on plates and spoon mushrooms and sauce over top.

188.   Haddock Fish Fillets With Wine Sauce Dated 1943 Recipe

Serving: 2 | Prep: | Cook: 30mins | Ready in:

Ingredients

- 2 tablespoons minced onion
- 1 tablespoon oil
- 2 tablespoons flour
- 1-1/2 teaspoons salt
- 1/8 teaspoon pepper
- 1/2 cup cream
- 1/2 cup sauterne wine
- 1 pound fresh haddock fillets
- 1 tablespoon chopped fresh parsley

Direction

- Sauté onion in hot oil in a heavy enameled pan or double boiler until tender.
- Stir in the flour, salt, and pepper blending well.
- Add milk stirring constantly and cook until thick.
- When thickened remove and very gradually stir in the wine.
- Put the fish in a baking pan and sprinkle with salt.
- Pour sauce over fish.
- Bake at 350 for thirty minutes basting often.
- Sprinkle with parsley and serve.

189.   Haddock Stew Recipe

Serving: 34 | Prep: | Cook: 20mins | Ready in:

Ingredients

- 1 lb haddock or other whitefish (frozen or fresh)
- 1 1/2 c cubed potatoes
- 1 c sliced celery
- 1 c sliced carrots
- 1 c sliced onions
- 2 Tbsp chopped green peppers
- 1 tsp salt (or to taste)
- 3 Tbsp butter
- 3 Tbsp flour
- 1/4 tsp poultry seasoning

Direction

- If frozen, thaw fillets enough to cut.
- Cook with vegs in water for 10 minutes.
- Drain and measure broth to make 1 1/2 cups. Use with rest of ingredients to make sauce.
- Pour over vegetables and fish.
- Bake at 425 degrees for 15-20 mins

190.   Heavenly Baked Haddock Recipe

Serving: 4 | Prep: | Cook: 20mins | Ready in:

Ingredients

- 1 1/2 lbs fresh or thawed haddock, cut into 2 fillets
- 1 cup New England style oyster crackers
- 1/2 stick butter melted
- ocean fish seasoning or salt and pepper
- fresh lemon
- mayonnaise , about T tbs
- gongonzolla blue cheese
- paprika

Direction

- Preheat oven to 425F.
- Coarse crumble crackers and then pour the butter over and mix till very well combined.
- Squeeze juice from a fresh lemon over fish and then season fish.
- Using enough mayo, spread evenly over fish.
- Press cracker mixture over fillets.
- Lay some slices of gorgonzola across the top of each fillet.
- Sprinkle with paprika.

- Bake fish until topping is golden and fish is cooked and done.
- Carefully split the 2 portions into 4 pieces.
- I find this easier to prepare instead of 4 smaller pieces.
- Serve at once.

191.   Jamie Oliver Style Fish Pie Recipe

Serving: 6 | Prep: | Cook: 1hours | Ready in:

Ingredients

- •5 large potatoes peeled and diced
- •2 eggs
- •250g spinach
- •1 onion finely chopped
- •1 carrot peeled and finely chopped
- •A little extra-virgin olive oil
- •1 tub creme fraiche
- •2 handfuls parmesan cheese grated
- •juice of 1 lemon
- •1 heaped tsp English mustard or French will do
- •1/2 pound haddock cod or other white fish, skinned, boned and sliced into strips
- •1/2 pound undyed smoked haddock , skinned, boned and cut into strips.
- •good grinding nutmeg to taste
- handful of flatleaf parsley, chopped
- •salt and pepper

Direction

- Preheat the oven to 230c degrees.
- Put the potatoes into a pan of salted, boiling water.
- Bring back to the boil for 2 minutes
- Add the eggs and boil for further 8 minutes. By which time potatoes should be cooked, if not fish out eggs and continue till done.
- Put eggs into cold water, then shell and quarter and set aside till later.

- Steam the spinach in a colander over the pan that has the potatoes.
- This will only take about a minute or two.
- When the spinach is done, remove from the colander and squeeze out excess water.
- Drain the potatoes in the colander.
- In a separate pan, slow-fry the onions and carrots in a little olive oil for about 8-10 minutes.
- Add the crème fraiche and bring just to a boil.
- Remove from the heat and add the cheese, lemon juice, chopped parsley and mustard.
- Put the spinach, fish and eggs in a suitable sized ovenproof serving dish.
- Pour over the creamy carrots and onion mix.
- Mash the cooked potatoes - adding a bit of olive oil, salt and pepper and nutmeg.
- Spread the potatoes on top of the fish.
- Place in the oven for 25 - 30 minutes.
- Enjoy!

192.   Light Broiled Haddock Recipe

Serving: 6 | Prep: | Cook: 25mins | Ready in:

Ingredients

- 2 lbs. haddock filets (I'm pretty sure this will work for just about any ocean whitefish!)
- 1/2 stick frozen (yep!) butter or low-fat butter replacement
- 1 lemon
- 1/2 -1 cup seasoned breadcrumbs
- 1 c. Miracle Whip Free
- 1/3 cup skim milk
- 1/4 tsp. marjoram
- 1/2 tsp. dried parsley flakes
- 1/2 c. slivered almonds

Direction

- Combine marjoram to 1/2 c. breadcrumbs.

- Butter or Pam 13x9x2 Pyrex baking pan (for crispier all-around filets, put a heavy cooling rack and foil on the bottom instead of butter).
- Finely coat bottom of baking pan with seasoned breadcrumbs (without marjoram), if you're not using the rack.
- Wash haddock (or whatever scrod you're using) well and then dry on paper towel.
- Whisk and combine 1/3 cup milk and Miracle Whip Free in mixing bowl--don't let it get too thick... add milk as necessary.
- Soak fish in milk /MWF in mixing bowl (salt if necessary--oddly enough, I never use salt in my recipes!).
- Roll filet in breadcrumb mixture (with marjoram).
- Placed breaded filet on breadcrumb coating (or rack).
- Grate frozen butter with cheese grater over breaded filets (substitute low-fat spray margarine ad. lib.).
- Sprinkle with parsley and slivered almonds.
- Place thinly sliced lemon on top of almonds and parsley.
- Bake for 20-25 minutes at 350.
- Serves nicely with stuffing, rice or grill-fried zucchini.

193. Maine Atlantic Top Stuffed Haddock Recipe

Serving: 4 | Prep: | Cook: 20mins | Ready in:

Ingredients

- 4 (6-8 oz) haddock or other white fish (firm)
- 4 oz canned crabmeat
- 4 oz can tiny shrimp
- 1 cup bread crumbs
- 2 tbsp thyme
- 1/3 cup olive oil
- 1/2 tsp lemon zest
- 1/2 stick butter melted**
- 2 tbsp olive oil**

- 1/4 cup white wine**
- salt & pepper

Direction

- In bowl:
- Toss bread crumbs, thyme, crabmeat, shrimp, oil (1/3 cup), zest, salt & pepper.
- Divide bread crumb mixture into 4 portions.
- Pat one portion on a piece of fish and continue with other 3 pieces of fish.
- Put in 9 x 13 pan.   Bake at 350-degree oven.
- Mix together: **
- 1/2 stick melted butter
- 2 tbsp olive oil
- 1/4 cup white wine
- Pour over fish before baking.
- Bake 10-15 minutes or till fish flakes.

194. Mediterranean Baked Salmon In A Parmesan Crust Recipe

Serving: 2 | Prep: | Cook: 40mins | Ready in:

Ingredients

- 2 x 180g/6oz fillets Salmon - skinned
- ½tsp Garlic - very finely chopped
- 100g/3½oz Cream cheese - "Philadelphia"
- 1 Lemon - zest only - to taste
- 2tbsp Parmesan Reggiano - grated
- Quantity Breadcrumbs
- 2tbsp fresh Dill - finely chopped
- Smoked Paprika - for sprinkling - to taste
- Salt and freshly ground black pepper

Direction

- Preheat the oven to 200C/400F/Gas 6.
- Season both sides of the salmon fillets and place on lightly greased kitchen foil in a roasting tin;
- In a small bowl, mix the cream cheese, garlic and lemon zest to taste;

- Season to taste with salt and pepper and spread the mixture on top of each fillet;
- Similarly, in a small bowl, mix the breadcrumbs, parmesan and dill and again season to taste;
- Sprinkle this mixture over the cream cheese one and then sprinkle paprika over the top;
- Bake in the oven for some 12 to 15 minutes or so or until the salmon is just cooked through;
- Serve

195. Parsley & Lemon Crusted Haddock Recipe

Serving: 4 | Prep: | Cook: 25mins | Ready in:

Ingredients

- 4 slices of haddock
- 100g Dried breadcrumbs
- zest of 1 lemon
- 3 tsp parsley
- 4 large tomatoes sliced thickly
- 1 onion sliced
- 1 tbsp balsamic vinegar
- 1 tbsp olive oil

Direction

- Heat the oven to 200c. In a bowl combined the tomato and onion with the balsamic vinegar and oil season to taste. Lay them on the bottom of an oven dish and roast for 10mins. Whilst it is cooking, combine the breadcrumbs, lemon zest and parsley; top each piece of fish with mixture and a drizzle of olive oil. Place the fish on top of the tomato and onion and cook for a further 15mins.

196. Peppered Haddock With Garlic Whipped Potatoes And Parsley Sauce Recipe

Serving: 12 | Prep: | Cook: 14mins | Ready in:

Ingredients

- 12 oz olive oil
- 1 oz lemon juice
- 1/2 cup Chopped parsley
- 1/2 tsp salt
- 3 1/2 lb haddock fillets cut into 5-oz portions
- 2 tbsp Crushed black peppercorns
- 2 1/2 oz garlic Whipped potatoes

Direction

- Prepare the sauce:
- Combine 10 oz. oil, lemon juice, chopped parsley, and salt in a blender.
- Process until the parsley is puréed.
- Coat the fish fillets evenly with a light sprinkling of crushed peppercorns.
- Season with salt.
- Heat 2 oz. olive oil in as many sauté pans as necessary to hold the fish in a single layer.
- Place the fish in the pans, presentation side down, and sauté over moderate heat until lightly browned and about half cooked.
- Turn over and finish the cooking.
- Place a 3-oz portion of potatoes in the center of each plate.
- Top with the fish fillet.
- Drizzle about 1 oz. sauce in a circle around the fish.
- ==========================
- Variations:
- Other firm-fleshed white fish, such as cod, sea bass, striped bass, red snapper, or grouper, may be substituted.

197.   Seafood Trio Recipe

Serving: 4 | Prep: | Cook: 1hours | Ready in:

Ingredients

- 2 Fillets of haddock
- 12 sea scallops
- 1 lb. Lump crab meat
- 1 Stick butter (melted)
- 1 Pk Ritz or Club crackers (crushed)
- 2 Tbsp butter
- 2 Tbsp flour
- 2 Cups Half & Half
- juice of 1 lemon
- Zest of Half the lemon
- 2 Tbsp pepper

Direction

- Preheat oven to 350°
- Butter or cooking spray an 8x12 casserole dish.
- Crush a package of crackers.
- Microwave the stick of butter to melt.
- Put crackers in a bowl, slowly add butter and stir until blended, but not too soft.
- In a pan, melt 2 tbsp butter and add flour and stir until blonde in color, slowly add half & half, stir until thickened.
- Add lemon juice, pepper and zest to roux, stir.
- Lay fish, scallops and crab into pan.
- Pour lemon sauce over all seafood.
- Crumble cracker mixture over seafood.
- Bake for 40 to 45 mins.
- Enjoy!!

198.   Smoked Haddock Creamy Stew With Shallots Spinach And Saffron Recipe

Serving: 6 | Prep: | Cook: 10mins | Ready in:

Ingredients

- 900g-1.25kg undyed smoked haddock fillets
- 8-10 shallots, peeled
- 3tbsp extra-virgin olive oil
- 600ml double cream
- 2 good pinches of saffron strands
- Freshly ground black pepper
- 100g fresh baby leaf spinach

Direction

- Feel the smoked haddock with your fingertips for bones and pull any out. Cut the filleted fish into chunks about 3cm wide.
- Chop the shallot very finely. Heat the olive oil in a large sauté pan and sauté the shallot until it is quite soft but not colored. Add the pieces of fish, cream and saffron and gently simmer. The fish will take about 3 minutes to cook, depending to a certain extent on the width of your sauté pan.
- Season with plenty of pepper – no salt will be needed for most tastes because the smoked haddock should be sufficiently salty. Add the spinach. It will be a high mound but cover the pan with a lid and the spinach will wilt very quickly
- When the spinach has wilted right down, carefully – so as not to break up the pieces of fish more than you can help – combine it evenly with the rest of the contents of the sauté pan. Ladle into warmed bowls to serve.
- You can prepare your fish hours in advance or even the previous day. Keep it in a covered bowl in the refrigerator. Similarly, you can chop and sauté the shallots well in advance, so all you need to do before eating is to assemble the ingredients and cook them.

199.   Smoked Haddock And Cucumber Salad Recipe

Serving: 2 | Prep: | Cook: 10mins | Ready in:

Ingredients

- 1 pound smoked haddock fillets skinned and sliced
- 1/2 cucumber cut into strips
- 4 spring onions chopped
- Rind and juice of 1 lime
- 1 tablespoon fresh chopped chives
- 1 teaspoon salt
- 1 teaspoon freshly ground black pepper
- 4 ounces natural yogurt

Direction

- Place fish in a suitable container then add 2 tablespoons water.
- Cover and cook in microwave on high for 2 minutes.
- Remove fish slices using a slotted spoon and leave to cool.
- Mix together the cucumber and spring onion then arrange in a pile on a plate.
- Mix together the yogurt, chives, lime rind and juice.
- Place fish on top of cucumber mixture and pour over yogurt mixture.

---

200. Smoked Haddock And Zucchini Lasagne Recipe

Serving: 4 | Prep: | Cook: 25mins | Ready in:

Ingredients

- 3/4 pint (15 fl. oz.) milk
- 12 oz. smoked haddock fillet. The important thing is to use real peat-smoked haddock (which isn't a very deep colour), and avoid the orange-dyed stuff that some fishmongers try to pass off as the real thing. It will just give you an allergic reaction to the food colour and the other additives. Actually I reckon you could use any suitable flaky smoked fish of your choice, as long as it's not artificially coloured.
- 1 oz. butter
- 6 oz. courgettes (zucchini), sliced

- 4 oz. onions, chopped
- 1 heaped teaspoon chopped fresh tarragon
- Another 1 1/2 oz. butter
- 1 1/4 oz. plain flour
- About 8 oz. dried lasagne sheets
- 4 oz. grated cheese

Direction

- Preheat oven to Gas 4 180C/350F.
- In a pan, put the fish and the milk.
- Bring to a very low simmer.
- Cook the fish through, lightly - about 7 minutes or thereabouts, depending on how thick the fillets are.
- Remove the fish from the milk and reserve the milk.
- In a frying pan, heat the 1 oz. butter.
- Add the courgettes (zucchini), the onions and the tarragon.
- Sauté but do not color. Drain.
- In a heavy saucepan, heat the 1 1/2 oz. butter.
- Blend in the flour. Cook a little but do not allow to color.
- Then gradually, but quickly, blend in the milk in which the fish was cooked.
- Bring to the boil and cook over a gentle heat for 15 minutes. Check the seasoning.
- Butter a 10 x 8" baking dish.
- Spread some sauce over the bottom.
- On top, put a layer of lasagne.
- Cover with half the courgette/onion mixture and half the fish, flaked.
- Top with some more sauce.
- Another layer of lasagne.
- The other half of the fish, courgette and onion.
- Some more sauce.
- Another layer of lasagne.
- The last of the sauce.
- Scatter the cheese over the top.
- Bake for 25 minutes.

201. Spicy Fried Haddock Recipe

Serving: 2 | Prep: | Cook: 10mins | Ready in:

Ingredients

- 1 pound haddock boned and filleted
- 2 cloves garlic finely sliced
- 1 teaspoon ground cumin
- 2 limes
- 3 ounces gram flour
- oil for frying

Direction

- Cut fish into 1" wide strips.
- Put in a shallow bowl and squeeze over juice of one of the limes then toss gently.
- Add all the other ingredients except oil and remaining lime and toss again.
- Heat oil in a frying pan to a depth of 1/2".
- Wait until it's really hot then add fish shaking off any surplus flour.
- Fry 2 minutes then drain well on paper towels and serve with lime wedges.

202. Stir Fried Haddock Recipe

Serving: 4 | Prep: | Cook: 30mins | Ready in:

Ingredients

- Haddock fish (or any big fish like salmon)
- cinnamon stick - 1 (small)
- cloves - 2
- Mustard seeds - 1/2 tsp
- Onion - 1 (chopped)
- Garlic - 10 (finely chopped)
- Curry leaves, coriander leaves
- Turmeric powder - 1/2 tsp
- Green chillies - 3 (finely chopped or slit lengthwise)
- black pepper powder - 1/4 tsp

Direction

- Boil the fish in a closed vessel with some turmeric powder and salt. Cook for 20 mins and then remove from flame.
- After cooling it down, drain the water and peel the skin off the fish.
- Shred the fish and set aside. .
- Heat oil in pan and add mustard seeds, cinnamon and cloves.
- Add onion, garlic, green chilies and turmeric powder. Fry till onions are translucent.
- Add the shredded fish and a pinch of salt. Keep frying until the color of fish changes.
- Finally add pepper and curry leaves and remove from flame.

203. Stuffed Haddock Fillets Recipe

Serving: 6 | Prep: | Cook: 40mins | Ready in:

Ingredients

- 6 haddock fillets or cod .
- butter or margarine
- 1/12 cups of soft bread crumbs
- 2 tbs. minced onion
- 2tbs minced fresh parsley, 1/2 tsp. summer savoury.
- salt and pepper hot chicken broth or water to moisten dressing

Direction

- Oven at 400 ---mix dry ingredients.
- Sprinkle fillets with some salt.
- Spread with the moistened dressing on each piece of fish.
- Roll up and secure with toothpicks.
- Bake for 30 mins.
- Good with tartar sauce and mashed potatoes and peas.

204.   Sweet And Spicy Haddock Explosions Recipe

Serving: 6 | Prep: | Cook: 30mins | Ready in:

Ingredients

- 6 haddock filets, 6 oz. each
- 1 cup carrot julienned
- 1 cup snow pea julienned
- 1/2 cup red pepper julienned
- 4 oz. dry white wine
- 1 tbsp. cayenne pepper
- 1 Alouette Sweet and Spicy pepper Medley Spreadable cheese
- 6 Sheets parchment paper 12x8 inches

Direction

- Heat oven to 425°F.
- Place 6 sheets of parchment paper on flat surface.
- Fold each sheet in half to form a crease and reopen.
- Place one piece of Haddock filet in the center of the parchment paper on one side of the crease.
- Divide and spread Alouette Sweet and Spicy Pepper Medley Spreadable Cheese over each one of the filets.
- Top with a sprinkle of cayenne pepper.
- Top the filets with the julienne of vegetables and a little white wine.
- Fold the parchment paper along the crease over the prepared fish filets and begin folding open ends. Overlap folds as you move along. Once you reach the end, tip and twist several times to secure tightly.
- Bake in the oven for 10 -12 minutes.
- Remove from oven and serve while fish is still hot. Open parchment carefully as to not burn yourself.

205.   Thai Fish Curry Recipe Wine & Dine With Jeff Recipe

Serving: 4 | Prep: | Cook: 35mins | Ready in:

Ingredients

- 4 six oz pieces of haddock fish fillet (you can also use Cod and Halibut)
- 2 tablespoons of grapeseed oil
- 1/2 cup of shallots diced
- 1 tablespoon of finely grated ginger
- 3 garlic cloves minced
- 3 tablespoons of red curry paste
- 1 tablespoon of brown sugar
- 1 1/4 cup of coconut milk (full of fat)
- 1 1/4 cup of chicken stock
- 1 lemongrass stock pounded out cut in half
- 1 tablespoon of fish sauce
- 2 tablespoons of cilantro
- 3 scallions diced green parts only
- Juice of 1 lime

Direction

- 1. Add your shallots, garlic and ginger to your sauté pan with the grapeseed oil on medium heat sauté for 3 minutes do not a brown mixture. This is a one pan dish use a pan large enough to hold all the liquids.
- 2. Incorporate the curry paste with the sautéed vegetables and sauté for one minute.
- 3. Stir in your wet ingredients coconut milk and chicken stock once incorporated add the brown sugar and fish sauce and simmer for 8 minutes the sauce will reduce about 1/2 cup.
- 4. Cut the root and stem off lemongrass and remove outer layers with mallet pound out lemongrass add to the sauce. After cooking remove lemongrass from the sauce.
- 5. Salt the fish fillets add them to the red curry sauce and place a lid on and simmer for 5 to 7 minutes depending on the thickness of your fish. Very important note the sauce should not be on a rolling boil just a slight simmer for poaching the fish.

- 6. In the last minute of cooking add the lime juice, cilantro, and scallions to the sauce.
- 7. Serve the Thai red curry fish on your favorite rice or sauté some fresh spinach with garlic and olive oil and serve on top of the spinach.

206. Traditional Style Kedgeree Recipe

Serving: 4 | Prep: | Cook: 2hours | Ready in:

Ingredients

- 450g/1lb Smoked Haddock fillets - all bones removed
- 60g/2oz Ghee or butter
- 1 clove Garlic - finely chopped
- 180g/6oz basmati rice
- 1½in/4cm fresh Ginger - grated
- 4tbsp Spring Onions - finely chopped
- 2tbsp medium Curry Powder
- 2 Tomatoes - peeled, deseeded and chopped
- 1tsp Dijon Mustard
- Handful fresh Coriander - torn and shredded
- 150ml?5fl oz chicken stock
- 1 Bay Leaf
- ½ Lemon - juice only - to taste
- 1 small fresh Red Chilli - seeds removed - finely chopped
- 2 large Eggs - hard boiled
- Salt and freshly ground black pepper

Direction

- Cook the rice, drain, cool and set aside.
- Boil the eggs for some 10 minutes or so, drain, cool and set aside.
- Place the fish and bay leaves and a little salt in a shallow pan and cover with milk/water or mixture of both.
- Bring to the boil, cover and, reducing heat, simmer for about 5 minutes or so or until fish just cooked through.
- Remove from pan and leave to cool.

- Remove the skin from fish, flake into chunks and set aside.
- Melt the butter in a pan over a low heat, add the ginger, onion and garlic and cook for some 5 minutes or so to soften.
- Add the curry powder and mustard, stir in well and cook for a further few minutes.
- Add the chopped tomatoes, chicken stock and lemon juice; stir in well and, increasing heat, bring to a boil.
- Reduce heat to gentle, add the fish and rice to the pan and, stirring gently, heat through.
- Shell and Quarter the eggs.
- Add the eggs, most of the coriander and the chili and stir gently to consistency desired.
- Serve on plates adding the rest of the coriander as garnish.

207. Haddock Croquettes Recipe

Serving: 4 | Prep: | Cook: 20mins | Ready in:

Ingredients

- 700g cooked potatoes
- 60g butter
- 30ml chopped fresh parsley
- salt & pepper to taste
- 3 eggs
- 350g smoked haddock, flaked
- 250ml grated cheddar
- 100ml seasoned flour
- 200g breadcrumbs

Direction

- Mash potatoes, butter, parsley, seasonings and one egg.
- Add flaked fish & cheese.
- Divide mixture into 8 oblong shapes.
- Roll in seasoned flour.
- Beat the remaining 2 eggs.
- Dip croquettes into egg and then breadcrumbs.

- Gently fry on all sides.
- Drain and serve.

208. Haddock Fillets With Shrimp Sauce Recipe

Serving: 4 | Prep: | Cook: 20mins | Ready in:

Ingredients

- 30 mls butter
- 30 mls flour
- 250 mls milk
- 2mls salt
- 1ml pepper
- 15mls lemon juice
- 170 mls canned shrimps drained
- 450g halibut fillets
- 150 mls grated mozzarella cheese
- praprika
- parsley

Direction

- In a measuring cup, combine butter, flour, milk, salt and pepper.
- Cook in microwave on high for 3-4 minutes, stirring every minute.
- Add lemon juice and shrimps.
- In a rectangular baking dish 15 x 20cm, place fish fillets and cover with paper towel.
- Cook on high for 3 minutes.
- Pour shrimp sauce over the fish.
- Sprinkle with cheese and paprika.
- Garnish with parsley.
- Cook a further 3-4 minutes longer.

209. Smoked Haddock Recipe

Serving: 4 | Prep: | Cook: 60mins | Ready in:

Ingredients

- 4 SMOKED PIECES OF haddock
- 400 ML OF milk
- 3 KNOBS OF butter
- 2 LBS potatoes PEELED AND QUARTERED
- 2 TEASPOONS WHOLEGRAIN mustard
- 4 TABLESPOONS extra virgin olive oil
- 1/2 PACK chives SNIPPED
- 4 FRESH LARGE eggs
- 12 SPEARS OF asparagus
- 2 TABLESPOONS creamed horseradish
- PICH OF SEASALT
- fresh ground black pepper
- 1 BUNCH OF scallions

Direction

- THIS IS A VERY LOVELY BRUNCH OF SUPPER ON SUNDAY AND EASY TO PREPARE. YOU CAN PREPARE THE MASHED POTATOES. POACH THE EGGS BEFOREHAND.
- IN A FRYING PAN, ADD A PIECE OF BUTTER; ADD MILK AND FISH, BRING TO BOIL, LOWER TEMPERATURE, COVER PAN AND SIMMER FOR ABOUT 10 MINUTES.
- IN A SMALL COOKING POT, PLACE THE CHOPPED SCALLION AND 6 TABLESPOONS OF THE POACHING MILK AND COOK FOR 3 MINUTES TILL SOFT.
- MASH THE BOILED POTATOES, ADD REMAINING BUTTER, Q TABLESPOON MUSTARD AND 2 TABLESPOON OF HORSERADISH AND THE SOFTENED SCALLIONS.
- TO POACH EGGS, SIMPLY BRING WATER TO BOIL, ADD FEW DROPS OF VINEGAR, WHIRL THE WATER AND DROP THE EGG AND BOIL FOR 3 MINUTES, REPEAT THE PROCESS.
- MIX THE OLIVE OIL WITH THE MUSTARD AND CHIVES.
- NOW ALL ITEMS ARE READY. SCOOP SOME OF THE MASHED POTATOES AT THE BOTTOM OF THE PLATE, PLACE ONE PIECE OF HADDOCK AND TOP WITH THE POACHED EGG AND DRIZZLE WITH THE MUSTARD OIL MIX.

- GOES SUPERBLY WELL WITH CHILLED WHITE WINE.

Chapter 5: Red Snapper Recipes

***

210. BAKED SNAPPER Recipe

Serving: 4 | Prep: | Cook: 256mins | Ready in:

Ingredients

- fresh parsley CHOPPED
- MINCED garlic
- RED MAGIC BLACKENED REDFISH
- fresh lemon
- fresh tomato
- PARMESAN cheese
- OR bread CRUMBS
- salt AND pepper
- butter

Direction

- PREHEAT OVEN TO 350 DEGREES
- PLACE PATS OF BUTTER OR BUTTER SPRAY AND GARLIC ON BOTTOM OF GLASS BAKING PAN
- PUT FRESH CHOPPED PARSLEY ON TOP OF BUTTER AND GARLIC
- PLACE SNAPPER FILETS ON TOP OF PREVIOUS INGREDIENTS
- SPRINKLE RED MAGIC OVER SNAPPER
- BAKE FOR 30 MINUTES
- PUT BROILER ON HI FOR 5 OR LOW FOR 10 MINUTES

- SLICE TOMATO AND PLACE OVER SNAPPER
- SPRINKLE PARMESAN OR BREAD CRUMBS OVER SNAPPER
- BROIL FOR DESIGNATED TIME
- SPRINKLE MORE PARSLEY AND SQUEEZE MORE LEMON ON TOP AND ENJOY!!!!!!!!!!!!!!!!!!

211. Baby Snapper Ceviche Recipe

Serving: 1 | Prep: | Cook: | Ready in:

Ingredients

- 60 g Fillet of Snappers sliced sashimi style into 3 pieces
- ½ Long green Chilli seeded removed and chopped
- ¼ small Green capsicum finely chopped
- ¼ red onion finely chopped
- ¼ small Lebanese cucumber finely chopped
- ¼ avocado finely chopped
- ½ Scud Chilli finely chopped
- ½ lime juiced
- ¼ tablespoon olive oil
- sea salt and freshly gound white pepper

Direction

- Mix all dressing ingredients together and add the salt and pepper to taste.
- Just prior to serving, marinate the sliced snapper pieces in the additional lime juice for 30 seconds.
- Remove and pat dry.

212. Baked Red Snapper Italian Style Recipe

Serving: 4 | Prep: | Cook: 60mins | Ready in:

Ingredients

- 3 pounds red snapper, whole fish (or bass)
- 1 clove garlic - chopped fine
- salt and black pepper to taste
- 1 small hunk hard Italian cheese (maybe 2 oz)
- 1 can crushed tomatoes
- 1 1/2 cups seasoned bread crumbs
- 1/4 cup parm or romano cheese grated
- 1 tablespoon vegetable oil
- 1 small onion sliced very thin
- 3 slices lemon
- 6-8 mint leaves

Direction

- Mix bread crumbs, grated cheese and 3 finely chopped mint leaves (optional).
- Stuff fish and close and fasten with toothpick(s).
- Grease baking pan with tablespoon of oil and place fish in it.
- Slit fish on upturned side and in each slit, place 1 small piece cheese, some thin slices of onion and 1 mint leaf.
- Pour tomatoes over fish and arrange 3 thin slices of lemon on top.
- Bake at 350 F. for 1 hr. basting regularly.
- Cover during last 15 minutes of cooking.

213. Baked Red Snapper With A Spinach Stuffing Recipe

Serving: 4 | Prep: | Cook: 55mins | Ready in:

Ingredients

- red snapper (leave whole): about 4 to 5 lbs
- 1 tsp cayenne
- 1 clove garlic, minced
- 1 tbs scallions, chopped
- 1 tsp salt
- 1 1/2 cups fish stock
- 2 oz butter, melted
- 1 lime, juiced

- 1 tsp cornstarch
- spinach Stuffing:
- 1-2 bunches fresh spinach
- 1/2 cup chives or spring onions, chopped
- 1 lime, juiced
- salt, to taste
- 1 tsp black pepper
- 1 cup white bread crumbs
- 3 tbs milk

Direction

- Directions for Fish:
- The fish should be scaled and cleaned thoroughly with the under portion slit to remove the gut.
- Dry properly and season with pepper, salt, scallions, garlic and lime juice. Let stand for 45 minutes.
- Fill the cavity of the fish with spinach stuffing.
- Place the fish in a baking-serving dish and brush with half of the butter. Pour the fish stock and rest of the butter into the dish. Heat oven to 375 degrees and bake for 45 minutes, basting whenever necessary.
- Remove dish from oven. Use a bulb baster or spoon to remove juices into a saucepan.
- Thicken sauce over medium heat with 1 tsp cornstarch dissolved in 1 tbsp water. Pour over fish. Garnish with cut lime wedges and serve.
- Directions for Spinach Stuffing:
- Remove hard stems from spinach and cook in boiling water for about 8 minutes until tender.
- Drain off water and set aside to cool. Squeeze spinach to remove excess water--until the mass is homogeneous and pulpy.
- In a skillet, melt the butter and cook the spinach to remove as much moisture as possible. Remove from heat and add the lime juice, bread crumbs, salt, milk and pepper. Blend well.
- Season with more lime juice and salt if necessary to correct flavor.

214. Baked Or Broiled Stuffed Red Snapper Recipe

Serving: 6 | Prep: | Cook: 45mins | Ready in:

Ingredients

- 6- 10oz red snapper fillets
- garlic powder
- lemon juice
- Seafood seasoning (any brand)
- crabmeat and shrimp Dressing:
- 4 cups chopped onion
- 2 cups chopped celery (I sometimes omit)
- 1 cup vegetable oil
- 1 lb lump crabmeat
- 1/2 lb cooked shrimp, coarsley chopped or whole salad shrimp
- 2 tbsp fresh parsley
- 1 tbsp dried basil
- 1 tbsp creole seasoning
- 6 cups of bread crumbs

Direction

- Preheat to 375 degrees F or Broil.
- In an 8-quart pot, simmer onions and celery in oil until translucent.
- Add crabmeat, shrimp, basil, and Creole seasoning, and simmer for 15 minutes longer.
- Remove from heat and stir in bread crumbs and parsley.
- Sprinkle filets with garlic powder and rub with lemon juice.
- Cut pocket in filet and stuff with dressing and sprinkle with seasonings.
- Bake at 375 degrees, 20 to 30 minutes, or until done, or Broil for about 10 minutes until fish flakes. 5-6" away from heat source.

215. Basil Stir Fried Snapper Fillet Recipe

Serving: 4 | Prep: | Cook: 15mins | Ready in:

Ingredients

- 4-6 fillets cut into smaller pieces
- 6 tbs oil (I use olive oil)
- 4 tbs oyster sauce
- 3-4 tbs of shredded galanga or ginger
- 4-5 cloves of finely chopped garlic
- 3-4 stems of chopped thai basil leaves
- 1-2 cayanne pepper(s) cut
- young pepper corn - you can find bottled peppercorn found in asian grocery stores...or you can just skip this
- fish sauce to taste

Direction

- Wash and dry the fillet and sprinkle with salt.
- Heat the oil in the wok and fry the fish.
- Once cooked, put the fish on kitchen paper towel to absorb extra oil.
- In the same oil (add more oil if required), stir fry the garlic and peppers.
- Add the fish and ginger; stir.
- Add the oyster sauce and fish sauce.
- Add basil and young pepper corn.
- Serve with rice.

216. Blackened Red Snapper Recipe

Serving: 4 | Prep: | Cook: 15mins | Ready in:

Ingredients

- 40z redsnapper fillets or other white fish fillets
- onioj powder
- garlic powder
- Dry mustard
- Ground thyme
- Quebrado chile

Direction

- Combine onion powder, garlic powder, ground thyme and pepper.
- Sprinkle one side of the filets with half of this mixture.
- Spray a non-stick pan and heat to until hot.
- Add fillets, seasoned-side down, cook 4 mins.
- Sprinkle remaining spices to the other side and let cook for about 4 minutes and wwwwwhall you are the master chef. You can do this to chicken, pork, all kinds of fish; I believe we were serving blackened wall paper. Peace! Hahahah

217. Blackened Snapper Cajun Style Recipe

Serving: 4 | Prep: | Cook: 10mins | Ready in:

Ingredients

- 1 tablespoon of sweet paprika
- 1 tablespoon of cayenne pepper
- 1 Teaspoon of black pepper
- 1 teaspoon of white pepper
- 1 teaspoon of cumin
- ½ teaspoon of thyme
- ½ teaspoon of oregano
- 1 teaspoon of salt
- Four 6 to 8 ounce snapper fillets
- Melted butter

Direction

- Dip snapper in melted butter and sprinkle on the Cajun spice.
- Pan Fry over high heat until cooked.
- Serve with a spicy salsa.

218. Broiled Red Snapper With Orange Butter Sauce Recipe

Serving: 3 | Prep: | Cook: 10mins | Ready in:

Ingredients

- 1/4 cup fresh orange juice
- 1 tablespoon butter
- 3 tablespoons olive oil
- 1 teaspoon salt
- 1 teaspoon freshly ground black pepper
- 1/2 cup diced peeled seeded plum tomatoes
- 1-1/2 pounds skinless red snapper
- 1/4 cup chopped fresh chives

Direction

- Preheat broiler to high.
- In a saucepan reduce the orange juice by half over high heat.
- Add butter, 2 tablespoons of the olive oil, salt and pepper then blend well with a wire whisk.
- Add tomatoes and set aside.
- Brush fish on both sides with the remaining olive oil.
- Sprinkle with salt and pepper and arrange fish in an unheated broiler pan.
- Broil fish 3 inches from the heat source for 4 minutes.
- Transfer fillets to a platter and pour the orange sauce over them and garnish with chives.

219. Broiled Snapper And Pear Bruschetta Recipe

Serving: 4 | Prep: | Cook: 20mins | Ready in:

Ingredients

- 1 pound skinless red snapper fillets
- 4 large slices sourdough bread (about 2-ounces each and about 3/4-inch thick)
- 4 medium pears, thinly sliced
- juice of 1 small orange
- 1 Tbl. olive oil (Extra Virgin preferred)
- 2 tsp. chopped fresh rosemary
- 1/8 tsp. kosher salt
- 1/8 tsp. pepper
- 1 large red bell pepper, finely diced

- 2 Tbs. sliced almonds

Direction

- Preheat the broiler.
- Rinse the fish and pat dry with paper towels.
- Cut fish into 1/2-inch pieces. Set aside.
- Put the bread on a baking sheet.
- Broil about 6-inches from the heat for 4 to 6 minutes, or until golden on both sides, turning over halfway through the broiling time.
- Remove the bread from the oven.
- Cover each slice with a layer of overlapping pears.
- Be sure the pears overhang the bread by 3/8 to 1/2-inch, or the sides of the bread will burn.
- Broil for 5 to 7 minutes, or until the pears begin to bubble and brown.
- Meanwhile, in a medium bowl, stir together the orange juice, oil, rosemary, salt, and pepper.
- Stir in the fish, bell pepper, and almonds.
- Spoon over the browned pears.
- Broil for 4 to 6 minutes, or until the fish flakes easily when tested with a fork.

---

220. Bucaneer Snapper With Ti Malice Sauce Recipe

Serving: 6 | Prep: | Cook: 20mins | Ready in:

Ingredients

- 2 pounds snapper with skin intact
- 1/2 teaspoon salt
- 1 teaspoon freshly ground black pepper
- 1/3 cup extra virgin olive oil
- 1/4 cup fresh lime juice
- 2 thyme sprigs
- 1/8 teaspoon dry mustard
- Sauce:
- 2 medium onions finely chopped
- 2 shallots finely chopped
- 1/2 medium red bell pepper seeded and diced

- 1 medium tomato peeled seeded and chopped
- 2/3 cup fresh lime juice
- 3 tablespoons olive oil
- 1/8 teaspoon cayenne pepper
- 1/4 teaspoon salt
- 1 teaspoon freshly ground black pepper

Direction

- Season fish with salt and pepper then place in a large dish.
- Combine oil, lime juice, thyme and dry mustard then pour over the fish.
- Cover and refrigerate for 1 hour turning once.
- Prepare a charcoal grill.
- When the coals burn with a dusty glow lightly oil the grill.
- Arrange the fillets skin side down on the grill and cook for 3 minutes.
- Turn and cook for 3 minutes on the second side.
- Serve with sauce.
- To make sauce combine all ingredients and allow to sit at least 15 minutes to blend flavors.

---

221. Cant Miss Red Snapper Recipe

Serving: 4 | Prep: | Cook: 15mins | Ready in:

Ingredients

- 4 red snapper fillets, 1/2" thk - (8 oz ea)
- 1 teaspoon salt
- 1/2 teaspoon freshly-ground black pepper
- 1 cup chopped onions
- 1 green bell pepper -- chopped
- 1/2 cup butter - (1 stick)
- 1 tablespoon worcestershire sauce
- 1 cup freshly-grated Parmesan

Direction

- Season the fish with the salt and pepper. Spread the onions and pepper in a 13- by 9-

inch glass baking dish and place the fish on top. Dot the fish with butter. Sprinkle with a little Worcestershire sauce.

- Bake for 12 minutes, then baste fish with pan juices. Sprinkle the fish with Parmesan and then place under the broiler for about 2 minutes or until the cheese browns.
- To serve, spoon the vegetables over the fish.

- Bring a large pan of water to the boil. Arrange the fish in a steamer lined with baking parchment or in a large sieve and place over the boiling water. Cover and steam for 10 minutes. Turn the fish over and steam for 10 minutes or until the fish is cooked.
- Drain the fish and transfer to serving plates. Garnish with wedges of lime and serve with stir fried vegetables.

---

222. Chilli And Crab Stuffed Red Snapper Recipe

Serving: 4 | Prep: | Cook: 20mins | Ready in:

Ingredients

- 4 red snappers, cleaned and scaled
- 2 tbsp dry sherry
- salt and pepper
- stir fried shredded vegetables, to serve
- wedges of lime and red chilli strips, to garnish
- Stuffing
- 1 small red chilli
- 1 garlic clove
- 1 spring onion
- ½ tsp finely grated lime rind
- 1 tbsp lime juice
- 100 g white crab meat, flaked

Direction

- Rinse the fish and pat dry on absorbent kitchen paper. Season inside and out and place in a shallow dish. Spoon over the sherry and set aside.
- Meanwhile, make the stuffing. Carefully halve, deseed and finely chop the chili. Place in a small bowl.
- Peel and finely chop the garlic. Trim and finely chop the spring onion. Add to the chili together with the grated lime rind, lime juice and the flaked crab meat. Season with salt and pepper to taste and combine. Spoon some of the stuffing into the cavity of each fish.

223. Citrus Grilled Snapper With Lime Rice Recipe

Serving: 3 | Prep: | Cook: 20mins | Ready in:

Ingredients

- $ hour Chill Time
- ------------------
- 1 1/2 lb red snapper
- 1 cup orange juice
- 1 cup grapefruit juice
- 1/4 cup lime juice
- 2 tbl Minced fresh cilantro
- 1/4 tsp cayenne pepper
- 2 tbl soy sauce
- 1 tbl Chopped garlic
- -----------------
- LIME rice
- -----------------
- 1 1/2 cup water
- 1 cup long-grain rice
- 1 tbl extra-virgin olive oil
- 2 1/2 tbl Fresh lime or lemon juice
- 3 tsp Grated zest, (for garnish)
- 1 tsp Ground white pepper
- 1/4 cup Chopped green onion or scallions, (for garnish)

Direction

- Combine the citrus juices, cilantro, cayenne pepper, chopped garlic and soy sauce in a shallow baking dish. Add the fish and refrigerate for 4 hours, turning the fish after 2 hours. Preheat the oven to 375. Remove the fish from the marinade and wrap in aluminum foil. Place the wrapped package on a sheet pan and bake for 15 to 20 minutes, or until the flesh flakes easily. Unwrap the fish and serve on a large platter.

224. Coconut Lime Red Snapper Recipe

Serving: 4 | Prep: | Cook: 15mins | Ready in:

Ingredients

- 1 large egg, beaten
- 1/3 cup coconut milk
- 3/4 cup bread crumbs
- 1/2 cup flaked coconut (sweetened or unsweetened)
- 1 teaspoon grated lime peel
- 4 red snapper fillets (approx 1.5lbs)
- 1/4 cup mayo
- 2 teaspoons Dijon mustard
- 2 teaspoons lime juice

Direction

- Preheat oven to 450F. Lightly grease a baking sheet.
- Combine egg and coconut milk in a shallow dish. Combine bread crumbs, coconut and lime peel in another shallow dish.
- Dip fillets in egg mixture, then dredge in coconut mixture.
- Arrange fillets on prepared baking sheet. Bake 15 mins or until fish flakes easily with a fork.
- Meanwhile, whisk mayo, mustard, and lime juice in a small bowl. Serve alongside fish.

225. Coconut Crusted Red Snapper Recipe

Serving: 4 | Prep: | Cook: 15mins | Ready in:

Ingredients

- Four 8 oz. red snapper fillets with skin (boned, rinsed, and patted dry)
- 1/2 cup shredded coconut (unsweetened)
- 1/2 cup flour
- 2 teaspoons curry powder
- 1 teaspoon ground coriander
- 1 teaspoon ground cumin
- 1 teaspoon black pepper
- 1 teaspoon salt
- 1 egg
- 1/2 cup milk
- 1 Tablespoon olive oil

Direction

- In a shallow bowl combine coconut, 1/4 cup flour, curry powder, coriander, cumin, black pepper, and salt.
- Mix the ingredients together until evenly combined.
- In another shallow bowl whisk together the egg and the milk.
- Place the remaining 1/4 cup flour in a shallow bowl.
- For each fillet: working with the skin side only, press each fillet into the flour, then into the egg/milk mixture, and then into the coconut mixture.
- Heat the 1 Tablespoon of olive oil in a large sauté pan until hot. Then add the fillets to the pan, coconut side down.
- Cook 3 minutes. Then turn and cook until done, about one minute more.

226. Cuban Broiled Snapper With Parsley Recipe

Serving: 4 | Prep: | Cook: 20mins | Ready in:

Ingredients

- 1 pound fresh or frozen skinless red snapper fillets
- 1/4 teaspoon salt
- 1/2 teaspoon freshly ground black pepper
- 2 tablespoons butter melted
- 3/4 cup soft bread crumbs
- 2 tablespoons snipped fresh flat leaf parsley
- 1 teaspoon finely shredded orange peel
- 1 tablespoon orange juice
- 1 clove garlic minced
- 1/4 teaspoon dried oregano crushed
- 1/4 teaspoon freshly ground black pepper
- 1/8 teaspoon salt
- orange wedges for garnish

Direction

- Thaw fish if frozen then preheat broiler and rinse fish then pat dry with paper towels.
- Cut fish into serving size portions then place on greased unheated rack of a broiler pan.
- Tuck under any thin edges then sprinkle lightly with salt and pepper.
- Brush 2 teaspoons of the butter over fish then broil fish 4" from heat 15 minutes.
- Combine remaining butter, crumbs, parsley, peel, juice, garlic, oregano, pepper and salt.
- Spoon mixture over broiled fish then broil 2 minutes more or until topping is lightly golden.
- Transfer fish to a serving platter then serve with orange wedges.

227. Curry Snapper Recipe

Serving: 2 | Prep: | Cook: 5mins | Ready in:

Ingredients

- 1 tablespoon flour
- 1 teaspoon curry powder
- salt
- 2 (6-ounce) snapper fillets
- 1 teaspoon grapeseed oil
- 1 teaspoon butter
- 1/2 cup prepared papaya salsa

Direction

- Mix the flour, curry powder and a pinch of salt together. Sprinkle over both sides of the fish (make sure you check for and remove any small pin-bones prior to seasoning the fish).
- Heat the oil and butter together in a large skillet over medium heat. Add the fish and cook until cooked through, about 2 - 3 minutes per side.
- Per Serving: 225 Calories; 7g Fat; 35g Protein; 4g Carbohydrate; trace Dietary Fiber; 68mg Cholesterol; 262mg Sodium.

228. Easy Baked Red Snapper Recipe

Serving: 2 | Prep: | Cook: 45mins | Ready in:

Ingredients

- 2 whole red snappers, fresh or frozen(thawed)
- 1 lg red onion, sliced or diced
- 1 large tomato thinly sliced
- 2 cloves garlic minced
- 2 tbs minced fresh parsley or oregano
- 2 Tbs olive oil
- 2 Tbs melted butter
- seasoning of choice: I use Spike brand (non salt, dried veges and herbs)

Direction

- Rinse fish in water and pat dry.
- Season fish liberally all over with desired seasoning.

- Place some onion, garlic, herbs in cavity of each fish.
- Melt butter and combine with olive oil and drizzle some over fish.
- Top fish with onion and tomato slices and drizzle with some more olive oil and butter and some more garlic and herbs.
- Bake in a 350F oven about 45 minutes or fish flesh is opaque and done.
- Serve with veggies of choice, rice also makes a good accompaniment with fish.

229.   Fried Fish With Hot Basil And Chili Sauce Recipe

Serving: 0 | Prep: | Cook: 22mins | Ready in:

Ingredients

- 1-1.5 lbs fish fillet (I used red snapper)
- 4 tablespoons flour, mixed with a pinch of salt and white pepper
- oil for deep-frying
- Hot basil and Chilli Sauce:
- 1 tablespoon oil
- 3 cloves garlic, minced
- 2 red chillies, sliced (I used bird eye but you can use anything you want)
- 1 tablespoon sugar
- 1 tablespoon oyster sauce
- 1 tablespoon fish sauce
- 1 tablespoon soy sauce
- 1 teaspoon white pepper
- 10 basil leaves
- spring onions, finely chopped to garnish

Direction

- To make the Hot Basil and Chili Sauce:
- Heat the oil in a wok or saucepan over medium heat. Add the garlic and chilies and stir-fry for about 1 minute until fragrant. Add the sugar, oyster sauce, fish sauce, soy sauce and pepper, and stir-fry for a further minute.

Finally add the basil leaves, mix well and quickly remove from heat. Set aside.
- Dip the fish in the flour mixture to coat thoroughly. Heat the oil in a wok over high heat. Deep-fry the fish for 3 to 5 minutes until golden brown and crispy. Remove and drain the excess oil on paper towels. Place on a serving platter.
- Pour the Hot Basil and Chili Sauce over the deep-fried fish, garnish with spring onions and serve hot with steamed rice.

230.   Fried Fish With Schezwan Sauce Recipe

Serving: 2 | Prep: | Cook: 22mins | Ready in:

Ingredients

- fish slices - 6 nos (Sliced & Boneless) (I used red snapper)
- eggs - 2
- green chili paste - 1 tsp
- ginger - 1 tsp
- garlic - 1 tsp
- Chopped cilantro - 2 tsp
- pepper powder - 1 tsp
- corn flour - 2 tsp
- All purpose flour - ½ cup
- spring onion - 1 tsp
- Chilly Sauce - 1 tsp
- soya sauce - 1 tsp
- lemon juice - 1 tsp
- salt to taste
- vegetable oil
- For the sauce:
- 1/4 cup sesame oil
- 3-4 whole red peppers
- 3/4 onions-chopped fine + 1 tbsp garlic+ 1 tbsp ginger ground to a paste
- 1/2 tsp cayenne pepper
- 2 tbsp corn flour mixed in a cup of water
- 1 tbsp vinegar
- 1 tsp soya sauce

- 1 tsp chilli sauce
- salt to taste
- chopped spring onions and green peppers to garnish

Direction

- Make a batter with egg, flour, ginger, garlic, finely chopped spring onions, chilies, pepper, salt, soya sauce, chili sauce, lemon juice, cilantro and corn flour mixed with little water.
- Dip the fish in the batter. Deep-fry them till they turn golden brown.
- Serve with Schezwan sauce (recipe as follows):
- Heat oil in a wok; add whole red peppers and sauté over high heat till they darken a bit. Add the onions, garlic and ginger mix and stir-fry over high heat till glossy.
- Add the corn flour mix and bring to a boil.
- Lower the heat and add the chili powder, vinegar, soya sauce, chili sauce and salt and mix well.
- Cook till well blended for about a minute.
- Garnish and serve with fish.

231.   Gas Grill Red Snapper Recipe

Serving: 4 | Prep: | Cook: 8mins |Ready in:

Ingredients

- 2Tbs. sweet paprika
- 2tsp onion powder
- 2tsp garlic powder
- 3/4tsp ground coriander
- 3/4tsp table salt
- 1/4tsp cayenne pepper
- 1/4tsp black pepper
- 1/4tsp white pepper
- 2Tbs unsalted butter
- Large aluminum disposable baking pan
- 4 red snapper fillets,6-8oz. each,3/4" thick
- veg. oil for grill rack

Direction

- Combine paprika, onion powder, garlic powder, ground coriander, salt and peppers in small bowl. Melt butter in 10" skillet over med. heat. When foaming subsides, stir in spice mixture. Cook, stirring frequently, till fragrant and spices turn a dark rust color, 2-3 mins. Transfer mixture to pie plate and cool, stirring occasionally, to room temp., about 10 mins. Once cooled, use fork to break any clumps.
- Turn all burners to high, cover, and heat grill till very hot, about 15 mins. Use grill brush to scrape clean.
- Meanwhile, pat fillets dry on both sides with paper towels. Using sharp knife, make shallow diagonal slashes every inch along skin side of fish, being careful not to cut flesh. Place fillets skin side up on rimmed baking sheet. Using fingers, rub spice mixture in thin even layers on top and side of fish. Flip fillets over and repeat on other side (use all spice mixture). Refrigerate till needed.
- Lightly dip wad of paper towel in oil; holding with tongs, wipe cooking grate. Place fish perpendicular to grill grates, skin side down on grill. Leaving burners on high, grill uncovered until very dark brown and skin crisp, 3-4 mins. Using thin metal spatula, flip fish and continue to grill till dark brown, beginning to flake, and center is opaque but still moist, about 5 mins longer.
- This is great with remoulade sauce or pineapple or mango salsa.

232.   Grilled Creole Snapper Recipe

Serving: 4 | Prep: | Cook: 30mins |Ready in:

Ingredients

- 2 medium tomatoes, cut crosswise in half
- 1 medium onion, cut into fourths
- 1/2 medium green bell pepper, cut in half

- 4 medium green onions, thinly sliced (1/4 cup)
- 1 1/2 tablespoons red wine vinegar
- 1/2 teaspoon dried thyme leaves
- 1/2 teaspoon salt
- 1/4 teaspoon red pepper sauce
- 1 1/2 pounds red snapper, sole or flounder fillets, about 1/2 inch thick
- cooking spray
- 2 tablespoons chopped fresh parsley
- Hot cooked rice, if desired

Direction

- Heat coals or gas grill for direct heat. Spray large piece of heavy-duty aluminum foil with cooking spray. Place tomatoes, onion and bell pepper on foil. Wrap foil securely around vegetables. Cover and grill foil packets, seam sides up, 4 to 6 inches from medium heat 6 minutes, turning once.
- While vegetables are grilling, mix green onions, vinegar, thyme, salt and pepper sauce in medium bowl; set aside.
- Spray fish and hinged wire grill basket with cooking spray. Place fish in basket; add to grill with vegetables. Cover and grill fish 7 to 8 minutes, turning once, until fish flakes easily with fork.
- Place fish on serving platter; keep warm. Coarsely chop grilled vegetables. Toss vegetables, parsley and green onion mixture; spoon over fish. Serve with rice.

---

233. **Grilled Red Snapper Over Swiss Chard, Broccolini , Carrots, And Asparagus Medley Over Arroz Amarillo With A Red Peppper Demi Glace Recipe**

Serving: 2 | Prep: | Cook: 40mins | Ready in:

Ingredients

- 4 red snapper fillets (about 2" x 4")
- 6 swiss chard stems (leaves removed)
- 6 Broccolini florets
- 4 carrot sticks
- 4 asparagus stems
- 1 tablespoon red pepper flakes
- 1 pinch salt
- 1 pinch pepper
- Arroz Amarillo Ingredients
- 1 cup Extra long grain rice
- 2 tbsp. extra virgin olive oil
- ½ medium yellow onion, finely chopped (about ½ cup)
- ¼ green bell pepper, finely chopped (about ¼ cup)
- 1 medium tomato, finely chopped, (about ½ cup)
- 1 tbsp. Achiote Seeds (also called "Annato")
- 1 packet Sazón with coriander and Annatto (a seasoning mix sold by GOYA)
- 2 tbsp. Sofrito (a tomato, onion, pepper mixture often sold by GOYA)

Direction

- VEGGIES
- Simply julienne Swiss chard, carrots, asparagus, and broccolini florets. Blanche and set aside. Add salt and pepper to taste. The blanching process will maintain the vegetables' color and crisp texture for the best look and effect.
- FISH
- Add salt and pepper to fish fillets. Cut into mini steaks then grill in pan.
- Cut fish fillets into mini rectangular shaped steaks. Add salt and pepper to both sides.
- Pan-fry fish in oiled pan until it begins to flake when tested with a fork (indicating that it's done).
- RICE
- This rice is best made in a flat, wide frying pan and spatula.
- Add achiote seeds and oil to frying pan. Heat pan and coat seeds thoroughly until the oil turns a deep, burnt red color and seeds are blackened. Reduce flame and remove seeds from oil.

- Immediately add rice to oil in pan. Coat rice thoroughly until it achieves a translucent reddish color (in about 2 mins).
- Add 1 packet of Sazon to rice and mix thoroughly again until an even deeper red-yellow-orange color is achieved.
- Immediately add sofrito, onions, tomatoes and peppers, mix thoroughly then add 2 cups of water.
- Bring rice mixture to a boil. Lower heat to medium-low and simmer, covered, until rice is tender and water is absorbed completely, about 25 minutes. Fluff rice with a fork and let it sit, covered, for 5 minutes before serving.

234. Grilled Red Snapper With Avocado Papaya Salsa Diabetic Friendly Recipe

Serving: 4 | Prep: | Cook: 10mins | Ready in:

Ingredients

- Ingredients:
- 1 tsp. ground coriander
- 1 tsp. paprika
- ¾ tsp. salt
- ¼ tsp. ground red pepper
- 1 Tbs. olive oil
- 4 skinless red snapper or halibut fish fillets (5 to 7oz each)
- ½ cup diced ripe avocado
- 2 Tbs. cilantro chopped
- 1 Tbs. fresh lime juice
- 4 Lime wedges

Direction

- 1) Prepare grill for direct grilling. Combine coriander, paprika, salt and red pepper in a small bowl or cup; mix well.
- 2) Brush oil over fish. Sprinkle 2 ½ tsp. Spice mixture over fish fillets; set aside remaining spice mixture. Place fish skin side down on

oiled grid over medium-hot heat. Grill 5 minutes per side or until fish is opaque.
- 3) Meanwhile, combine avocado, papaya, cilantro, lime juice and reserved spice mixture in a medium bowl; mix well. Serve fish with salsa and garnish with lime wedges. Makes 4 servings.
- Nutritional Values: Calories per serving: 221, Fat 9g, Carbohydrate 5g, Cholesterol 51mg, Sodium 559mg
- Note: This is a Diabetic Friendly recipe.

235. Grilled Red Snapper With Creole Sauce Recipe

Serving: 0 | Prep: | Cook: 30mins | Ready in:

Ingredients

- Grilled Red Snapper:
- 1 whole fish (clean and gutted) if possible otherwise fish fillet
- chilies crushed (optional)
- Virgin coconut oil
- garlic paste
- ginger paste
- lime juice
- Soy sauce
- tomato sauce
- Salt- to taste
- Pepper- to taste
- CREOLE SAUCE FOR FISH:
- 1kg fresh tomatoes
- 1 onion sliced
- 1 sachet of bouquet garni or fresh herbs
- 6 tsps coconut oil
- salt
- pepper

Direction

- For the Grilled Fish:
- Score the whole fish. Blend all the spices together and insert in the slices of the fish or simply baste the fish fillet in the sauce and

leave to marinade in the fridge. Add some more oil on the fish to help it marinade better. Grill the fish in the oven or on a BBQ grill. Turn over regularly to ensure both sides are cooked evenly.
- For Creole Sauce:
- Heat oil in pan. Stir in onions and tomatoes until really soft. Add some water, bouquet garni or the fresh herbs. Cover and simmer until the sauce reduces. Add salt and pepper to taste. If sauce is too thick, let it reduce some more and if sauce is too dry, add a little more water. Serve with grilled fish.

---

236. Grilled Redfish On The Half Shell Recipe

Serving: 0 | Prep: | Cook: 1hours | Ready in:

Ingredients

- Grilled Redfish on the Half-Shell
- thx to BBqGuys .com
- 2 red fish fillets on the half shell (one side still has the skin and scales intact)
- marinade:
- 1/4 cup- Worcestershire sauce
- 1/4 cup- extra virgin olive oil
- 1/4-1/2 teaspoon- cayenne pepper
- 1/4 teaspoon- dried thyme
- 1 Tablespoon- paprika
- Sea salt and fresh ground black pepper to taste
- 1 yellow onion
- 1 lemon
- 2 whole garlic cloves
- 1 bunch - parsley
- 1/2 stick (unsalted/diced)- butter

Direction

- - Lay red fish fillets in a bowl flesh side up.
- - Pour marinade ingredients over the fillets, rub in well, and set aside.
- - Thin slice the onion, garlic, and half of a lemon.

- - Squeeze the reserved half a lemon over the fish.
- - Lay the thin sliced onion and garlic over the fish and allow the fillets to marinade for 30 minutes.
- - Preheat your grill to medium heat, and place the fillets on the grill flesh side down, reserving the sliced onions and garlic.
- - After the flesh side has nice color and grill marks, turn the fillets flesh side up, and add the reserved onion and garlic slices from earlier.
- - Once fish has been cooking for a total of about 20 minutes, place a cast iron sauce pan on the grill.
- - Add in butter, once it is half way melted remove the pan from the grill and add parsley.
- - Season sauce with sea salt to taste and a squeeze of lemon.
- - Remove the red fish from the grill and pour sauce over the top. Garnish the top of the fillets with thin sliced lemon, parsley and enjoy!

---

237. Grilled Whole Red Snapper / Charred Tomato Jalapeno Vinaigrette. Recipe

Serving: 0 | Prep: | Cook: 2hours | Ready in:

Ingredients

- Grilled Whole red snapper / Charred tomato jalapeno vinaigrette.
- from Grillin and Chillin
- 1 1/2 lb whole red snapper -- scaled : & gutted 4 TB olive oil : salt : freshly ground black pepper Prepare a wood or charcoal grill and let it burn down to embers.
- Rub each fillet with 1 tablespoon of the olive oil. season to taste with salt and pepper. Grill for 7 minutes on each side or until cooked. Serve with Charred tomatoJalapeno vinaigrette.

Direction

- Charred Tomato, Jalapeno Vinaigrette
- Yield: 1 Serving
- Ingredients:
- 1   2 whole tomatoes
- 1   2 jalapeno peppers
- Instructions:
- 2 TB olive oil
- 2 TB red onion -- diced
- 1 TB garlic -- minced
- 1 TB Dijon mustard
- 1 TB red wine vinegar
- 1 TB rice wine vinegar
- 1 c olive oil
- 1 TB sesame oil
- 2 TB basil chiffonnade
- 1 TB Ancho chile powder
- Salt
- Freshly ground black pepper
- As soon as the snapper comes off the grill, sprinkle it with the vinaigrette (which has to be at room temperature). The vinaigrette heats up on the fish and all the flavors spring to life.
- Brush the jalapenos and tomatoes with olive oil, and cook on the grill until the skin is charred. Let the peppers and tomatoes cool and then coarsely chop the tomatoes and slice the jalapenos thin.
- In a large mixing bowl, combine the remaining ingredients, including the salt and pepper to taste, with the jalapenos and tomatoes, and whisk until blended. Bring to room temperature before serving.
- Spoon the vinaigrette, to taste, over the fish as soon as you take it off the grill and serve immediately.
- Yield: 2 cups

238.   Jamaican Grilled Fish Recipe

Serving: 3 | Prep: | Cook: 40mins | Ready in:

Ingredients

- * 3 Medium Snappers
- * salt to taste
- * pepper to Taste
- * Powder onion
- * pimento (all spice) branches or aromatic wood
- * Red Stripe beer and water
- * lemon

Direction

- 1. Cut fish in slices and add salt, pepper, powdered onion and pimento
- 2. Squeeze lemon over the fish
- 3. Marinate for about 2 hours in the refrigerator.
- 4. Mix a solution of half water and half beer (salt is optional)
- 5. Grill the fish on a low fire.
- 6. Sprinkle the fish occasionally with Beer/water solution to keep it moist and keep the fire low.
- 7. Cook for approximately 25-35 mins.
- 8. Serve with 4.

239.   Jamaican Red Snapper With Vegetables Recipe

Serving: 6 | Prep: | Cook: 55mins | Ready in:

Ingredients

- 2 lbs whole snappers, cleaned and scaled
- (or substitute 1.5lb snapper fillets)
- 1/2 cup fresh lime juice
- salt & freshly ground black pepper
- 1/2 cup olive oil
- 1 large onion, thinly sliced
- 1 teaspoon fresh thyme
- (or substitute 1/2 teaspoon dried thyme)
- 1/2 teaspoon fresh oregano
- 1 bay leaf, crumbled
- 1 medium onion, diced

- 3 carrots, peeled and sliced
- 8 oz calaloo or spinach, washed w/tough stems discarded
- 2 cloves garlic, minced
- 1 scotch bonnet or jalapeno chili, deseeded and minced
- 1 tablespoon chopped fresh parsley

Direction

- Step 1: Rub the fish inside and out with the lime juice, season it with salt and pepper, and set aside to marinate.
- Step 2: Pour 6 tablespoons of the olive oil into a large roasting pan or baking dish and arrange the onion slices on the bottom of the pan. Sprinkle them with thyme, oregano, and bay leaf and additional salt and pepper.
- Step 3: Drain the fish, saving the lime juice; pour the preserved lime juice over the onions in the pan. Place the snapper on top of the bed of onions.
- Step 4: Heat the oven to 400F.
- Step 5: Heat the remaining 2 tablespoons of olive oil in a skillet over medium heat and sauté all of the remaining ingredients for 3 minutes.
- Step 6: Place the sautéed vegetables around the fish and bake, uncovered, until the fish flakes easily when tested with a fork (about 20 to 30 minutes).

---

240. Lemon Red Snapper With Herbed Butter Recipe

Serving: 4 | Prep: | Cook: 40mins | Ready in:

Ingredients

- • Four 6-8 oz. red snapper or other firm white fish fillets.
- • 2 large lemons.
- • 1 Tbs. olive oil.
- • ¼ tsp. salt.
- • ¼ tsp. smoked paprika.

- • ¼ tsp. FG black pepper.
- • 2-3 Tbs. butter, softened.
- • 1 1/2 tsp. finely chopped fresh herbs of choice, such as rosemary, thyme, basil, parsley, etc.
- • Fresh herb sprigs (optional).

Direction

- 1. Preheat oven to 425° F. (220° C).
- 2. Cut 1 lemon into 8 slices. Place slices, in pairs, on a rimmed baking sheet you've brushed with olive oil. Grate remaining lemon to get 1 tsp. lemon zest; set aside. Reserve lemon for lemonade.
- 3. Place 1 fillet on top of each pair of lemon slices. Combine salt, paprika, and pepper; sprinkle evenly over fish. Bake at 425° for 12-13 minutes or until fish flakes easily when tested with a fork or until desired degree of doneness; DO NOT OVERCOOK!
- 4. While fish bakes, combine reserved lemon zest, softened butter, and herbs in a small bowl.
- 5. Place fish and lemon slices on individual serving plates; top each fillet with herbed butter, spreading to melt.
- 6. Garnish with herb sprigs, if desired.
- I sautéed a mixture of zucchini, red bell pepper, broccoli florets and Enoki mushrooms in butter and steamed some Basmati rice as sides. A 2012 Babich Sauvignon Blanc from NZ was perfect.

---

241. Lemony Red Snapper Fillets Recipe

Serving: 4 | Prep: | Cook: 45mins | Ready in:

Ingredients

- 4 red snapper fillets
- 1/2 cup sliced carrots
- 1/2 cup sliced celery
- 1 cup largely diced potatoes

- 1/2 cup chopped parsley
- 1 teaspoon minced garlic
- 3/4 cup extra virgin olive oil
- 1 cup white wine
- 1 teaspoon chopped fresh basil
- 1/2 cup ready cut tomatoes
- 1 tablespoon salt
- 1 teaspoon freshly ground black pepper
- 1 large lemon sliced into rounds

Direction

- Place the fish on a large sheet of foil or parchment paper.
- Make sure the foil is large enough to completely cover the fish when folded.
- Place vegetables around fish then shake wine and olive oil together in a jar to make an emulsion.
- Pour this over the fish then sprinkle fish with parsley, basil, garlic, salt and pepper.
- Garnish top of fish with lemon slices.
- Fold over foil all around fish and make sure it has a tight fit so liquid will not boil out.
- Bake at 325 for 45 minutes.

242. Limed Snapper Recipe

Serving: 2 | Prep: | Cook: 20mins | Ready in:

Ingredients

- 1/3 cup chopped scallions
- 2 tablespoons butter
- 2 chopped ripe tomatoes
- 3 tablespoons fresh lime juice
- 2 tablespoons chopped green chilies
- 1 tablespoon chopped parsley
- 1/8 teaspoon salt
- 1/8 teaspoon garlic salt
- white pepper
- 1 pound red snapper fillets
- lime wedges

Direction

- Sauté scallions in butter until tender.
- Add remaining ingredients except snapper and lime wedges then bring to boil.
- Reduce heat and simmer 10 minutes.
- Put snapper in sauce then spoon over fish.
- Cover and simmer 10 minutes longer.
- Serve on heated platter surrounded by lime wedges.

243. Louisiana Court Bouillon Recipe

Serving: 0 | Prep: | Cook: 2hours | Ready in:

Ingredients

- Louisiana Court Bouillon
- thanks to Leah Chase
- (some people turn this into a thick seafood stew , like Gumbo. and others make it soupy, find the one that works for you. I make my Gumbo like a thick stew. I would more than likely do the same with this recipe.)
- Preparation time: 35 minutes
- Cooking time: 1 hour, 45 minutes
- 1 redfish (4 to 5 pounds), or any other firm whole fish like red snapper
- 1 bay leaf
- 1 rib celery, coarsely chopped
- 1 medium-size carrot, scraped and coarsely chopped
- 1 medium-size onion, coarsely chopped
- 1 clove garlic, peeled and lightly crushed
- 4 to 5 cups water
- 1/2 cup vegetable oil
- 2 tablespoons flour
- 1/2 cup chopped onion
- 1/2 cup chopped green pepper
- 1 tablespoon chopped garlic
- 3 cups whole tomatoes, peeled and coarsely chopped
- 1 teaspoon fresh thyme leaves
- 1 tablespoon salt, or to taste
- 1/2 teaspoon cayenne pepper

- 1 whole dried red pepper
- 1 tablespoon minced parsley.

Direction

- 1. Have your fishmonger scale, gut and fillet the fish, saving the head and bones. Cut each fillet in three pieces and set aside.
- 2. In large stock pot, place fish head and bones with bay leaf, celery, carrot, the coarsely chopped onion and the crushed garlic. Add water, enough to just cover the fish bones. Bring to a boil over medium heat, reduce heat to bare simmer, cover and simmer for about an hour, until the stock is well flavored with fish.
- 3. Remove bones and vegetables from stock and discard. Strain stock through a fine sieve and set aside until ready to use. (Stock may be prepared ahead of time and refrigerated or frozen until ready to use.)
- 4. In a Dutch oven or other large casserole, heat vegetable oil. When it is hot, add flour and cook, stirring constantly with a wooden spoon, until flour is light tan. Add chopped onion and cook, stirring, until translucent, about 10 minutes. Add green pepper and chopped garlic, and cook 5 more minutes, continuing to stir.
- 5. Add the tomatoes and 3 cups of fish stock. Stir well. Add thyme, salt, cayenne pepper, whole red pepper and parsley. Let gravy come to a boil, then lower heat to simmering.
- 6. Add fish pieces to simmering gravy. Simmer for 20 minutes or until fish is flakes. Serve immediately over plain boiled rice.
- Yield: 4 to 6 servings.

244. Mexican Orange Snapper Recipe

Serving: 2 | Prep: | Cook: 10mins | Ready in:

Ingredients

- 3 tablespoons flour

- 1/4 teaspoon salt
- 1/2 teaspoon freshly ground black pepper
- 1 pound snapper fillets
- 1 teaspoon olive oil
- 1/2 cup chopped red onion
- 2 garlic cloves crushed
- 1/2 cup orange juice
- 4 orange slices for garnish

Direction

- Place flour on a plate and season with salt and pepper.
- Rinse fillets and pat dry with a paper towel.
- Dip into seasoned flour making sure both sides are coated then shake off excess.
- Heat olive oil in medium nonstick skillet on medium high.
- Add fish, onion and garlic then brown 3 minutes per wide.
- Remove to a plate and season with salt and pepper.
- Add orange juice to skillet stirring to scrape up brown bits.
- Lower heat to medium and return fish to skillet then cover and cook 5 minutes.

245. Mexican Red Snapper Recipe

Serving: 4 | Prep: | Cook: 8mins | Ready in:

Ingredients

- 2 pounds red snapper filets or orange roughfy
- 2 cups pico de gallo
- 3 cups flour
- 2 limes
- 1 tablespoon red pepper
- 1 tablespoon black pepper
- 1 tablespoon salt
- 3 cups water
- 1/2 cup olive oil

Direction

- Soak filets in lime juice, salt and water for 2 hours.
- Drop in flour, red and black pepper.
- Sauté in olive oil.
- Cook until light brown.
- Serve with Pico de Gallo.

246. Mushroom Baked Snapper Fillets Recipe

Serving: 2 | Prep: | Cook: 20mins | Ready in:

Ingredients

- olive oil spray
- 3/4 pound snapper fillets
- 1 teaspoon olive oil
- 4 ounces sliced mushrooms
- 1 tablespoon chopped fresh thyme
- 1/2 teaspoon salt
- 1 teaspoon freshly ground black pepper
- 1/4 cup white wine

Direction

- Preheat the oven to 450.
- Line baking tray with foil and spray with olive oil spray.
- Place tray in the oven while oven preheats.
- Rinse fish and pat dry.
- Remove tray from oven and place fish on it.
- Brush fillets with olive oil then spoon mushrooms over top.
- Sprinkle with thyme, salt and pepper.
- Pour wine over fish and cover tray with foil then bake 10 minutes.
- Place fish on plates and spoon mushrooms and sauce over top.

247. Mustard Roasted Snapper Recipe

Serving: 4 | Prep: | Cook: 1hours | Ready in:

Ingredients

- • Four 8oz. (225 g) Snapper fillets.
- • Kosher salt and freshly ground black pepper.
- • 8 oz. (235 ml) creme fraiche.
- • 3 Tbs. Dijon mustard.
- • 1 Tbs. whole-grain mustard, more or less to taste.
- • 2 Tbs. minced shallots.
- • 2 tsp. drained capers.

Direction

- 1. Preheat the oven to 425 F (220 C).
- 2. Line a sheet pan with parchment paper.
- 3. Place the fish fillets skin side down on the sheet pan.
- 4. Sprinkle generously with salt and pepper.
- 5. Combine the creme fraiche, 2 mustards, shallots, capers, 1 tsp. salt, and 1/2 tsp. pepper in a small bowl.
- 6. Spoon the sauce evenly over the fish fillets, making sure the fish is completely covered.
- 7. Bake for 10 to 15 minutes, depending on the thickness of the fish, until it's barely done. (The fish will flake easily at the thickest part when it's done.) Be sure not to overcook it!
- 8. Serve hot or at room temperature with the sauce from the pan spooned over the top.
- A watercress salad. Some crusty bread. . And a bottle of nice, Aussie, Pouilly Fume work very well. .

248. Oregenata Crusted Snapper Recipe

Serving: 1 | Prep: | Cook: 17mins | Ready in:

Ingredients

- 6 (6-ounce) red snapper fillets
- 5 idaho potatoes, peeled and grated
- 1/2 cup melted butter
- 1 cup oregenata-spices crust
- 1 tablespoon salt
- 3/4 tablespoon freshly ground black pepper
- 1 cup grated Asiago
- 1 tablespoon finely minced lemon zest
- Preheat oven to 425 degrees F.

Direction

- Bring a large pot of lightly salted water to boil. Add grated potatoes, boil for 30 seconds, and then drain. Plunge into an ice bath and drain immediately. Spread the potatoes on a plate or baking sheet to dry. Toss with the melted butter, salt, pepper, cheese, and lemon zest. Coat each filet with potato, lightly pressing with fingertips.
- Place the fish on a lightly oiled baking sheet and roast for 15 to 20 minutes in the oven until lightly browned and cooked through.

---

249.   Pan Fried Fish Recipe

Serving: 0 | Prep: | Cook: 17mins | Ready in:

Ingredients

- 500 gms red snapper fillet
- vegetable oil
- For the Marinade:
- salt
- black pepper
- juice of half a lime
- mustard paste 2-3 tbsps
- ginger garlic paste- 2 tsps
- green chilli chopped- to taste
- 1 egg
- rice/corn flour - 1 tbsp

Direction

- Stir in all the ingredients together for the marinade.
- Marinate the fillets in this mix and refrigerate for half an hour.
- Before frying, remove excess marinade.
- Heat oil in a pan, fry the fish pieces for 3-4 minutes each side till it turns golden brown.
- Drain excess oil on a paper towel and serve with salad or chips or both :)

---

250.   Pan Fried Red Snapper In A Coconut Cream Sauce With Spinach And Red Pepper Topping Recipe

Serving: 4 | Prep: | Cook: 30mins | Ready in:

Ingredients

- 675   grams (4 fillets) boneless red snapper
- -- fillets
- 4   teasp. Whatever Whenever rub
- 1   tablesp. olive oil for fish & rub
- 2   tablesp. olive oil for pan-frying
- 2   tablesp. salted butter for pan-frying
- SAUCE
- 1   can Asian coconut milk (not the one used in
- -- cocktails)
- 3   sprigs green onions
- 1   stalk lemon grass
- 1/2   tablesp. Grated ginger
- 1/2   tablesp. Whatever Whenever rub
- 3/4   teasp. salt
- TOPPING
- 1/2   large red pepper
- 3   garlic cloves
- 4   cups baby spinach leaves
- 1   tablesp. olive oil
- 1   tablesp. salted butter
- 1/8   teasp. Grated nutmeg
- 1/4   teasp. salt
- WHATEVER WHENEVER RUB

- 1 1/2 tablesp. paprika
- 2 tablesp. brown sugar
- 1 tablesp. garlic powder
- 1/2 tablesp. black pepper
- 1 tablesp. onion powder
- 1 tablesp. thyme leaves
- 1 tablesp. oregano leaves
- 1/2 tablesp. cayenne pepper
- 1/4 tablesp. turmeric
- 1/2 tablesp. cumin powder
- 1 1/2 tablesp. salt

Direction

- Red bell pepper - Halve, then quarter one half. Slice into strips, 1/4" thick.
- Green onions - Discard root tips & chop the onions including green parts.
- Lemon grass - Use only the bottom 7". Cut into 3 lengths, crush with a mallet & set aside.
- Ginger - Use a fine grater & grate.
- Garlic cloves - Peel, slice cloves & set aside.
- Spinach - If pre-washed then measure out 4 cups & set aside
- Fish - Place the fish on 2 layers of kitchen paper towels and thoroughly. Gently press the fish with another paper towel to dry on both sides. Drizzle a total of 1/2 tbsp olive oil on one side of the fish. Sprinkle a total of 2 tsp rub, shared equally between the fillets. Rub with clean fingers, working the rub into the fish. Flip over the fillets & repeat on the other side with another 1/2 tbsp olive oil & 2 tsp rub. Set aside.
- Cooking Method
- Sauce
- In a sauce pan, add the coconut milk, lemon grass, grated ginger, chopped green onions, 3/4 tsp salt & 1/2 tbsp rub. On medium heat, bring to simmer. This should take a couple of minutes. Turn off heat. Do not boil or allow the coconut milk & its natural oils to separate. Taste & adjust seasonings. Set aside so the seasonings infuse the sauce. Remove lemongrass stalks before serving.
- Spinach topping

- In a sauté pan, on medium heat, heat olive oil till fuming, add the butter. Once the butter melts, immediately add the garlic & red pepper strips. Sauté for 2-3 minutes. Add the baby spinach leaves. Turn with tongs and let wilt, 2 or 3 min. Add 1/4 tsp salt & 1/8 tsp grated nutmeg. As soon as the spinach wilts take pan off the heat. Do not cover set aside & get working on the fish.
- Fish
- In a heavy flat bottom frying pan, preferably a sat iron pan if you have one, on medium - high heat, (gas mark 8 in my case, shy of high heat) heat olive oil till fuming, add the butter. Once the butter melts, immediately add fish fillets in a single layer. Pan-fry for about 3 or 4 minutes without touching or flipping over. You will be able to tell when the fish is ready to flip - the sides turn from pink to flaky white. Very gently with a spatula, turn the fish over & continue to cook about another 2 minutes. By this time the fish meat should be flaky white & surface slightly blackened. Immediately remove to plates & assemble
- Assembly
- To assemble, place the fish on the plate. Pour about 1/2 cup sauce over and around the fish. Divide the spinach topping into 4 parts. Place one portion of the topping over the fish.
- Serve Immediately. Enjoy!
- Whatever - Whenever Dry Rub
- Place all ingredients, one by one in a screw top glass jar or any plastic container with tight lid. Close lid tightly and shake for 30 seconds vigorously to combine all above ingredients in a thoroughly dry airtight container.
- Store in a dry and cool place.

---

251.   Pan Grilled Fish Over Citrus Dijon Orzo Recipe

Serving: 6 | Prep: | Cook: 30mins | Ready in:

Ingredients

- 3lbs fish fillets
- couple T Old Bay Seasoning
- olive oil
- 2 cups dry orzo
- 3 cups chicken or veggie stock
- 1 large shallot, diced small
- 1 lemon, juiced
- 1/2 orange, juiced
- 1/4 cup Dijon
- about 3T fresh dill, minced or sub 1-2T dry dill weed
- kosher or sea salt and fresh ground pepper

Direction

- Prepare orzo per package directions, subbing stock for some or all of the water called for. When done, drain and keep warm.
- In medium bowl, whisk together orange juice, juice from 1 lemon, Dijon, dill and shallots until well combined.
- Slowly add oil, whisking constantly, until well mixed.
- Add salt and pepper and give another quick whisk to combine.
- Add half of the dressing to the warm orzo and toss well. Set aside slightly warm or at room temp while preparing the fish.
- Heat a grill pan or other heavy pan over medium high heat.
- Sprinkle both sides of the fillets with Old Bay and a lil salt and pepper and grill for 2-4 minutes on each side.
- Serve the fish over the orzo salad, and drizzle with a little more of the dressing.

252.   Pan Seared Scarlet Red Snapper Crispy Polenta With Roasted Shallot Vinaigrette Recipe

Serving: 2 | Prep: | Cook: 10mins | Ready in:

Ingredients

- For the Crispy polenta
- 1 pre cooked polenta loaf sliced into ¾ inch rounds
- 4 tablespoons olive oil
- 2 tablespoons butter
- cilantro for garnish
- parsley for garnish
- lemon wedges
- cajun seasoning
- roasted shallot Vinaigrette:
- 4 shallots, peeled
- 1 cup olive oil
- 3 tablespoons balsamic vinegar
- 2 tablespoons chopped fresh chives
- salt and pepper
- For the red Snapper:
- 2 one inches of fresh Snapper about 6 oz each
- cajun seasoning
- 6 tablespoons of olive oil infused with shallots

Direction

- To make the crispy polenta, cut slices polenta loaf and sauté them in oil and butter.
- In a skillet, heat half the oil and half the butter. When the butter melts, fry the polenta slices without crowding over medium high heat, turning often, until they are golden brown and crisp. Fry the remaining slices in the same way.
- Remove from pan and lightly sprinkle with Cajun seasoning.
- Place in a warm oven.
- Directions for Vinaigrette:
- To prepare the vinaigrette: Place the shallots and 3/4 cup of the olive oil in a small ovenproof pan and cover tightly. Bake at 350 degrees for 50 to 60 minutes, or until the shallots are soft. Let the shallots cool in the olive oil, and then remove, reserving the oil. Julienne the shallots and put them in a bowl. Add the balsamic vinegar and slowly whisk in the reserved olive oil. Add the chopped chives and season to taste with salt and pepper.
- Directions for the Scarlet red Snapper:
- Sprinkle some Cajun seasoning on Snapper.
- In a fry pan, heat the oil until it shimmers.

- Add the Snapper skin side down and fry until it is browned and releases from the pan, about 4 minutes.
- Lower heat to medium, turn over and cook until browned remove and let rest.
- In a plate, spread some vinaigrette with shallots on each plate.
- Add the Crispy Polenta then top with the Snapper.
- Squeeze some fresh lemon on fish if desired.
- Top fish with more vinaigrette and garnish with parsley.
- Add the Salsa Verde on the side.
- Add tomato salsa and garnish with cilantro.
- Garnish with fresh lemon wedges and parsley.

253. Pan Seared Snapper With Spicy Lime Butter Recipe

Serving: 4 | Prep: | Cook: 7mins | Ready in:

Ingredients

- 4 tablespoons softened butter
- 1/4 cup finely chopped shallot
- 1 tablespoon lime zest
- 2 teaspoons fresh lime juice
- 1 red chili, minced
- 3/4 teaspoon salt
- 2 tablespoons olive oil
- 4 Snapper filets

Direction

- In a small bowl, mix together butter, shallot, lime zest, lime juice, red chili, and 1/4 teaspoon salt.
- In a large nonstick skillet, heat olive oil over medium-high heat. Pat snapper fillets dry, then season with 1/2 teaspoon salt and cook the fillets, skin side down, until golden and crisp, about 4 minutes. Turn fish once and cook about 3 more minutes.
- Top fish with some of the spicy lime butter, reserving the rest for another use.

254. Pan Fried Red Snapper Fillet With Corn Cream Creole Sauce Recipe

Serving: 2 | Prep: | Cook: 30mins | Ready in:

Ingredients

- 2 tablespoons achiote oil
- 2 tablespoons onions, finely chopped
- 3 tablespoons red and green peppers, finely chopped
- 1 small tomato, peeled, seeded, and chopped
- 2 sweet chile peppers (Serrano or Anaheim), finely chopped
- 2 cloves garlic, finely chopped
- 2 sprigs fresh cilantro, plus extra sprigs, for garnish
- 1 bay leaf
- salt and pepper
- 4 cups fresh corn, cut from cobs
- 1 cup fish stock
- 1/2 cup evaporated milk
- 2 teaspoons cornstarch
- 1 tablespoon water
- 1 tablespoon butter, softened
- 2 pounds fresh red snapper fillet, cut into 4 pieces
- 4 tablespoons olive oil
- Lightly toasted and crushed coriander seeds, for garnish

Direction

- In a large saucepan, heat the achiote oil over medium heat. Add the onions, bell peppers, tomato, chile peppers, garlic, cilantro, bay leaf, salt, and pepper, and stir-fry for about 4 minutes. Add the corn and fish stock and cook over medium heat for about 6 minutes. Remove from the heat and let cool slightly. Transfer to a blender process until smooth on high speed.* Pour the sauce through a fine strainer into a saucepan, add the evaporated milk, and warm over low heat.

- Dilute the cornstarch with 1 tablespoon water. Add to the saucepan, mix well, and incorporate the butter with a whisk. Taste for seasoning and cook for about 5 minutes. Keep warm.
- Generously season both sides of the fish with salt and pepper. In a large nonstick skillet, heat the oil over high heat. When oil is hot, place the fillets in the skillet, skin side down, and cook for 3 minutes, without turning. Flip onto other side and cook for about 2 minutes. Remove from heat to a platter.
- Spoon the warm sauce in the center of each dinner plate. Top with a fish portion. Garnish with cilantro sprigs and the toasted and crushed coriander seeds.

255. Pecan Crusted Red Snapper Recipe

Serving: 4 | Prep: | Cook: 30mins |Ready in:

Ingredients

- 1 lb red snapper fillets
- 2 T olive oil
- 1 T cajun seasoning
- 2 t lemon juice
- 1 t thyme
- 1/3 C pecans, chopped
- 2 T parmesan cheese
- 1 T bread crumbs
- 1 T chopped parsley

Direction

- Set oven to 425 F.
- Spray a baking dish with pan release spray.
- Put fish into the pan.
- Combine the next 4 ingredients, brush 1/2 of the mixture onto the fish.
- Add remaining ingredients and combine.

- Spoon evenly over the fish. Bake for 10 - 15 mins until fish is flaky.

256. Potato Crusted Snapper With Bell Pepper Salsa Recipe

Serving: 0 | Prep: | Cook: 25mins |Ready in:

Ingredients

- For salsa:
- 1 large yellow bell pepper, roasted (see directions)
- 1/2 cup chopped onion
- 1/2 cup chopped seeded plum tomato
- 1 tablespoon thinly sliced fresh basil
- 1 tablespoon chopped fresh parsley
- 1 tablespoon fresh lemon juice
- 1 1/2 teaspoons capers
- 1 teaspoon extra-virgin olive oil
- 1/8 teaspoon salt
- For fish:
- 1 cup shredded, peeled potato
- 3 tablespoons grated fresh parmesan cheese
- 2 teaspoons chopped fresh parsley
- 1/2 teaspoon salt, divided
- 1/4 teaspoon freshly ground black pepper
- 2 (6-ounce) red snapper or other firm white fish fillets
- 2 teaspoons olive oil, divided

Direction

- Preheat broiler.
- To prepare salsa, cut bell pepper in half lengthwise; discard seeds and membranes. Place pepper halves, skin sides up, on a foil-lined baking sheet; flatten with hand. Broil 8 minutes or until blackened. Place in a zip-top plastic bag; seal. Let stand 10 minutes. Peel and coarsely chop. Combine bell pepper, onion, and next 7 ingredients.
- Preheat oven to 375°.
- To prepare fish, combine potato, Parmesan, parsley, 1/4 teaspoon salt, and black pepper.

Sprinkle both sides of fillets with 1/4 teaspoon salt. Spread 1/4 cup potato mixture over 1 side of each fillet; press mixture onto fish. Heat 2 teaspoons oil in a large nonstick skillet over medium-high heat. Add fish fillets, potato side down, to pan. Cook 3 minutes, or until browned. Turn fish potato side up in the pan.

- Bake for 5 minutes, or until fish flakes easily when tested with a fork. Serve with salsa.
- Enjoy!

---

257.   Red Lobsters Lemon Basil Snapper Recipe

Serving: 4 | Prep: | Cook: 10mins | Ready in:

Ingredients

- * 4 each 5–6 oz. skinned salmon fillet
- * 24 each 26–30 count peeled shrimp
- * 4 each bamboo skewers (soaked in water for 10–15 minutes)
- * 8 each fresh pineapple half moons (super sweet variety)
- * olive oil
- * salt and pepper to taste
- * sweet chili sauce (choose your favorite brand, but make sure it is sweet)

Direction

- 1. Brush both sides of salmon with olive oil and season with salt and pepper.
- 2. After soaking the skewers, slide 6 shrimp onto each skewer, leaving room on either end. Brush both sides with olive oil and season with salt and pepper.
- 3. Cut the fresh pineapple into slices approximately half inch in diameter and then cut in half. Brush both sides with olive oil.
- 4. On a medium heated grill, place the salmon flesh side down. Grill approximately 6–7 minutes per side or until the fish reaches 150 degrees.

- 5. Grill shrimp approximately 3–4 minutes per side or until 150 degrees.
- 6. Grill pineapple for 2–3 minutes per side or until there is good caramelization.
- 7. Brush all items generously with the sweet chili sauce.
- 8. To serve, place the pineapple at the top of each plate and crisscross. Top the pineapple with a scoop of your favorite rice. Crisscross the salmon and the shrimp skewer on top of the rice. Sprinkle with fresh parsley and serve with your favorite vegetable.

---

258.   Red Snaper Ceviche With Squash Blossoms Recipe

Serving: 4 | Prep: | Cook: 25mins | Ready in:

Ingredients

- 8 oz Red Snaper or other firm white fish
- juice of 2 large limes
- 6 Tablespoons of fresh diced tomato
- 2 Tablespoons of diced red onion
- 1 Tablespoon of diced Serrano chile
- 2 teaspoons of virgin olive oil
- Thin slices of avocado
- 2 Tablespoons of diced cilantro
- Fresh squash blossoms

Direction

- Cut the fish into quarter-inch dice.
- In a small non-reactive bowl, combine the fish and the lime juice, allow the fish to marinate for 10 to 15 min in the refrigerator.
- Dice and add the tomatoes, onion, chilies and cilantro and olive oil to the fish and lime.
- Season to taste with coarse ground pepper and sea salt and gently stir to combine, place back into the refrigerator while preparing squash blossoms.
- Use a veggie clean spray or carefully wash your blossom and let dry.

- Open the petals of a squash blossom and place a thin slice of avocado inside the blossom and spoon enough ceviche into each to fill, if you like re-chill for another 10 mins.

259.   Red Snapper Baked Filets With Mushroom Recipe

Serving: 2 | Prep: | Cook: 20mins | Ready in:

Ingredients

- olive oil spray
- 3/4 pound red snapper fillets
- 1 teaspoon olive oil
- 4 ounces sliced mushrooms
- 1 tablespoon chopped fresh thyme
- 1/2 teaspoon salt
- 1 teaspoon freshly ground black pepper
- 1/4 cup white wine

Direction

- Preheat the oven to 450.
- Line baking tray with foil and spray with olive oil spray.
- Place tray in the oven while oven preheats.
- Rinse fish and pat dry.
- Remove tray from oven and place fish on it.
- Brush fillets with olive oil then spoon mushrooms over top.
- Sprinkle with thyme, salt and pepper.
- Pour wine over fish and cover tray with foil then bake 10 minutes.
- Place fish on plates and spoon mushrooms and sauce over top.

260.   Red Snapper En Papillote Recipe

Serving: 4 | Prep: | Cook: 16mins | Ready in:

Ingredients

- 4 red snapper filets, 4-6 oz each
- 2 cups prepared couscous
- 1 bunch Italian parsley (cilantro is a good substitute)
- 1 lemon, thinly sliced
- 1/2 red onion, thinly sliced
- 1/2 cup white wine
- olive oil
- kosher salt
- pepper

Direction

- Prepare couscous according to package instructions.
- Preheat oven to 400 degrees F.
- Cut out four large heart shapes out of parchment paper.
- On one side of the heart, lay out 1/2 cup of couscous so that you have a mound of couscous.
- Sprinkle with salt.
- Lay a filet on top of the couscous.
- Lay one or two lemon slices on top of the fish.
- On top of the lemon, arrange a few stems of parsley and a few rings of red onion.
- Drizzle with olive oil and white wine.
- Sprinkle salt and pepper on top.
- Fold the other half of the parchment paper over the fish and roll up the sides. A stapler is handy, but not necessary.
- Repeat with the remaining fish filets.
- Arrange the papillotes (the parchment paper pouches) on a baking sheet.
- Bake for 15-16 minutes.
- To serve, carefully cut open the papillote. Watch out for steam!
- You can use any white flaky fish. I've used tilapia when I couldn't find fresh snapper, and it's just as good.

261.   Red Snapper Livornesa Recipe

Serving: 4 | Prep: | Cook: 20mins |Ready in:

Ingredients

- 4 red snapper fillets
- 15 oz Italian plum tomatoes, crushed with juices
- 1/2 cup white wine
- 1 cup chicken broth
- 12 gaetta olives, pitted and chopped
- 2 tablespoons of capers
- 1 medium onion, chopped
- 1/4 cup of olive oil

Direction

- Preheat oven to 350 degrees.
- Heat olive oil in large sauté pan over medium heat.
- Add olives, onion and capers, cook until onion is translucent.
- Add tomatoes and simmer for 5 minutes.
- Place red snapper fillets in pan.
- Add wine, broth and salt & pepper to taste.
- Place in oven and bake for 15 to 20 minutes.
- Serve fillets with sauce spooned over top.

262.   Red Snapper Mediterranean Style Recipe

Serving: 4 | Prep: | Cook: 20mins |Ready in:

Ingredients

- 4 x 6oz Skin on Fillets Of American Red or Pacific Snapper
- 12 pieces Baby fennel
- 2 cups chicken stock
- 1 # spinach, cleaned
- 8 Vine Ripe tomatoes, peeled, seeded and diced 2 lemons
- 1/8 cup

- sugar
- 1/4 cup olive oil
- Cracked black peppercorns
- sea salt
- Chopped fresh herbs (parsley, chervil, tarragon and basil)

Direction

- Method
- Braise the baby fennel in the chicken stock until tender. Keep fennel in the broth and cool.
- Toss diced tomatoes with sea salt and pepper to taste.
- Peel the lemon zest and blanch in cold water making sure the peel is only the yellow and not the white pith.
- Boil the water with sugar and make a heavy syrup. Cook lemon peel in the syrup until the peel is candied and translucent. Set aside to cool and then finely julienne the peel. Reserve the syrup.
- Season the red snapper fillets. Heat a heavy sauté pan and sear the fish in half the amount of olive oil. Cook flesh-side first and give the fish a good color. Cook fish in the skin and crisp the skin. Cook fish until tender, about 8 minutes.
- Wash spinach thoroughly. Place spinach leaves on a plate. Place fish on top of spinach. Sauté the tomatoes in the remaining olive oil. Add the fennel bulbs which have now been split in half lengthwise. Add two spoons of chopped fresh herbs and the lemon zest. Taste for seasonings.
- Finish dish with a tablespoon of the lemon syrup and a quarter cup of the fennel braising broth.
- Heat up plates in the oven. Arrange six pieces of fennel on each plate. Spoon tomato relish on top of the fish and lightly drizzle the broth over the top. Garnish with sprigs of tarragon and chervil.

263. Red Snapper Parmigiana Recipe

Serving: 4 | Prep: | Cook: 15mins | Ready in:

Ingredients

- 1/2 c. chablis or other dry white wine
- 1/2 tsp dried whole thyme
- 1/4 tsp crushed red pepper
- 3 cloves garlic, crushed
- 4 (4-ounce) red snapper fillets (1-inch thick)
- 1/4 c. all-purpose flour
- 1/4 c. grated fresh Parmesan or romano cheese
- 1/4 tsp salt
- 1/4 tsp pepper
- cooking spray
- 1 1/2 tsp olive oil
- lemon wedges

Direction

- Combine first 4 ingredients in a large zip-top heavy duty plastic bag. Add fish; seal bag, and marinate in refrigerator for 30 minutes, turning bag occasionally. Remove fish from bag; discard marinade. Set fish aside.
- Combine flour and next 3 ingredients in a large zip-top plastic bag. Add fillets; seal bag and shake to coat fillets with flour mixture.
- Coat a large skillet with cooking spray; add oil, and place over medium heat until hot. Add fish, and cook 6 minutes on each side or until fish flakes when tested with a fork. Serve with lemon wedges.

264. Red Snapper Royale Recipe

Serving: 6 | Prep: | Cook: 28mins | Ready in:

Ingredients

- 6   Nice sized red snapper or fresh bass fillets
- -   dry white wine
- 1/2   lemon, quartered
- 4tbs   chopped fresh basil divided
- 2 1/2 lb.   Fresh spinich, Chopped   (no frozen stuff)
- 2 1/2 Tbs. unsalted organic butter
- 2   shallots, finely chopped
- 2 Tbs all purpose flour
- 1 pt.   whipping cream
- 3 Tbs. sun-dried tomato paste
- add sea salt and fresh ground pepper to taste.
- 1/4 cFresh grated parmesan cheese
- 1/8 c. dry white wine
- 4Tbls   organic salted butter

Direction

- In a shallow pan over medium heat, (poach) fish fillets in wine to half cover.
- Add lemon and 2 tsp. basil to wine and fish and let cook until fish has turned white.
- Remove fish from pan and break into large chunks, be careful to remove all bones. Set aside.
- Sauté spinach in 1/8 cup dry white wine and 4 tbsp butter until just turning a bright green; remove immediately and drain. Set aside.
- Then take your shallots and 2 tsp fresh basil and sauté in butter over med. heat till tender then add your flour and cook, stirring constantly, until a light sand-colored.
- Blend in whipping cream and whisk until thickened.
- Remove from heat and whisk in tomato paste and 2 tsp fresh basil chopped finely.
- Add your salt and fresh pepper to taste.
- Preheat oven to 350.
- Spread spinach over bottom of a large, greased baking dish, then layer fish pieces on spinach.
- Pour sauce over top fish and spinach and top with cheese.
- Bake for at least 20 min.
- Enjoy.
- Goes great with some nice steamed broccoli and a nice balsamic Vinaigrette salad with glazed walnuts and Feta Cheese.

265. Red Snapper Soup Recipe

Serving: 6 | Prep: | Cook: 120mins | Ready in:

Ingredients

- 1 1/2 to 2 lbs red snapper fillet, cut in chunks
- 1 can whole tomatoes (28 oz) cut up with liquids
- 1 large onion chopped
- 10 ounce package frozen cut okra unthawed
- 1/2 cup chopped green onions
- 1 cup beef broth
- or
- 1 cup water and 2 Tbs. beef bouillon paste
- 1/4 cup sherry or vermouth
- salt, pepper,
- fresh thyme for garnish

Direction

- Red snapper can be an expensive fish so try to buy it on sale.
- The soup is stew like and has wonderful flavor.
- We make it for special occasions.
- Recipe may be made in a slow cooker cooked on high for several hours or in a simmer in a stockpot.
- Simply combine all and cover and cook.
- Garnish soup bowls with fresh thyme.

266. Red Snapper Veracruz Recipe

Serving: 0 | Prep: | Cook: 1hours | Ready in:

Ingredients

- red snapper Veracruz
- Recipe by Emilio Allende Hernandez, Pardinos Restaurant, Veracruz, Mexico.
- Ingredients:

- 1 whole red snapper (approx. 1 1/2 kg - 3.3 lbs.)
- 4 plum tomatoes
- ½ cup freshly made tomato puree (water, tomatoes & a dash of olive oil)
- 12 green olives, whole
- 8 green olives pitted and crushed
- 6 pickled chillies
- 1 onion, sliced
- 2 laurel leaves
- 1 pinch of oregano
- 1 tablespoon capers
- parsley
- oil
- salt
- For the marinade:
- 3 cloves of garlic, chopped
- juice of two limses
- 4 tablespoons water
- 1 pinch of clove
- 1 pinch of pepper

Direction

- Directions
- Clean the fish without cutting off either the head or the tail. With a sharp knife, score the fleshy part of the snapper and pour over the garlic and lime marinade. Allow the marinade to penetrate the snapper for half an hour.
- Pour a tablespoon of oil into a hot pan and sear the fish for a few minutes on both sides. Add a ladle of chicken broth and begin to add your ingredients. Firstly, add the sliced onion, then the laurel or bay leaves and two pinches of oregano.
- Next, pour in the fresh tomato puree, followed by the whole plum tomatoes. The pickled chilies are then added, with crushed olives and capers. Season with salt and continue simmering for 15 minutes.
- Before serving, sprinkle the whole olives and chopped parsley over the snapper and serve on a large dish.

267. Red Snapper Veracruz Style Huachinango A La Veracruzana Recipe

Serving: 6 | Prep: | Cook: 35mins | Ready in:

Ingredients

- For Sauce:
- 1 28-ounce can diced tomatoes in juice, well drained, juices reserved
- 1/4 cup extra-virgin olive oil
- 1/4 cup finely chopped white onion
- 3 large garlic cloves, chopped
- 3 small bay leaves
- 2 tablespoons chopped fresh parsley
- 1 teaspoon dried Mexican oregano
- 1/4 cup chopped pitted green olives
- 2 tablespoons raisins
- 2 tablespoons drained capers
- ~~~~
- 6 4- to 5-ounce red snapper fillets
- 3 pickled jalapeño chiles, halved lengthwise

Direction

- Make Sauce:
- Place drained tomatoes in medium bowl. Using potato masher, crush tomatoes to coarse puree. Drain again, reserving juices.
- Heat oil in heavy large skillet over medium-high heat.
- Add onion and stir 30 seconds. Add garlic and stir 30 seconds.
- Add tomato puree and cook 1 minute. Add bay leaves, parsley, oregano, and 1/4 cup reserved tomato juices. Simmer until sauce thickens, about 3 minutes.
- Add olives, raisins, capers, and all remaining reserved tomato juices. Simmer until sauce thickens again, stirring occasionally, about 8 minutes.
- Season sauce to taste with salt and pepper. (Can be made 1 day ahead. Cover and refrigerate.)
- ~~~~
- Cook Fish:

- Preheat oven to 425°F.
- Spread 3 tablespoons sauce in bottom of 15x10x2-inch glass baking dish.
- Arrange fish atop sauce. Sprinkle fish lightly with salt and pepper.
- Spoon remaining sauce over.
- Bake uncovered until fish is just opaque in center, about 18 minutes.
- Using long spatula, transfer fish with sauce to plates. Garnish with pickled jalapeño halves.

268. Red Snapper With Garlic And Herbs For Two Recipe

Serving: 2 | Prep: | Cook: 12mins | Ready in:

Ingredients

- 2 red snapper fillets, about 6 to 8 ounces each
- 4 Tbs. butter
- 1 medium clove garlic, minced
- 1/4 tsp. worcestershire sauce
- 1/2 tsp. Creole or cajun seasoning blend
- 1/8 tsp. fresh ground black pepper
- 1 to 2 tsp. fresh minced parsley
- 1 tsp. snipped fresh chives
- 3 to 4 Tbs. plain or seasoned bread crumbs

Direction

- Preheat oven to 400F.
- Place snapper fillets in a baking dish which has been sprayed with baking spray.
- In a skillet, melt butter with garlic, Worcestershire sauce, seasoning blend, pepper, parsley and chives. Cook on low for two minutes, just to blend flavors. Brush both sides of the fish fillets with the butter and herb mixture. Toss bread crumbs in the remaining butter mixture and sprinkle over the fillets. Bake for about 12 minutes, depending on the thickness of the fillets, until fish flakes easily.

269.   Red Snapper With Garlic And Lime Recipe

Serving: 0 | Prep: | Cook: 12mins | Ready in:

Ingredients

- 2-6 (8oz) snapper fillets
- 1/2 cup chopped cilantro
- 1.5 tablespoons minced garlic
- 1.5 tablespoons finely grated fresh lime zest
- 6 tablespoons extra-virgin olive oil
- 3/4 teaspoon black pepper
- 1 teaspoon salt

Direction

- Preheat your broiler and prepare a shallow baking pan with a small amount of oil.
- Pat the fish dry and place with skin side up into the pan. Take 3 teaspoons of olive oil and brush *both* sides of the fish. Sprinkle a little salt and pepper on top.
- Place the fish *6 inches* away from the heat source. Broil for about 10 minutes.
- While that is cooking, toss up cilantro, garlic and zest in a bowl.
- Remove fish and sprinkle with the cilantro-garlic-zest mixture. You can optionally drizzle a little olive oil on top at the end.

270.   Red Snapper With Peaches, Baby Spinaches, Spicy Yogurt & Balsamic Syrup Recipe

Serving: 2 | Prep: | Cook: | Ready in:

Ingredients

- 2 Filets of red snapper
- 1 peach peeled and pitted.
- 3 basil leaves
- balsamic vinegar

- 1 Bunch of baby spinach
- extra virgin olive oil
- lemon wedge
- salt & pepper
- Spicy yogurt
- 7 oz. Plain Greek yogurt
- 3 Tbsp. peach nectar
- 1 Tsp. cayenne pepper

Direction

- Reduce 1 cup of balsamic vinegar over med high heat to a syrup like consistency.*
- Cut peach into small bites (to your liking). Combine in a Ziploc bag with about a teaspoon of olive oil, basil and salt and pepper. Press as much air out as possible and seal. Gently massage the bag to incorporate the flavors. Alternatively you could use a food saver for this as well. Let sit while cooking the fish.
- Season filets with salt and pepper and sauté in a skillet over med high heat about 2-3 min. per side until done. Set aside to rest.
- Combine yogurt, cayenne pepper and peach nectar. Stir and season with salt if desired.
- Toss baby spinach in 1 part Balsamic vinegar, 2 parts Extra Virgin olive Oil and seasoning to taste.
- To Serve: Spread a small amount of spicy peach yogurt in the middle of the plate. Scatter peaches around plate, drizzle reduced balsamic vinegar around plate. Plate fish in middle of plate and top with baby spinach mixture. Squeeze lemon wedge over fish and spinach.
- *Balsamic syrup can also be purchased at some grocery stores. If reducing turn on a vent or open a window.

271.   Red Snapper With Pecan Banana Butter Recipe

Serving: 4 | Prep: | Cook: 20mins | Ready in:

Ingredients

- 1/2 cup flour
- 2 teaspoons hot paprika
- 1/4 teaspoon dried thyme
- 1/2 teaspoon salt
- 1/2 cup milk
- 3 tablespoons canola oil
- 4 red snapper fillets
- 4 tablespoons butter
- 1/3 cup finely chopped pecans
- 1/4 teaspoon nutmeg
- 1/8 teaspoon salt
- 1 large ripe banana diced
- 2 tablespoons fresh lime juice
- 2 tablespoons minced fresh cilantro

Direction

- Stir together flour, paprika, thyme and salt on a large plate.
- Pour milk into a shallow bowl.
- Heat oil in a large skillet over medium heat until hot but not smoking.
- Dip fish in milk then flour mixture and cook in hot oil in batches until browned on bottom.
- Turn fillets and brown other side 4 minutes then remove to platter and keep warm.
- Drain cooking oil and wipe skillet with paper towels.
- Heat butter over medium heat and add pecans, nutmeg and salt.
- Cook stirring until pecans are lightly browned about 3 minutes.
- Add bananas and cook stirring 1 minute or just until heated through.
- Remove from heat and stir in lime juice and cilantro.
- Place fillets on warm plates then spoon some sauce over each and serve immediately.

272.   Red Snapper With Tomatoes, Olives And Onions Recipe

Serving: 4 | Prep: | Cook: 25mins | Ready in:

Ingredients

- 1/4 cup extra-virgin olive oil
- 1 medium yellow onion, peeled and slivered
- 4 8-oz. center-cut skinless red snapper filets
- 1/4 cup dry white wine
- 1 14-oz. can diced tomatoes
- 1/4 cup black olives, pitted and halved
- 1/2 bunch parsley, chopped
- Pinch red pepper flakes
- salt

Direction

- Heat oil in a large skillet over medium heat, add onions, and cook, stirring occasionally, until onions are fragrant and slightly soft, about 2 minutes. Add snapper, skinned side up, and cook until lightly golden, about 2 minutes. Turn fish and cook other side another 2 minutes.
- Add wine, tomatoes, olives, half the parsley, and red pepper flakes to the pan with the fish. Season to taste with salt and bring to a simmer over medium heat. Reduce heat to medium-low and simmer, partially covered, until fish is just cooked through, 10–15 minutes, spooning sauce over fish as it cooks. Uncover and simmer until sauce has thickened slightly, about 3 minutes. Adjust seasonings and sprinkle with remaining parsley.

273.   Red Snapper With Vegetables Recipe

Serving: 4 | Prep: | Cook: 20mins | Ready in:

Ingredients

- 4 red snapper fillets with skin
- 1/2 teaspoon salt
- 1 teaspoon freshly ground black pepper
- 1/4 cup milk
- 1/4 cup all purpose flour
- 3 tablespoons extra virgin olive oil
- 1/2 lemon
- 2 cups thinly sliced zucchini
- 2 cups yellow peppers cored seeded and sliced into 1/4" strips
- 1/4 cup finely chopped shallots
- 1 sprig fresh rosemary
- 1/2 cup cherry tomatoes

Direction

- Season fish fillets with salt and pepper then dip in milk then four tapping to remove excess.
- Heat 1 tablespoon of the olive oil in a large skillet over medium high heat.
- When the oil is sufficiently hot add fillets skin side up and brown.
- Turn and cook the second side.
- Sprinkle with lemon juice and transfer to a warm platter.
- Heat remaining olive oil in a skillet then add zucchini.
- Season with salt and pepper and cook stirring constantly for 2 minutes.
- Add yellow peppers and simmer stirring constantly for 2 additional minutes.
- Add shallots and rosemary then continue to cook without browning.
- Add cherry tomatoes and cook until they are warmed but not wilted.
- To serve place each fillet on a plate and garnish with sautéed vegetables.

---

274.   Red Snapper With Balsamic Sauce Recipe

Serving: 4 | Prep: | Cook: 10mins | Ready in:

Ingredients

- 4 red snapper fillets
- 1/4 teaspoon salt
- 1/2 teaspoon freshly ground black pepper
- 2 tablespoons all purpose flour
- 1 tablespoon olive oil
- 1 tablespoon minced garlic
- 16 ounces tomatoes drained
- 3/4 cup chicken broth
- 1/2 cup balsamic vinegar
- 1/3 cup dry white wine
- 1 tablespoon basil

Direction

- Preheat oven to 375 then sprinkle fillets with salt and pepper then with flour.
- Heat oil in large skillet over high heat then snapper skin side up and cook 2 minutes.
- Turn fish over then add garlic, chopped tomatoes, chicken broth, vinegar and wine.
- Bring to boil then transfer skillet to oven and roast 10 minutes until fish is opaque.
- Transfer snapper to plates and keep warm.
- Continue cooking tomato mixture on stove over high heat until thickened about 10 minutes.
- Stir in basil then spoon sauce over fillets.

---

275.   Red Snapper With Lemon Caper Butter Sauce Recipe

Serving: 4 | Prep: | Cook: 15mins | Ready in:

Ingredients

- 3 Tbsp. extra-virgin olive oil
- 4 each 6-ounce red snapper fillets
- salt and freshly ground pepper
- 2 Tbsp. butter, cut into 4 pieces
- 1 shallot, finely chopped
- 2 Tbsp. drained capers
- 1/4 cup lemon juice
- 1 tablespoons finely chopped Italian parsley

Direction

- In a large nonstick skillet, heat 2 tablespoons of the oil until shimmering. Season the fish with salt and pepper. Add it to the skillet and cook over moderately high heat, turning once, until golden and cooked through, about 6 minutes. Carefully transfer the fish to plates and keep warm.
- Wipe out the skillet and add the remaining oil. Add the shallots and capers and cook over moderate heat until the shallots are softened and the capers are slightly crisp, about 3 minutes. Add the lemon juice and simmer until slightly reduced. Add the butter and whisk until incorporated. Season with salt and pepper and stir in the parsley. Spoon the sauce over the fish and serve right away.

276.   Red Snapper With Matah (bali) Recipe

Serving: 5 | Prep: | Cook: 15mins | Ready in:

Ingredients

- Grill fish :
- 1 tail (500 grams) of red snapper, cleaned, gerat both sides of the body
- 2 tablespoons cooking oil
- salt to taste
- Sambal Matah :
- 6 cloves garlic
- 10 grains of red onion
- 15 small red chilies
- 1 tablespoon shrimp paste cooked (fried)
- 3 lime leaves, discard the bones, chopped fine
- 2 stalks lemongrass, white part thinly sliced
- lime juice, take the water.

Direction

- Brush fish with oil and salt, then grill.
- Make Your Sambal:

- Thinly sliced garlic, red onion and red chili. Set aside.
- Blend the fried shrimp. Mix with garlic, onion, red chili, lemon grass and salt. Add the lime juice. Stir well. Serve with grilled fish.

277.   Red Snapper With Tarragon Sauce Recipe

Serving: 4 | Prep: | Cook: 30mins | Ready in:

Ingredients

- 2 medium carrots, sliced
- 2 stalks celery, sliced
- 1 medium onion, sliced
- 1 cup dry white wine
- 2 lemon slices
- 1 bay leaf
- 3 whole black peppers
- 1 pound fresh red snapper
- tarragon Sauce (recipe follows)
- tarragon Sauce:
- 2 tablespoons butter or margarine
- 1 tablespoon flour
- 3/4 teaspoon snipped fresh tarragon
- 1/2 teaspoon sugar
- Dash of salt
- 3/4 cup reserved broth
- 1 egg yolk, beaten
- 1 teaspoon lemon juice

Direction

- For the fish:
- In a large soup pot, combine vegetables, wine, lemon slices, bay leaf, peppers, 8 cups water and 2 teaspoons salt. Bring to a boil. Reduce heat. Cover; simmer broth for 30 minutes.
- Strain broth through cheesecloth.
- In a skillet, bring 1 cup broth to boiling; add snapper fillets. Add more broth to half-cover fish, if needed. Return to boiling. Reduce heat; simmer, covered, until fish flakes easily with a

fork. Remove fish, reserving poaching broth; keep fish warm. Strain broth, reserving 3/4 cup for sauce.

- Prepare Tarragon Sauce. Spoon some sauce over fish, and pass the remaining sauce.
- For the sauce:
- In a saucepan, melt the butter or margarine, stir in flour, tarragon, sugar and salt. Add reserved broth all at once. Cook and stir until thick and bubbly. Cook and stir for 1 minute more. Gradually stir half of the hot mixture into the egg yolk. Return all to the saucepan. Cook and stir till bubbly. Reduce heat, then cook and stir for 1 to 2 minutes more. Stir in lemon juice.
- Makes 3/4 cup.

278.   Red Snapper With Orange Plum Sauce Recipe

Serving: 4 | Prep: | Cook: 20mins | Ready in:

Ingredients

- 4 red snapper fillets
- 2 Tbsp soy sauce
- 1/2 cup all-purpose flour
- 1/4 tsp salt
- 1/8 tsp black pepper
- 2 to 3 Tbsp plus 1 tsp peanut oil
- 1/2 cup orange juice
- 1 tsp cornstarch
- 2 Tbsp minced garlic
- 1 jalapeno pepper, seeded & minced
- 1/2 cup plum sauce
- 2 Tbsp rice wine
- 1 Tbsp chili garlic sauce
- 1 Tbsp minced green onion, green part only (optional)

Direction

- Combine snapper fillets and soy sauce in Ziploc; turn to coat all sides. Let stand 30 minutes

- Combine flour, salt & pepper on shallow plate. Remove fish from soy sauce; coat with flour mixture
- Heat 2 Tbsp oil in large nonstick skillet. Place fish and cook over medium-high heat 4 to 5 minutes per side.
- Remove fish from skillet and keep warm.
- While fish is cooking, stir orange juice into cornstarch in small bowl; mix well.
- Heat 1 tsp oil in small saucepan over medium-high heat. Add garlic & jalapeno pepper; cook and stir 1 to 2 minutes.
- Add cornstarch mixture, plum sauce, rice wine and chili garlic sauce; cook and stir a couple minutes or until slightly thickened.
- Arrange fish on plates and top with sauce; garnish with green onion.

279.   Roasted Red Snapper With Lemon Parsley Crumbs Recipe

Serving: 4 | Prep: | Cook: 12mins | Ready in:

Ingredients

- 1 cup panko
- 3 tbsp melted butter
- 3 tbsp chopped parsley
- 2 tsp lemon zest, plus rest of lemon
- salt and pepper
- 1 large red snapper fillet (enough to fed four)

Direction

- Preheat oven to 425, with the rack in the middle.
- In a bowl, combine panko, butter, parsley, lemon zest, salt and pepper.
- Stir to combine.
- Oil a rimmed baking sheet (or use parchment paper).
- Season fish with salt and pepper.

- Place panko topping all over the top of fish and bake for 10-12 minutes.
- Throw under the broiler for about 30 seconds to really crisp up the top.
- Squeeze lemon juice over the top.

280. Roasted Snapper With Tomato Relish Recipe

Serving: 6 | Prep: | Cook: 15mins | Ready in:

Ingredients

- 2 tablespoons olive paste
- 1 tablespoon Dijon mustard
- 6 snapper fillets skinned
- 2 tomatoes seeded and diced
- 2 tablespoons fresh basil chopped
- Combine olive paste and mustard then mix well.

Direction

- Preheat oven to 500 then grease a jellyroll pan.
- Fold ends of fillets under so each fillet forms a square then place in pan.
- Spread olive paste mixture over fillets then bake 15 minutes.
- Combine tomatoes, basil and 1/4 teaspoon each salt and pepper.
- Mix and spoon over fillets.

281. Saucey Red Snapper Recipe

Serving: 8 | Prep: | Cook: 30mins | Ready in:

Ingredients

- 6-8 red snapper fillets
- 1 lb. crawfish tails
- 6-roma tomatoes
- 1 small can black olives
- 1 lemon
- 4 tlbs. olive oil
- 1-2 cups shredded Italian cheese
- 1bunch green onions
- 1-tlbs. butter
- cajun seasoning
- 1-tsp. garlic powder
- 1/2 tsp. celery salt
- 1 pinch of ground bay leaf

Direction

- Rinse fish thoroughly, if fillets are real thick, you may want to half them lengthwise.
- Spray baking dish with non-stick spray.
- Arrange fish in dish and sprinkle generously with Cajun seasoning.
- Squeeze lemon over fish and bake 15 minutes @ 350.
- Remove and top with crawfish sauce and cheese.
- Mince onions, tomatoes, and crayfish. Heat olive oil and 1 tbsp butter.
- Add tomatoes and onions, sauté until onions wilt.
- Add crayfish tails, olives, celery salt, garlic powder, bay leaf, and sprinkle with Italian seasoning. Cook until tomatoes melt.

282. Sauteed Red Snapper Fillets With Lemon Asparagus Puree Recipe

Serving: 4 | Prep: | Cook: 20mins | Ready in:

Ingredients

- 1 pound asparagus trimmed
- 1 large boiling potato
- 4 red snapper fillets with skin
- 2 teaspoons olive oil
- 2 teaspoons fresh lemon juice

Direction

- Cut tips off asparagus spears and reserve.
- Cut all spears into 1/2" pieces and cook in saucepan of salted boiling water for 6 minutes.
- Transfer cooked asparagus with a slotted spoon to a blender.
- Purée with 1 cup cooking liquid reserving remaining cooking liquid in pan.
- Keep purée warm in a small saucepan.
- Have ready a bowl of ice and cold water.
- Return reserved cooking liquid to a boil and blanch reserved asparagus tips until just tender.
- Drain tips and immediately transfer to ice water to stop cooking.
- Drain tips and reserve for garnish.
- Scrub potato and cut lengthwise into four thick slices.
- In saucepan, cook potato slices in salted boiling water to cover until tender about 5 minutes.
- Transfer with a slotted spoon to a bowl then keep potatoes warm and covered.
- Pat snapper dry and season with salt and pepper.
- In large non-stick skillet, heat oil over moderate heat until hot but not smoking.
- Cook fish skin sides down about 3 minutes or until skin is golden brown.
- Turn fish over and cook 2 minutes more or until just cooked through.
- Whisk lemon juice, salt and pepper to taste into asparagus purée.
- Spoon some sauce onto 4 plates and top each portion with a potato slice and a fish fillet.
- Garnish fish with asparagus tips and serve remaining sauce on side.

283.   Sensational Snapper With Pineapple Peach Salas Recipe

Serving: 2 | Prep: | Cook: 15mins | Ready in:

Ingredients

- 2 red snapper fillets skin on
- 1/4 cup fresh orange juice
- 1-1/2 teaspoons olive oil
- 1-1/2 teaspoons salt
- 1/4 teaspoon freshly ground black pepper
- 1/4 teaspoon paprika
- 3 garlic cloves minced
- Salsa:
- 1 fresh pineapple sliced cored and peeled
- 2 medium peaches peeled halved and pitted
- 1 small red onion diced
- 2 jalapeno peppers seeded and diced
- 8 sprigs fresh cilantro chopped
- 1 teaspoon salt
- 1/4 teaspoon sugar
- 1 teaspoon fresh lime juice
- Mango Guacamole:
- 3 ripe mangos
- 1/2 small white onion very finely chopped
- 1 jalapeno chili seeded and finely chopped
- 1 ripe tomato cored and finely chopped
- 1 garlic clove minced
- 2 teaspoons chopped fresh mint
- 1/2 teaspoon salt
- 5 sprigs parsley chopped

Direction

- Rinse fish and pat dry.
- Combine orange juice, oil, salt, pepper, paprika and garlic in a plastic bag.
- Add fish and seal bag tightly then turn to coat fish and marinate in refrigerator 2 hours.
- Make salsa by placing pineapple rings and peach halves in center of cooking grate.
- Grill 7 minutes turning once halfway through cooking.
- Remove from grill and allow to cool.
- Dice fruit and place in a small bowl then add onion, jalapeno and cilantro mixing well.
- Season with salt, sugar and lime juice then allow to rest 30 minutes so flavors can blend.
- Make guacamole by peeling mangos and cut fruit off each side and ends of the pit.

- Mash mango and combine with remaining ingredients until well mixed but still lumpy.
- Chill until ready to serve.
- Remove fish from marinade and blot on a paper towel.
- Lightly brush both sides of fish with oil to prevent sticking to cooking grate.
- Place fish skin side down in center of cooking grate then grill 10 minutes.
- Turn once halfway through grilling time then remove from grill.
- Serve with salsa, guacamole and tortillas.

284.   Sexy Fish Stew

Serving: 1 | Prep: | Cook: 1mins | Ready in:

Ingredients

- 2 tablespoons butter
- 1 large leek, cleaned and thinly sliced
- ½ cup sliced shallots
- salt
- ¾ cup white wine
- 1 ¼ cups chicken broth
- ½ cup thinly sliced fennel bulb
- 1 pound baby red potatoes, trimmed
- salt and freshly ground pepper to taste
- 1 pinch cayenne pepper, or more to taste
- ½ cup heavy whipping cream
- 1 pound boneless rockfish filets, cut into 1-inch pieces
- 1 tablespoon chopped fresh tarragon

Direction

- Melt butter in a large saucepan over medium-low heat. Cook and stir leek, shallots, and 1/2 teaspoon salt in the melted butter until softened, 10 to 15 minutes.
- Stir wine into leek mixture, increase heat to medium, and cook for 2 minutes. Add chicken broth and bring to a simmer.
- Mix fennel and potatoes into leek mixture and simmer, stirring occasionally, until potatoes

are nearly tender, about 10 minutes. Season with salt, black pepper, and cayenne pepper. Add cream and stir to combine.

- Stir fish and tarragon into soup, cover and cook for 3 minutes. Stir gently, reduce heat to medium-low and cook until fish flakes easily with a fork, about 5 minutes. Season with salt and black pepper.
- Cook's Note:
- If you can't find rockfish, red snapper, or any other white fish works well in this recipe.
- Nutrition Facts
- Per Serving:
- 382.4 calories; protein 26.2g 53% DV; carbohydrates 29.6g 10% DV; fat 13.9g 21% DV; cholesterol 79.4mg 27% DV; sodium 735.9mg 29% DV.

285.   Snapper Burger With Mango Ketchup Recipe

Serving: 4 | Prep: | Cook: 20mins | Ready in:

Ingredients

- 1 pound fresh red snapper fillets
- 3 large egg whites
- 1-1/2 teaspoons kosher salt
- 1/4 teaspoon cayenne pepper
- 1 tablespoon Thai fish sauce
- 2 tablespoons chopped scallions
- 1 teaspoon chopped fresh dill
- 1/4 cup fresh bread crumbs
- 2 tablespoons olive oil
- 1 loaf French bread quartered
- 1 cup spinach cleaned and dried
- mango ketchup:
- 4 medium mangos
- 2 ounces vinegar
- 1 tablespoon ginger
- 1 dash cinnamon
- 1 teaspoon salt
- 1/2 cup raw sugar
- 1/2 cup white wine

- 1/2 teaspoon allspice
- 1/2 teaspoon cayenne pepper
- 1 whole clove

Direction

- Chop red snapper by hand then place in large stainless steel bowl.
- Add egg whites, salt, cayenne, fish sauce, scallions and dill then mix well.
- Add enough bread crumbs to bind all together then form into 4 burgers.
- Chill in refrigerator for 30 minutes before grilling.
- Heat a grill or broiler until very hot.
- Drizzle a little olive oil over the burgers just before grilling.
- Grill over high heat for 2 minutes on each side being careful not to overcook.
- Serve burgers immediately on the bread with spinach leaves and a tablespoon of mango ketchup.
- To make mango ketchup peel and clean mango then remove pulp.
- Put pulp in food processor fitted with stainless steel blade.
- Add remaining ingredients and pulse together.
- Cook mixture over low heat for 1 hour in heavy saucepan then remove from heat and cool.
- Strain through five sieve

286. Snapper Ceviche Recipe

Serving: 3 | Prep: | Cook: 240mins | Ready in:

Ingredients

- 1/2 pound snapper meat, skinned and deboned, cut into 1/2' pieces
- 1/2 green jalapeño, brunoise
- 1/2 red jalapeño, brunoise
- juice of 2 limes
- juice of 1 lemon

- 1 T minced cilantro
- 1/2 t sugar
- kosher salt and pepper, as needed
- cilantro leaves, chiffonade (for garnish)
- tortillas

Direction

- Combine the snapper, jalapeño peppers, lemon juice, lime juice, cilantro, sugar, salt and pepper, in a non-reactive bowl.
- Cover and place in the refrigerator to marinate for three to four hours or until the fish turns white and opaque.
- Stir the mixture occasionally to evenly distribute the marinade.
- Serve with some fresh deep fried flour tortillas.

287. Snapper Cooked In Wine And Bourbon Recipe

Serving: 2 | Prep: | Cook: 20mins | Ready in:

Ingredients

- 2 slices white onion
- 1 carrot sliced
- 1/2 cup red wine
- 2 snapper fillets
- 1/4 cup mayonnaise
- 1 tablespoon fresh lemon juice
- 1 tablespoon bourbon
- Several sprigs of watercress

Direction

- Place onion, carrot, wine and 2 cups water in medium saucepan and bring to a boil.
- Boil 5 minutes to make court bouillon then rinse fish and place in court bouillon.
- Liquid should completely cover fish if not add water.
- Bring to a simmer and gently cook 5 minutes then remove to individual plates.

- Whisk mayonnaise, lemon juice and whiskey together in a small bowl and spoon over fish.
- Place several sprigs of watercress on the side and serve immediately.

288. Snapper Jack Recipe

Serving: 4 | Prep: | Cook: 30mins | Ready in:

Ingredients

- red snapper
- seasoning
- olive oil
- crawfish Etouffee
- vidalia batter mix
- non stick skillet

Direction

- Put oil into skillet.
- Make a batter out of the batter mix.
- 1 cup of mix with 1 cup of water.
- Season snapper.
- Dip into batter then place into hot skillet; fry on one side, 6 minutes.
- Then on the other 6 minutes.
- Place on your plate and guest plates.
- Then top with crawfish Etouffee.
- Serve with Salad Baked Potato Rolls.
- Bon Appétit!

289. Snapper Pontchartrain Recipe

Serving: 4 | Prep: | Cook: 10mins | Ready in:

Ingredients

- 2 tablespoons olive oil, divided
- 1/2 cup diced red onions
- 1 cup sliced mushrooms
- 1/4 cup white wine
- 8 shrimp, peeled and deveined
- 1/2 pound jumbo lump crab meat, picked over but not broken
- 1 tablespoon butter
- 4 (4- to 6-ounce) snapper fillets
- salt and pepper
- 1/4 cup all-purpose flour
- 1/4 cup heavy cream

Direction

- Preheat oven to 500 degrees. In a skillet over medium-high heat, add 1 tablespoon oil. Sauté red onions until translucent. Add mushrooms and cook for 5 minutes. Add wine and cook until almost dry. Add shrimp and cook until just done. Add crab meat and butter and heat until butter is melted.
- Meanwhile, season snapper with salt and pepper, Dredge fish in flour, then cream, then flour again. In a large oven-safe skillet over high heat, sear fish on both sides. Transfer to oven and cook for 4 to 7 minutes (depending on thickness) or until just done. Do not overcook.
- Serve topping over snapper.

290. Snapper With Ginger Salsa Recipe

Serving: 4 | Prep: | Cook: 30mins | Ready in:

Ingredients

- 3 medium tomatoes peeled and diced
- 2 tablespoons scallions chopped
- 2 tablespoons cilantro chopped
- 2 tablespoons jicama chopped
- 3 tablespoons fresh lime juice divided
- 2 tablespoon jalapeno peppers minced
- 2 teaspoons fresh ginger chopped
- 4 snapper filets
- 2 cups dry white wine

Direction

- Combine tomatoes, onion, cilantro, jicama, 2 tablespoons lime juice, jalapeno and ginger in bowl.
- Cover and let sit for at least one hour then preheat oven to 425.
- Place snapper in shallow pan and cover with wine and remaining lime juice.
- Cover pan with foil and bake 25 minutes.
- Arrange fish on serving plate and spoon salsa on top.

---

291. Snapper With Pineapple Peach Salsa And Mango Guacamole Recipe

Serving: 2 | Prep: | Cook: 20mins | Ready in:

Ingredients

- 2 red snapper fillets skin on
- 1/4 cup fresh orange juice
- 1-1/2 teaspoons olive oil
- 1-1/2 teaspoons salt
- 1/4 teaspoon freshly ground black pepper
- 1/4 teaspoon paprika
- 3 garlic cloves minced
- Salsa:
- 1 fresh pineapple sliced cored and peeled
- 2 medium peaches peeled halved and pitted
- 1 small red onion diced
- 2 jalapeno peppers seeded and diced
- 8 sprigs fresh cilantro chopped
- 1 teaspoon salt
- 1/4 teaspoon sugar
- 1 teaspoon fresh lime juice
- Mango Guacamole:
- 3 ripe mangos
- 1/2 small white onion very finely chopped
- 1 jalapeno chili seeded and finely chopped
- 1 ripe tomato cored and finely chopped
- 1 garlic clove minced
- 2 teaspoons chopped fresh mint

- 1/2 teaspoon salt
- 5 sprigs parsley chopped

Direction

- Rinse fish and pat dry.
- Combine orange juice, oil, salt, pepper, paprika and garlic in a plastic bag.
- Add fish and seal bag tightly then turn to coat fish and marinate 2 hours in refrigerator.
- Place pineapple rings and peach halves in center of the cooking grate.
- Grill 7 minutes turning once halfway through cooking time.
- Remove from grill and allow to cool then dice fruit and place in a small bowl.
- Add onion, jalapeno and cilantro then mix well and season with salt, sugar and lime juice.
- Let rest 30 minutes so flavors can blend.
- Make guacamole by peeling mangos and cut fruit off each side and ends of pit.
- In medium bowl mash mango with fork and combine with remaining ingredients.
- Mix until well mixed but still lumpy then chill until ready to serve.
- Remove fish from marinade and blot on a paper towel.
- Lightly brush both sides of fish with oil to prevent sticking to cooking grate.
- Place fish skin side down in center of cooking grate then grill 10 minutes.
- Turn halfway through grilling then remove from grill.
- Serve with salsa and guacamole.

---

292. Snapper With Sausage Recipe

Serving: 4 | Prep: | Cook: 20mins | Ready in:

Ingredients

- 4 6 ounces fresh, skinless red snapper fillets, 1/2- to 3/4- inch thick
- 3 Tbs. olive oil

- 1 tsp. smoked paprika
- 1/4 tps. salt
- 1/4 tps. groung cardamom
- 1/4 tps. groung black pepper
- 1-1/4 pounds sweet potatoes (3 medium), pelled and thinly sliced (4 cups)
- 1 20 oz. can pineapple chunks (juice pack), drained
- 6 ounces pepperoni, diced (1-3/4 cups)
- 2 Tbs. snippped fresh cilantro

Direction

- In a small bowl, combine olive oil, paprika, salt, cardamom, and pepper; set aside.
- Cut four 18X12-inch pieces of heavy foil. Fold in half to make 18x12-inch rectangles. Arrange 1 cup sweet potato slices in the center of each piece of foil.
- Rinse fish; pat dry. Top sweet potatoes with a fish fillet, tucking under thin edges of fillets. Top fish with pineapple and pepperoni. Drizzle with oil. Bring together 2 opposite edges of foil; seal with a double fold. Fold remaining edges together to enclose mixture, leaving space for steam to build.
- For gas grill, preheat. Reduce heat to medium. Place packets on grill rack. Cover and grill for 20-25 minutes or until fish flakes easily when tested with a fork and potatoes are tender.
- To serve, carefully open packets. Transfer mixture with juices to 4 shallow bowls. Sprinkle with cilantro.

293. Snapper With Ginger Salsa Recipe

Serving: 4 | Prep: | Cook: 25mins | Ready in:

Ingredients

- 3 medium tomatoes peeled, diced
- 2 tablespoons scallions, spring or green onions chopped
- 2 tablespoons cilantro fresh, chopped

- 2 tablespoons jicama chopped
- 3 tablespoons lime juice fresh, divided
- 1 tablespoon jalapeno peppers minced
- 2 teaspoons ginger fresh, chopped
- 4 each red snapper fillets 1 pound
- 1 cup white wine dry

Direction

- Salsa: Combine tomatoes, onion, cilantro, jicama, 2 T lime juice, jalapeno and ginger in bowl. Cover and let sit for at least one hour.
- Fish: Preheat oven to 425 degrees. Place fillets in a shallow pan and cover with wine and remaining 1 T. lime juice. Cover pan with aluminum foil and bake for 25 minutes or until fish flakes when poked with a fork. Arrange fish on a serving plate and spoon salsa on top.

294. Snapper With Sour Cream Recipe

Serving: 4 | Prep: | Cook: 30mins | Ready in:

Ingredients

- 1 pound snapper fillets, cut into serving-sized pieces
- 4 ounces fresh mushrooms, sliced
- 1 small onion, chopped
- 1 tablespoon margarine or butter
- 1/2 teaspoon salt
- 1 8 teaspoon pepper
- 1/2 cup dairy sour cream
- 3 tablespoons grated parmesan cheese
- 2 tablespoons dry bread crumbs
- paprika
- Snipped parsley

Direction

- Pat fish dry with paper towels; arrange in ungreased rectangular baking dish, 12x7x2 inches. Cook and stir mushrooms and onion in margarine until mushrooms are golden, about

3 minutes. Spoon mushroom mixture over fish; sprinkle with salt and pepper.

- Mix sour cream and Parmesan cheese; spread over mushroom mixture. Sprinkle with bread crumbs. Bake uncovered in 350° F. oven until fish flakes easily with fork, 25 to 30 minutes. Sprinkle with paprika and parsley.

295. Southern Fried Red Snapper Recipe

Serving: 4 | Prep: | Cook: 10mins | Ready in:

Ingredients

- 2 pounds red snapper fillets
- 3/4 cup yellow corn mill
- 1/3 cup all purpose flour
- 1 teaspoon paprika
- 1/2 teaspoon salt
- 1/2 teaspoon pepper
- 1/3 teaspoon celery salt
- 1/4 teaspoon dry mustard
- 1/4 teaspoon onion powder
- 3/4 cup buttermilk
- olive oil

Direction

- In a medium bowl, mix all of the dry ingredients together.
- Dip the red snapper fillets in the buttermilk then coat each side with the dry mixture.
- Fry the fillets in hot oil for 5 minutes on each side until fish flakes easily when tested with a fork.
- Pat fillets dry with a paper towel and serve.

296. Spicy Molasses Snappers Recipe

Serving: 48 | Prep: | Cook: 8mins | Ready in:

Ingredients

- 2/3 cup sugar
- 1/4 cup brown sugar
- 1 cup shortening
- 1 cup blackstrap molasses
- 1/3 cup eggnog
- 1/2 tbsp vanilla
- 1 tbsp apple cider vinegar
- 3 cups flour
- 2 cups spelt flour
- 2 tsp baking soda
- 2 1/2 tsp pumpkin pie spice

Direction

- Cream sugars and shortening until fluffy.
- Add molasses, eggnog, vanilla and vinegar, beating in well.
- Whisk together dry ingredients in another bowl. Beat into creamed mixture.
- Wrap dough well in plastic and chill 8 hours, or up to 36.
- Preheat oven to 375F.
- Roll dough out on a floured board and cut into shapes, placing on parchment-lined sheets. Decorate if desired.
- Bake 8 minutes, do not overbake!

297. Steamed Snapper With Ginger And Spring Onions Recipe

Serving: 3 | Prep: | Cook: 15mins | Ready in:

Ingredients

- 1 whole red snapper
- 1 tbsp of chopped garlic
- 2cm thick ginger, peeled, slice into matchsticks
- 3 stalks spring onions – chopped
- cooking oil
- SAUCE:
- 1 tbsp shaoxing wine/ Chinese cooking wine (optional)

- 2 tbsp light soy sauce
- 1 tbsp oyster sauce
- 1 tsp sugar
- ½ tsp salt
- ½ tsp sesame oil
- 100ml water

Direction

- Clean and cut 2 slits on each side of the fish.
- Arrange fish on a steaming tray, add in one table spoon of cooking oil and Sprinkle the fish with half the ginger.
- Steam at high heat for 10 minutes or until the fish flakes easily when tested with a fork.
- Removed and discard fishy and cloudy fish juice and transfer the fish to a large serving platter.
- Heat up with pan with 2 table spoon of oil, sauté remaining ginger and garlic until fragrant.
- Add in sauce and bring to boil and dish up.
- Pour sauce over steamed fish and sprinkle with chopped spring onion and serve immediately.

---

298. Tasty Red Snapper With Fresh Herbs Garlic And Olive Oil Recipe

Serving: 4 | Prep: | Cook: 20mins | Ready in:

Ingredients

- 2 pound red snapper cleaned but with head and tail
- 1/3 cup olive oil
- 2 teaspoons fresh lemon juice
- 2 large cloves garlic finely minced
- 1 teaspoon fresh rosemary crumbled
- 1 teaspoon fresh thyme crumbled
- 1 teaspoon salt
- 2 teaspoons freshly ground black pepper
- lemon wedges for garnish

Direction

- Preheat oven to 450.
- Pat dry fish and rub inside and out with oil, juice, garlic, rosemary, thyme, salt and pepper.
- Arrange fish in an oiled baking dish and bake 20 minutes.
- Transfer to a serving plate and pour juices around fish.
- Garnish with lemon wedges.

---

299. Tom Yum Baked Snapper Recipe

Serving: 3 | Prep: | Cook: 25mins | Ready in:

Ingredients

- 1 whole red snapper
- 2 tbsp of Tom Yum paste
- ½ onion cut into slices
- 1 lemon juice
- mint leaves to garnish
- Tom Yum Sauce
- 2 tbsp Tom Yum paste
- 1 tsp sugar
- 1 tbsp fish sauce
- 100ml water
- (if you prefer soupy, add more water and adjust the taste accordingly)

Direction

- 1. Clean and cut 2 slits on each side of the fish.
- 2. Line a baking tray with a sheet of aluminum foil with length enough to wrap the fish.
- 3. Pre-heat oven at 200 degree Celsius.
- 4. Arrange the fish on the tin foil, sprinkle with onion
- 5. Pour Tom Yum sauce over the fish and wrap it all up and seal the tin foil tightly.
- 6. Put the baking tray in the oven and bake for 20 minutes.
- 7. Removed and test fish with skewer, if skewer comes out clean, fish is done.

8. Squeeze lemon juice over, garnish with mint leaves and serve immediately.

300. Tuscan Fish Stew

Serving: 1 | Prep: | Cook: | Ready in:

Ingredients

- 3 cups cherry tomatoes, halved
- 1 cup clam juice
- 4 tablespoons olive oil, divided
- ¼ cup sliced green onions
- 4 cloves garlic, sliced
- 1 anchovy fillet
- 2 pinches red pepper flakes
- 12 ounces halibut, cut into 2-inch pieces
- 1 pound shrimp, peeled and deveined
- salt to taste
- 1 tablespoon chopped fresh parsley
- ½ tablespoon chopped fresh basil
- ½ tablespoon chopped fresh oregano
- 1 pinch minced fresh rosemary

Direction

- Puree cherry tomatoes and clam juice in a blender until smooth. Press mixture through a fine-mesh strainer into a bowl.
- Combine 3 tablespoons olive oil, green onions, garlic, anchovy, and 1 pinch red pepper flakes in a cold plan. Place over medium heat. Cook and stir until garlic and onions just start to soften, about 3 minutes. Stir in the tomato mixture. Bring to a simmer over medium-high heat. Reduce heat to medium and simmer stew until color deepens, about 10 minutes.
- Add halibut and shrimp to the stew. Season with salt. Increase heat to high. Cover pan and cook until fish flakes easily with a fork, about 5 minutes. Stir in parsley, basil, oregano, and rosemary. Pour stew into a warm bowl. Drizzle in remaining olive oil and sprinkle 1 pinch red pepper flakes on top. Serve with crusty bread.

- Chef's Notes:
- Any tomato product will work in this, but I really like cherry tomatoes here, since they provide a fragrant freshness you just won't get with a can or jar. You do need to strain them after blending, but the few extra minutes of work will be well worth the effort.
- Fish stock or chicken broth can be substituted for the clam juice.
- Use any mix of white fish and shellfish that works best for you. If your shrimp is small, add it after larger chunks of seafood have already started cooking.
- You can use 2 tablespoons of any combination of the Italian herbs mentioned.
- Nutrition Facts
- Per Serving:
- 672 calories; protein 76.3g 153% DV; carbohydrates 14.3g 5% DV; fat 34.1g 52% DV; cholesterol 405mg 135% DV; sodium 922.4mg 37% DV.

301. Vera Cruz Red Snapper Recipe

Serving: 2 | Prep: | Cook: 15mins | Ready in:

Ingredients

- 2 pounds red snapper fillets
- juice of 1 lime
- 1 teaspoon salt
- 2 tablespoons olive oil
- 1 medium white onion chopped
- 1 bell pepper julienned
- 1 tablespoon garlic chopped
- 2 medium tomatoes chopped
- 1/4 cup green olives sliced
- 1 tablespoon capers
- 2 pickled jalapeno peppers

Direction

- Preheat oven to 450.
- Sprinkle fish with lime juice and salt.

- Set aside.
- Sauté onion, bell pepper, garlic and tomatoes in oil until softened.
- Simmer sauce until most of liquid is evaporated.
- Place fish in baking dish then top with sauce, olives, capers and chili peppers.
- Cover with foil and bake 15 minutes.

302.   Zesty Snapper Fillets Recipe

Serving: 4 | Prep: | Cook: 15mins | Ready in:

Ingredients

- 8 ounces whole tomatoes drained and chopped
- 2 tablespoons finely chopped white onion
- 1 tablespoon finely chopped fresh ginger
- 1 clove garlic finely chopped
- 1 teaspoon finely chopped jalapeno
- 1 teaspoon salt
- 4 red snapper fillets

Direction

- Preheat oven to 400 then tear off 4 large sheets of aluminum foil.
- Combine tomatoes, onion, ginger, garlic, jalapeno and 1/2 teaspoon salt then set aside.
- Sprinkle fillets with remaining salt then place 1 fillet on each piece of foil.
- Top each fillet with 2 tablespoons salsa then seal packets tightly folding edges over twice.
- Heat a large baking sheet in heated oven about 2 minutes.
- Place packets on heated baking sheet then bake 8 minutes or until fish is cooked through.

Chapter 6: Swordfish Recipes

***

303.   Baked Swordfish With Olive Relish Recipe

Serving: 4 | Prep: | Cook: 15mins | Ready in:

Ingredients

- 1/3 cup green olives, pitted and chopped
- 1/3 cup kalamata or black oil cured olives, pitted and chopped
- 1/4 cup roasted red pepper, chopped (you can do these yourself or you can use bottled, I use bottled)
- 1 tablespoon fresh parsley, minced
- 2 anchovies, drained and minced (this really gives a good flavor to the relish, so try to use them and don't go yuck)
- 2 teaspoons capers, drained
- 1 teaspoon red wine vinegar
- 1 large clove garlic, minced
- 2 tablespoons olive oil, divided
- 4 (6-ounce) swordfish steaks

Direction

- Combine the olives, peppers, parsley, anchovies, capers, vinegar and garlic in a small bowl. Stir in 1 tablespoon olive oil. Season with salt and pepper, allow to sit for a while to let the flavors blend, 1 hour would be great. (LindySez Party Tip: Make this the day before and let it sit overnight covered in the refrigerator. Bring to room temperature before serving.)
- Preheat the oven to 400 degrees F. Brush the swordfish on both sides with olive oil; season with salt and pepper. Heat an oven proof skillet over medium high heat until hot; add

the fish and sear on both sides until brown; then pop the pan in the oven to finish the cooking process; cook until done, about 10 minutes more.

- Put the fish on a warm plate, top with the relish.
- Per Serving: 338 Calories; 20g Fat (3g Sat, 9g Mono, 2g Poly); 34g Protein; 3g Carbohydrate; 1g Dietary Fiber; 68mg Cholesterol; 653mg Sodium.

304. Baked Swordfish With Salsa Verde Recipe

Serving: 4 | Prep: | Cook: 45mins | Ready in:

Ingredients

- 4x200g swordfish or marlin or tuna or kingfish or barramundi
- salsa verde
- 2 tbsp. olive oil
- 1 large onion finely chopped
- 1 garlic gloves finely chopped
- 1 large green capsicum (pepper)
- 40 g. (1 1/2 oz) jalapeno chilies
- 2 tbsp. roughly chopped coriander (cilantro) leaves

Direction

- Preheat the oven to 180C (350F / gas 4).
- Put the fish steaks in a large rectangular ovenproof dish.
- To make salsa verde:
- Heat 1 tbsp of the oil in a small saucepan and when hot, add the onion and garlic and cook for 10 minutes or until the onion has softened.
- Allow to cool for a few minutes.
- Blanch the capsicum in boiling water for 8 minutes then drain.
- Put the softened onion and garlic in a food processor with the capsicum, chili, coriander and remaining oil.
- Blend to puree and season with salt.

- Alternatively, finely chop the ingredients by hand and mix together well.
- Spread the salsa verde on top of the fish steak, diving it equally.
- Bake in the preheated oven for 20-25 minutes or until the fish is firm and opaque.
- Served with crispy baked potato chunks

305. Broiled Swordfish Steak With Toasted Almonds Allfreshseafoodcom Recipe

Serving: 1 | Prep: | Cook: 15mins | Ready in:

Ingredients

- 6 swordfish steaks, center cut, 6-7 oz. each
- 4 oz. Amaretto
- 2/3 c. white wine
- 1 c. crushed tomatoes
- 1/2 c. almonds
- 2 tbsp. olive oil
- 1/2 fresh lemon (juice)

Direction

- Marinade swordfish in Amaretto, lemon juice and white wine for 1/2 hour in refrigerator. In baking dish (large enough to broil fish), spread crushed tomatoes. Remove swordfish from marinade and place on top of crushed tomatoes. Preheat oven on broiler. Season each steak with salt and pepper and lightly brush with olive oil. Broil for 10 minutes (half way cooked). Then pour Amaretto and white wine marinade on top and sprinkle with almonds. Continue baking for another 15 minutes at 350 degrees.

306.   Broiled Swordfish Steak With Toasted Almonds Recipe

Serving: 1 | Prep: | Cook: 15mins | Ready in:

Ingredients

- 6 swordfish steaks, center cut, 6-7 oz. each
- 4 oz. Amaretto
- 2/3 c. white wine
- 1 c. crushed tomatoes
- 1/2 c. almonds
- 2 tbsp. olive oil
- 1/2 fresh lemon (juice)

Direction

- Marinade swordfish in Amaretto, lemon juice and white wine for 1/2 hour in refrigerator. In baking dish (large enough to broil fish), spread crushed tomatoes. Remove swordfish from marinade and place on top of crushed tomatoes. Preheat oven on broiler. Season each steak with salt and pepper and lightly brush with olive oil. Broil for 10 minutes (half way cooked). Then pour Amaretto and white wine marinade on top and sprinkle with almonds. Continue baking for another 15 minutes at 350 degrees.

307.   Grilled Swordfish With Avocado Lime Sauce Recipe

Serving: 4 | Prep: | Cook: 10mins | Ready in:

Ingredients

- 1 lime
- 1 large avocado
- 3/4c. water
- 1/2tsp. sea salt, divided
- 1/2tsp. freshly ground pepper, divided
- 1/2tsp. ground cumin
- 1/3c. loosely packed fresh cilantro
- 1/2 jalapeno pepper, unseeded

- 4 garlic cloves
- 4(1 inch thick) swordfish steaks
- 2tsp. olive oil

Direction

- Peel lime with a vegetable peeler, reserving green rind only; remove and discard pith. Cut lime into fourths, and place in a blender; add rind.
- Cut avocado in half, and scoop pulp into blender; add 3/4 cup water, 1/4tsp. salt, 1/4tsp. pepper, cumin and next 3 ingredients. Process until sauce is smooth, stopping once to scrape down sides.
- Brush fish with oil, and sprinkle with remaining 1/4tsp. salt and remaining 1/4tsp. pepper.
- Grill, covered with grill lid, over high heat (400F to 500F) 5 minutes on each side or until fish flakes easily with a fork.
- Serve immediately with sauce.... Enjoy....

308.   Pan Seared Swordfish With Nectarine Salsa Recipe

Serving: 4 | Prep: | Cook: 20mins | Ready in:

Ingredients

- 2 nectarines or peaches, diced
- 1/2 cup diced red onion
- 1/2 cup chopped fresh cilantro
- 3 tablespoons lime juice
- 1/2 teaspoon sea salt, divided
- 6 lightly packed cups baby arugula
- 3 1/2 teaspoons extra-virgin olive oil, divided
- 2 (12-ounce) swordfish steaks, about 1 inch thick
- 1/4 teaspoon ground black pepper

Direction

- Combine nectarines, onion, cilantro, lime juice and 1/4 teaspoon salt in a small bowl. In a separate medium bowl, combine arugula and 1 teaspoon oil. Heat remaining 2 1/2 teaspoons oil in a large skillet over medium-high heat. Cut fish into portions, sprinkle with pepper and remaining 1/4 teaspoon salt and add to skillet. Cook, turning once, until browned and almost opaque in the center, 7 to 8 minutes, being careful not to overcook. Divide greens between plates; top greens with fish and salsa.

309. Pescespada Stemperata Swordfish Stemperata Recipe

Serving: 4 | Prep: | Cook: 10mins |Ready in:

Ingredients

- 1/4 cup extra virgin olive oil
- Four 6 to 8-ounce swordfish steaks (3/4 inch thickness)
- All purpose flour
- 1 onion, finely chopped
- 1 and 1/3 cups pitted Spanish green olives, quartered lengthwise
- 1/2 cup golden raisins
- 1/4 cup drained capers
- 1/4 cup white wine vinegar
- 1/4 cup minced fresh mint

Direction

- Heat olive oil in heavy large skillet over high heat.
- Season fish with salt and pepper. Coat fish in flour and add to skillet. Cook until brown, about 2 minutes per side. Transfer fish to plate.
- Add onion to same skillet, reduce heat to medium and cook until golden, about 4 minutes.
- Add olives, raisins and capers. Reduce heat to low; cook 2 minutes, stirring frequently.
- Return fish to skillet.

- Spoon sautéed ingredients over. Add vinegar and half of mint; cook until fish is cooked through, about 2 minutes.
- Season with salt and pepper.
- Transfer fish to plates, spooning sautéed ingredients over. Sprinkle with remaining mint.

310. SWORDFISH NICOISE ON PASTA Recipe

Serving: 6 | Prep: | Cook: 20mins |Ready in:

Ingredients

- 5 T. high quality olive oil
- 2-3 swordfish steaks
- ½ c. chopped pitted kalamata or nicoise olives
- 3-4 large tomatoes
- 6 T. finely chopped flat-leaf parsely
- 2 T. capers, chopped fine
- 2 flat anchovy fillet, minced (or 2 t. puree)
- 2 cloves garlic, mashed into a paste with ½ t. salt
- 4 T. minced scallion
- 3 T. balsamic or red-wine vinegar
- 1 lb. penne or similar pasta

Direction

- Boil water for pasta. Grill swordfish steaks and chop into bite-sized pieces. Mix with remaining ingredients (except pasta).
- Cook pasta (in salted water) to just done (al dente) then add sauce and mix.

311. Swordfish With Ginger Lemongrass Recipe

Serving: 4 | Prep: | Cook: 4mins |Ready in:

Ingredients

- Swordfish With ginger & lemongrass
- This recipe comes from The Ultimate Chinese & Asian Cookbook. A special friend gave me this cookbook and I absolutely love it and use it often. Swordfish is a firm-textured, meaty fish that cooks well in a wok if it has been marinated as steaks rather than cut strips. tuna is a good substitute for swordfish if you can not find swordfish at your local grocery.
- Ingredients:
- (serves 4)
- 1 lime leaf
- 3 tbsp salt
- 5 tbsp light brown sugar
- 4 swordfish steaks(8 oz each)
- 1 lemongrass stalk, sliced
- 1-inch piece fresh ginger, cut into thin strips
- 1 lime
- 1 tbsp vegetable oil
- 1 large ripe avocado, peeled and pitted
- salt and ground black pepper
- 1

Direction

- 1. Bruise the lime leaf by crushing slightly to release the flavor.
- 2. To make the marinade, process the salt, brown sugar and lime leaf in a food processor or blender until thoroughly blended.
- 3. Place the swordfish steaks in a bowl. Sprinkle the marinade over them and add the lemongrass and ginger. Set aside in the refrigerator for 3-4 hours to marinate.
- 4. Rinse off the marinade and pat the fish dry with paper towels.
- 5. Peel the lime. Cut the peel into very thin strips. Squeeze the juice from the fruit.
- 6. Heat a wok, then add the oil. When the oil is hot, add the lime rind and then the swordfish steaks. Stir fry for 3-4 minutes. Add the lime juice. Remove the wok from the heat. Slice the avocado and add to the fish. Season to taste and serve.

312. Swordfish With Mango Scotch Bonnet Sauce Recipe

Serving: 4 | Prep: | Cook: 10mins | Ready in:

Ingredients

- 4 swordfish steaks
- olive oil
- 1 teaspoon salt
- 1 teaspoon freshly ground black peppers
- 2 chayotes cut into 1/4" slices
- mango Scotch Bonnet Sauce:
- 2 green bell peppers halved and seeded
- 2 red bell peppers halved and seeded
- 4 fresh peeled tomatoes halved and seeded
- 3 ripe mangoes peeled and chopped
- 1 white onion chopped
- 5 cloves garlic minced
- 2 scotch bonnet peppers cut in half
- 3/4 cup cider vinegar
- 1 cup brown sugar
- 1/4 cup molasses
- 1/4 cup Dijon mustard
- 1/4 cup tamarind pulp
- 2 tablespoons cinnamon
- 1 tablespoon cumin
- 1 tablespoon thyme leaf
- 1 tablespoon marjoram
- 1/2 teaspoon salt
- 1 teaspoon freshly ground black pepper
- 1 cup water
- avocado Butter:
- 2 ripe avocados
- juice of 1/2 lime
- 1/4 cup extra virgin olive oil
- 1/2 teaspoon salt
- 1 teaspoon freshly ground black pepper

Direction

- Brush swordfish with olive oil and sprinkle with salt and pepper then set aside.
- Prepare medium fire in a grill.
- Brush chayote with olive oil and grill over medium heat for several minutes until tender.
- Remove and set aside.

- Combine all ingredients in large saucepan then simmer gently for 1 hour.
- Remove from heat and let cool slightly then puree in blender and pour through mesh strainer.
- Grill swordfish continually basting with sauce.
- To serve arrange chayote slices in circles on dinner plates then place swordfish in center.
- Garnish each piece of fish with a tablespoon of avocado butter and serve at once.
- To make avocado butter cut avocados in half and scrape out flesh.
- Puree flesh in blender with lime juice slowly adding olive oil salt and pepper then set aside.

313. Swordfish With Zucchini And Orange Recipe

Serving: 4 | Prep: | Cook: 20mins | Ready in:

Ingredients

- 1 (12-ounce) swordfish steak, about 1 inch thick
- 2 zucchini, thinly sliced
- 1 large orange, peeled and diced
- 1/3 cup pitted black olives, chopped (optional)
- 2 garlic cloves, finely chopped
- 1/4 teaspoon ground black pepper
- 2 tablespoons white wine or orange juice
- 2 cups cooked barley

Direction

- Preheat oven to 425°F. Cut 4 pieces of parchment paper, each about 12 inches square. Cut swordfish into 4 portions and place a piece of fish in the middle of each piece of paper; top fish with zucchini, orange and olives (if using). Sprinkle evenly with garlic, pepper and wine. Fold up parchment like a package, making sure the seam is at the top, to seal the ingredients inside; tuck under the ends.

- Transfer to a baking sheet and bake until fish is almost opaque in the center and zucchini is tender, about 10 minutes. Be careful not to overcook; you can carefully unwrap parchment to check doneness. Unseal packets and slide onto plates. Serve with barley.

314. Swordfish And Sketti Recipe

Serving: 4 | Prep: | Cook: 20mins | Ready in:

Ingredients

- 1 pound whole-wheat spaghetti
- 1/4 cup water
- 1/2 large onion, peeled and diced
- 1 1/2 pounds peeled ripe tomatoes, diced
- 1 pound kale (preferably Tuscan-style or curly), chopped
- 1 pound swordfish, skinned and cubed into 1/2" pieces
- salt and pepper, to taste
- 1/4 cup arugula, minced

Direction

- In a large pot of boiling, salted water, cook spaghetti until just shy of "al dente" - about 5-6 minutes. Drain and keep warm.
- Heat water in a large skillet.
- Add the onion and sauté 6-7 minutes.
- Add tomatoes and cook 10 minutes.
- Add the kale and swordfish, season to taste, and cook 3 minutes.
- Stir in arugula and cooked spaghetti, tossing well to coat.
- Serve immediately.

315. Swordfish With Golden Sauce Recipe

Serving: 4 | Prep: | Cook: 20mins | Ready in:

Ingredients

- 2 small lemons peeled and cut into thin rounds
- 1 tablespoon ground turmeric
- 1/4 teaspoon salt
- olive oil
- 4 cloves garlic minced
- 1/2 teaspoon saffron threads crushed and steeped in 1/4 cup warm water
- 1 bunch fresh cilantro stemmed and chopped divided
- 4 swordfish fillets
- 1/2 teaspoon freshly ground black pepper
- 1 cup pitted green olives
- 1/8 teaspoon ground cumin

Direction

- Place lemon slices in a shallow bowl or on a platter and sprinkle with turmeric and salt.
- Press down on the lemon slices with a fork to extract some juice.
- Drizzle with a bit of olive oil then set aside.
- In large sauté pan heat 1 tablespoon olive oil over medium heat and sauté garlic 3 minutes.
- Stir in saffron infusion then arrange lemon slices on bottom of pan reserving accumulated juices.
- Sprinkle with half the chopped cilantro then arrange fish fillets on top.
- Sprinkle with salt, pepper, reserved lemon juice, remaining cilantro and olives.
- Bring to a boil then reduce heat to low and cover then simmer 10 minutes.
- Sprinkle with cumin then serve hot or warm.

316. Swordfish With Bananas Recipe

Serving: 4 | Prep: | Cook: 20mins | Ready in:

Ingredients

- 2 tbsp.   oil
- 1 onion   thinly sliced
- 1 small   green capsicum (pepper) sliced
- Pinch of dried chili flakes
- Pinch of freshly grated nutmeg
- 2 tomatoes
- 2 bananas
- 4x200 gm.(7 oz) swordfish steaks
- 250 ml. (1 cup) coconut milk
- coriander leaves for garnish

Direction

- Heat the oil in a large deep pan frying or sauté pan then add the onion.
- Cook for 5 minutes then add the green capsicum, chili and nutmeg.
- Cook for a further 3-4 minutes or until the onion and pepper are soft.
- Meanwhile, score a cross in the base of each tomato.
- Cover with boiling water for 30 seconds, thin plunge into cold water.
- Drain and peel the skin away from the cross.
- Cut each one into quarter.
- Peel the bananas and cut into chunk on the diagonal.
- Put the swordfish steak in the pan on top of the onion and capsicum.
- Scatter the tomato quarters and bananas over the top.
- Pour the coconut milk into the pan and season with salt and pepper.
- Cover and cook gently for 15 minutes or until the fish is cooked.
- Garnish with coriander leaves and serve with rice.

317. Swordfish With Olives And Caramelized Onions Recipe

Serving: 4 | Prep: | Cook: 25mins | Ready in:

Ingredients

- 4 swordfish steaks (about 8 oz. each)
- 2 Tbl. extra virgin olive oil
- 2 large red onions, cut in half and thinly sliced
- 1 Tbl. orange zest
- 2 Tbl. ripe (black) olives, coarsely chopped
- 6 whole ripe olives, sliced in half
- 1 tsp. oregano
- 1/2 cup fresh squeezed orange juice
- salt and pepper to taste

Direction

- Toss the onions and orange zest in the oil.
- Place the onion mixture in a baking dish and bake at 400 degrees for 25 minutes.
- Stir in all the olives and oregano and transfer to a bowl, set aside.
- Arrange the swordfish steaks in a baking dish.
- Pour the orange juice over the steaks and season with salt and pepper.
- Spoon the onion mixture over the steaks.
- Bake at 400 degrees for 15 - 20 minutes.
- Serve.

Chapter 7: Sole Fish Recipes

***

318. A Classic Sole Veronique Recipe Recipe

Serving: 8 | Prep: | Cook: 25mins | Ready in:

Ingredients

- 8 Fillets of Sole
- white wine
- 1 onion
- peppercorns & a Bay Leaf
- 8 oz (225g) White grapes
- 1 oz (25g) butter
- 1 oz (25g) Plain flour
- 1/2 pint (300ml) milk
- parsley

Direction

- Lay the Sole Fillets in a buttered dish and cover with White Wine. Add a slice of Onion, a Bay Leaf and several Peppercorns. Poach the Fish for 15 minutes at 300F / 150C / Mark 2. Peel and pip the Grapes. Remove the Fillets from the stock when cooked and reduce the liquid to a strong concentrated stock (1/4 pint / 150ml). Melt the Butter in a saucepan and stir in the Flour, adding the Milk and fish stock by degrees until the sauce is bubbling. Check the seasoning and add the Grapes. Arrange the Fish on an oval dish and spoon over the sauce. Garnish with Parsley. Serves 8.

319. Asian Garlic Sesame Sole Recipe

Serving: 4 | Prep: | Cook: 10mins | Ready in:

Ingredients

- 1 lb sole fillets
- 2 tbsp cornstarch
- 1/8 tsp salt
- ½ tsp pepper
- 4 green onions

- 10 cloves garlic, minced
- ½ cup water
- 1 cup fish or clam stock
- 1 tbsp clear honey
- 1-1/2 tsp rice wine vinegar
- 1 tsp low-sodium soy sauce
- 1 tsp toasted sesame oil

Direction

- Cut sole into wide strips; toss with cornstarch, salt and pepper. Cut onions into 1-inch lengths; set aside.
- In nonstick skillet, heat a spritz of non-stick spray over medium heat.
- Sauté garlic and green onions 2 minutes.
- Add water, stock, honey, rice vinegar and soy sauce.
- Bring to boil and add fish, carefully separating pieces.
- Cook until fish flakes easily, about 2 to 3 minutes. Carefully stir in sesame oil without breaking up fish.

---

320.   Baked Romano Sole Recipe

Serving: 4 | Prep: | Cook: 15mins | Ready in:

Ingredients

- 1-2 pounds sole fillets
- 1/3 cup flour
- 1/8 teaspoon pepper
- 1/8 teaspoon ground nutmeg
- cayenne pepper to taste
- 4 teaspoons olive oil
- 1 clove garlic, crushed
- 1 can (28 oz) tomato puree
- 4 ounces mozzarella cheese, shredded
- 1 teaspoon minced fresh oregano
- 2 teaspoons minced fresh parsley
- 2 tablespoons freshly grated romano cheese

Direction

- In a shallow bowl, combine flour, pepper, nutmeg and cayenne. Dredge fillets in seasoned flour, coating both sides.
- In a large skillet, heat 3 teaspoons oil. Add fillets and quickly brown over medium-high heat for 1 minute on each side. Drain on paper towels.
- Rub garlic clove and remaining oil on the surface of a large baking dish. Discard garlic clove. Spread 1 cup tomato puree evenly over bottom of dish. Arrange fillets on puree in one layer and sprinkle with mozzarella. Spoon remaining puree over mozzarella and sprinkle with oregano, parsley and Romano.
- Bake at 400° F. for 15 minutes, or until sauce bubbles.

---

321.   Baked Sole With Mango Recipe

Serving: 4 | Prep: | Cook: 10mins | Ready in:

Ingredients

- 2 tsp. soy sauce
- 1 clove garlic, minced
- 1-1/2 lbs. sole fillets
- 1 cup chopped mango or peaches
- 1 tsp. grated ginger root
- 2 Tbsp. lemon juice
- 1 tsp. sugar
- 1/4 tsp. salt
- dash white pepper

Direction

- Preheat oven to 375 degrees.
- Place fillets in a single layer in glass baking dish. Mix soy sauce with garlic and spread over fish. Let stand at room temperature for 30 minutes to marinate.
- Combine mango, ginger, lemon juice, and salt and pepper. Spread this mixture over the fish and bake at 375 degrees for 10 minutes, or until fish flakes easily when tested with fork.

322. Broccoli Stuffed Sole Recipe

Serving: 4 | Prep: | Cook: 35mins | Ready in:

Ingredients

- 4 4-ounce fresh or frozen skinless sole, flounder, or other fish fillets, about 1/4 inch thick
- 1 cup frozen cut broccoli, thawed
- 1 beaten egg
- 1 8-ounce container soft-style cream cheese with chives and onion
- 1/4 cup grated parmesan cheese
- 3/4 cup herb-seasoned stuffing mix
- 2 tablespoons milk
- 2 tablespoons dry white wine

Direction

- Thaw fish, if frozen. Rinse fish and pat dry with paper towels.
- For stuffing, drain broccoli, pressing out excess liquid. Combine egg, half of the cream cheese, and the Parmesan cheese. Stir in broccoli and stuffing mix.
- Spoon one-fourth of the stuffing onto an end of each fillet. Roll up, securing rolls with wooden toothpicks.
- Place fish in a greased 2-quart square baking dish. Bake, covered, in a 350-degree F oven for 30 to 35 minutes or until fish flakes easily with a fork and stuffing is hot.
- Meanwhile, for sauce, in a small saucepan cook remaining cream cheese, milk, and wine until heated through, stirring often.
- Serve sauce over fish.

323. Broiled Filet Of Sole With Green Olive Paste Recipe

Serving: 8 | Prep: | Cook: 10mins | Ready in:

Ingredients

- 1 large garlic clove
- 5 ounces stuffed green olives
- 1/4 cup olive oil
- 1/4 cup grated parmesan cheese
- 8 small sole fillets

Direction

- Preheat broiler.
- Place garlic clove in a food processor or blender and process until finely chopped.
- Drain olives and add them to the processor then pulse several times to chop them.
- Add olive oil and cheese then process until olive paste is fairly smooth.
- Arrange slices of sole on a broiler pan in a single layer.
- Spread a thin layer of the olive paste over each fish fillet then broil 4 inches from heat without turning for 4 minutes.

324. Broiled Sole Mediterranean Recipe

Serving: 4 | Prep: | Cook: 8mins | Ready in:

Ingredients

- 4 ounces french baguette, cut into 1/2-inch cubes (about 2 cups)
- vegetable oil spray (olive oil preferred)
- 4 Italian plum tomatoes, seeded and coarsey chopped
- 1/2 pound asparagus spears, trimmed, cut into 1-inch pieces, tips reserved seperately
- 1/2 medium onion, diced
- 2 tsp. olive oil
- 1 Tbs. fresh lemon juice

- 1/8 tsp. pepper
- 4 sole fillets (about 4-ounces each)
- 1/2 medium red bell pepper, minced
- 8 kalamata olives, minced

Direction

- Preheat the broiler.
- Put the bread in a 13X9X2-inch baking pan.
- Lightly spray with vegetable oil spray.
- Toss the bread gently.
- Lightly spray again.
- Add tomatoes, asparagus pieces (not the tips), and onion.
- Stir to distribute evenly.
- With the oven door slightly ajar, broil about 6-inches from the heat for 3 minutes, or until the bread begins to brown.
- Stir and broil for 2 minutes.
- Meanwhile, in a shallow dish or pie pan, stir together the olive oil, lemon juice, and pepper.
- Rinse the sole and pat dry with paper towels.
- Dip the sole in the mixture, turning to coat.
- Place the sole on the broiled vegetables, overlapping as necessary.
- Sprinkle the bell pepper, olives, and asparagus tips over the sole.
- Broil for 4 minutes.
- Turn off the oven and leave the pan in the oven for 3 minutes, or until the sole flakes easily when tested with fork.

325. Cheese Stuffed Sole Recipe

Serving: 6 | Prep: | Cook: 40mins | Ready in:

Ingredients

- 1/3 cup butter
- 1-1/2 teaspoons garlic powder
- 1-1/2 teaspoons basil leaves
- 2 tablespoons chopped green onions
- 6 fresh sole filets cut in half

- 1 large ripe tomato sliced
- 12 slices pepper jack cheese
- 2 tablespoons grated parmesan cheese

Direction

- Preheat oven to 350 then melt butter in rectangular baking dish.
- Stir in garlic, basil and green onions.
- Dip both sides of filet halves into seasoned butter.
- Set half the filets aside and place the other half in pan.
- Layer 2 slices of cheese and a sliced tomato.
- Cover with remaining filet half and sprinkle with parmesan cheese.
- Bake 35 minutes.

326. Classic Sole Meuniere Recipe

Serving: 0 | Prep: | Cook: 11mins | Ready in:

Ingredients

- FISH:
- 1/2 C all purpose flour
- 4 Sole filets (3-4 oz each)
- Coarse kosher salt
- fresh ground black pepper
- 2 TBS veggie/canola oil
- 2 TBS unsalted butter
- SAUCE:
- 1/4 C (1/2 stick) unsalted butter, cut into 4 pieces
- 2 TBS parsley
- 1 TBS fresh lemon juice
- lemon wedges

Direction

- FISH: Place flour in a pie dish. Rinse fish and pat dry. Sprinkle both sides with S&P. Dredge fish in flour and shake off the excess. Set aside.

- Heat oil in a large skillet over medium-high heat until oil is hot and simmers. Add butter, give the skillet a swirl to coat. When the foam subsides add fish and cook until golden on bottom, about 2-3 mins. Carefully turn fish over and cook until the center is opaque and bottom is golden, about 1-2 minutes. Divide fish between 2 plates and set aside, pour off drippings from skillet and wipe with paper towel.
- SAUCE: Place skillet back on medium-high heat, add butter, cook until golden, about 1-2 mins. Remove from heat, stir in parsley and lemon juice. Spoon over fish and serve with lemon wedges.
- Remove from heat and add crabmeat, crushed saltines, and parsley.
- Spread mixture on each fillet. Roll up and place, seam side down, in prepared casserole. (You may use toothpicks to secure fillet rolls)
- Melt butter in a small saucepan. Whisk in flour and salt. Add milk and stir until smooth. Add sherry and stir for 3-5 minutes until sauce thickens.
- Pour sauce over filets and bake, uncovered at 350 degrees for 20 minutes or until sauce bubbles.
- Sprinkle with grated cheese and paprika and bake 5 minutes more, or until cheese melts.
- Wine: California Johannisberg Riesling
- Note: Don't forget to remove toothpicks, if used.

327.   Crab Stuffed Sole Recipe

Serving: 0 | Prep: | Cook: 45mins | Ready in:

Ingredients

- 1/4 cup butter
- 1/4 cup chopped onions (I prefer shallots)
- 3/4 cup chopped mushroms
- 13 ozs crabmeat (can use frozen or canned)
- 1/2 cup crushed saltine crackers
- 2 tbs chopped fresh parsley
- 8 fillets of sole (about 2 pounds)
- 3 tbs butter
- 2 tbs flour
- 1/4 tsp salt
- 1 1/2 cups milk (whole)
- 1/3 cup dry sherry
- 4 ozs swiss cheese, grated
- 1/2 tsp paprika

Direction

- Preheat oven to 350 degrees. Lightly grease a 9"x13" casserole.
- Melt butter in skillet and saute onions until translucent. Add mushrooms and sauté until tender.

328.   Dilly Sole Fillets Recipe

Serving: 4 | Prep: | Cook: 15mins | Ready in:

Ingredients

- 1-1/2 pounds sole fillets
- 3 cups white bread crumbs
- 1 tablespoon chopped fresh tarragon
- 2 eggs lightly beaten
- Sauce:
- 2/3 cup mayonnaise
- 1 tablespoon capers drained
- 1 tablespoon gherkins drained
- 1/2 teaspoon salt
- 1/2 teaspoon freshly ground black pepper

Direction

- Cut fillets into strips then preheat oven to 425.
- Stir bread crumbs and tarragon together until thoroughly mixed.
- Dip fish into egg and then bread crumb mixture and continue until all crumbs have been used up.
- Place on a greased baking sheet and cook in preheated oven for 10 minutes.

- Roughly chop capers and gherkins then stir into mayonnaise.
- Season with salt and pepper then dollop over fillets.

329. Dover Sole Piccatta Recipe

Serving: 24 | Prep: | Cook: 15mins |Ready in:

Ingredients

- 1 lb Sole filets
- 2 tablespoons flour
- Freshly ground salt & pepper (to taste)
- ¼ cup extra virgin olive oil
- ½ cup white wine (I used a good chardonnay)
- 3 cloves finely minced garlic (to taste)
- 3 tablespoons finely minced shallots
- ¼ cup juice from fresh lemon
- 1 tablespoon chopped fresh Italian parsley, plus extra for garnish
- 6 tablespoons butter
- 2 tablespoons capers

Direction

- Combine the flour, salt, & pepper in a flat bottomed, medium sized dish.
- Heat the olive oil in a large skillet over medium heat almost to its smoking point.
- Pat the Sole filets dry with a paper towel, dredge through the flour mixture, shaking off any excess, and place into hot oil. When the filets have browned on one side, flip it and brown on the other. Be patient and allow each side to fully brown. Transfer to a warm platter.
- Deglaze the skillet with the wine. Add garlic, shallots, & lemon juice and reduce by half. Slowly mix in the butter until it's creamy. Add parsley, salt, pepper, & capers.
- Spoon sauce over fish & garnish with fresh sprigs of parsley.

330. Filet Of Sole In White Wine Recipe

Serving: 4 | Prep: | Cook: 20mins |Ready in:

Ingredients

- 8 ounce bottle clam juice
- 1/2 cup dry white wine
- 1/2 bay leaf
- 6 whole black peppercorns
- 1/2 teaspoons salt
- 1 bunch fresh parsley
- 1 clove garlic split
- 2 pounds fillets of sole
- 1/4 cup lemon juice
- Chopped parsley

Direction

- Combine clam juice, wine, bay leaf, peppercorns, salt, parsley, garlic, and 1/2 cup water.
- Bring to boiling and reduce heat then simmer uncovered 15 minutes.
- Preheat oven to 350.
- Wipe fillets with damp paper towels and sprinkle with lemon juice.
- Arrange in shallow baking dish then pour claim juice mixture over fillets.
- Cover dish tightly with foil and poach fish in oven 15 minutes.
- Drain fillets reserving 1 cup liquid for sauce.
- Keep fillets warm on serving platter.
- When ready to serve pour reserved liquid over fillets and sprinkle with parsley.

331. Filet Of Sole Recipe

Serving: 4 | Prep: | Cook: 10mins |Ready in:

Ingredients

- 4 fresh filet of sole
- 4 slices smoked salmon
- 4 cleaned fresh shrimp
- 3 ounces butter
- 1 lemon peeled and thinly sliced
- 1 tomato blanched and thinly sliced
- 1/2 teaspoon salt
- 1 teaspoon freshly ground black pepper

Direction

- Dry sole between paper toweling.
- Place one slice of salmon and one shrimp on top of each filet.
- Roll filets jelly roll fashion and fasten with a toothpick.
- Heat one-half of the butter in a skillet and sauté rolled filets on all sides until brown.
- Preheat oven to 350.
- Place rolls in a baking dish and cover with foil.
- Bake 10 minutes.
- Lightly brown remaining butter.
- Remove fish from oven and garnish with lemon and tomato slices.
- Pour browned butter over fish.

---

332.   Filet Of Sole With Tartar Sauce Recipe

Serving: 4 | Prep: | Cook: 30mins | Ready in:

Ingredients

- 1 pound sole filets, cut in serving size pieces
- 1/2 teaspoon slat
- 1/2 teaspoon freshly ground black pepper
- 2 tablespoons butter melted
- 1 tablespoon lemon juice
- 1 teaspoon onion finely chopped
- Sauce:
- 1 cup mayonnaise
- 2 tablespoons dill pickle finely chopped
- 1 tablespoon fresh parsley snipped
- 2 teaspoons pimento chopped

- 1 teaspoon onion grated

Direction

- Preheat oven to 400.
- Combine all ingredients for sauce then set in refrigerator to blend flavors.
- Arrange filets in an ungreased baking dish and sprinkle with salt and pepper.
- Mix butter, lemon juice and onion together and drizzle over fish.
- Bake uncovered for 30 minutes then serve with tartar sauce.

---

333.   Fillet Sole Meuniere Recipe

Serving: 2 | Prep: | Cook: 30mins | Ready in:

Ingredients

- 2 filets of sole, about 6 oz each
- salt and pepper
- 1 tablespoon flour
- 2 tablespoons butter, divided
- 1/2 lemon, juiced

Direction

- Warm a serving plate or 2 dinner plates.
- Heat 1 tablespoon butter in a 12" skillet. Salt and pepper the filets, dust with flour and lay them flat in the skillet. Cook about 2 minutes on each side. Remove to warm plate.
- Add remaining butter to skillet and cook until foamy. Add lemon juice, scrape up any bits from the pan, and pour over fish. Serve hot. Serve with remaining 1/2 lemon cut into wedges, if desired.

334.   Fillets Of Sole Bonne Femme Recipe

Serving: 10 | Prep: | Cook: 1hours | Ready in:

Ingredients

- 2 tbsp salted butter
- 1/2 lb cremini mushrooms, sliced
- 1/4 lb oyster mushrooms, roughly torn
- 1 leek, white and light green parts, thinly sliced
- 1/4 tsp white pepper
- 2 1/2 lbs sole fillets
- 3/4 cup cold fish stock (or 1/2 cup water + 1/4 cup clam juice)
- 3/4 cup dry white wine
- 2 1/2 tbsp flour
- 3 tbsp salted butter
- 1 cup heavy cream
- salt and white pepper to taste
- lemon juice
- 1/4 cup finely grated Gruyère cheese

Direction

- Preheat the oven to 350°F.
- In a large, enameled cast iron Dutch oven, melt the butter and cook the mushrooms and leek for two minutes (don't let them brown). Pour into a bowl and season with salt and pepper, and set aside.
- Season the filets lightly and arrange them in one (somewhat overlapping) layer in the Dutch oven.
- Spread the mushroom mixture over top.
- Pour in the cold fish stock, wine and enough water so fish is barely covered.
- Place over low heat and bring almost to a simmer.
- Lay a piece of wax paper over the fish and place the Dutch oven in bottom third of the oven. Cook for 8 to 12 minutes, until a fork pierces the flesh easily. (Do not overcook the fish should not be dry and super-flaky).
- Place a cover over the dish and drain out all the cooking liquid into a saucepan.
- Place over high heat and boil until the liquid has reduced to 1 cup.
- Off the heat, beat the flour with the butter to form a paste.
- Beat this paste into the hot liquid off the heat, then whisk in 2/3 cup of the cream.
- Bring to a boil.
- Slowly add remaining cream, whisking, and cook just until it coats the spoon.
- Season to taste with salt, pepper, and drops of lemon juice.
- Spoon the sauce over the fish in the Dutch oven and sprinkle with cheese.
- Place dish under the broiler for 2 to 3 minutes to reheat fish and brown top of sauce lightly. Serve as soon as possible with slices of lemon.

335.   Fish With White Wine Recipe

Serving: 4 | Prep: | Cook: 30mins | Ready in:

Ingredients

- 1 whole fish, about 6-8 lbs.
- 1 1/2 c. white wine
- 1 c. water
- 2 onions, chopped
- 1 sprig parsley, chopped
- 1 sprig chervil or dill, chopped, or tbsp. ground
- 1 sprig thyme, chopped or tbsp. ground
- 2 bay leaves
- white pepper
- 6 oz. butter

Direction

- Heat oven 350. Rub fish with butter. Place fish in baking dish. Mix wine with water. Pour over fish. Place onion, parsley (or dill) under and over fish. Add bay leaves and thyme. Top with salt, white pepper and butter. Bake 25-30 minutes or until fish flakes with fork. (Dried herbs may be used for fresh, if needed.)

336. Fresh Fillet Of Sole With Lemon Cream Recipe

Serving: 4 | Prep: | Cook: 6mins |Ready in:

Ingredients

- 2 tablespoons butter
- 2 pounds sole fillets, cut to make 4 pieces
- 3/4 teaspoon salt
- 1/4 teaspoon fresh-ground black pepper
- 1/4 cup flour
- 3/4 cup heavy cream
- Grated zest of 1/2 lemon
- 1 tablespoon lemon juice
- 2 tablespoons chopped fresh parsley

Direction

- In a large nonstick frying pan, melt the butter over moderate heat. Sprinkle the sole with 1/2 teaspoon of the salt and the pepper. Dust the sole with the flour and shake off any excess. Put the sole in the pan and cook for 2 minutes. Turn and cook until just done, about 2 minutes longer. Remove the sole from the pan.
- Add the cream and lemon zest to the pan. Bring to a simmer and cook until starting to thicken, about 2 minutes. Stir in the remaining 1/4 teaspoon salt, the lemon juice, and parsley. Serve the sauce over the fish.
- Fish Alternatives: Other members of the flounder family, such as sand dab or fluke, will go well with the sauce, as will such mild fish fillets as trout, hake, or whiting.
- Wine Recommendation: A ripe, full-flavored chardonnay with oak overtones will be well suited to the richness of this creamy dish. Try a bottle from California or Australia.

337. Gourmet GOUJONS OF SOLE PARMESAN Recipe

Serving: 4 | Prep: | Cook: 10mins |Ready in:

Ingredients

- 1 1/2 - 2lb lemon or Dover sole fillets, skinned
- 2 tblsp seasoned flour
- 1 egg (beaten)
- 4 tblsp fresh breadcrumbs
- 2 tblsp parmesan cheese (grated)
- 3oz clarified butter or sunflower oil
- 2 small bananas
- 1/2 oz butter
- 1 lemon
- 2oz flaked almonds (toasted)

Direction

- Mix the breadcrumbs and Parmesan cheese and set aside.
- Cut the fillets of fish diagonally into finger-like strips.
- Coat the fish in seasoned flour, then the beaten egg and finally the breadcrumbs and Parmesan.
- Do a few pieces at a time making sure the fish is well coated at each stage.
- Fry the fish in clarified butter or sunflower oil until crisp and golden brown.
- Transfer to a serving dish and keep warm.
- Wipe the frying pan with absorbent paper.
- Peel the bananas, cut into thick slices on the diagonal and fry quickly in a knob of butter until golden brown.
- Arrange the bananas and almonds around the fish and serve immediately with lemon wedges.
- Any white fish is suitable for this recipe. If preferred, you can omit the banana and almonds and serve the goujons simply with lemon wedges and tartare sauce

338. Italian Sole For Your Soul Recipe

Serving: 6 | Prep: | Cook: 20mins | Ready in:

Ingredients

- 2 1/2 lbs fillet of sole
- 1/4 c olive oil
- 1 clove garlic flattened
- 1/4 c diced onion
- 3 tbl diced green pepper
- 1/4 c diced celery
- 1 1/2 c crushed tomatoes
- 1/4 c sherry wine
- 1 bay leaf
- 2 tbl diced prosciutto
- 3 tbl grated parmesan cheese
- 1 c bread crumbs
- 3 tbl butter
- salt and freshly ground pepper

Direction

- Heat the oil and brown the garlic-discard garlic.
- Sauté diced onions, peppers and celery for 5 minutes.
- Add tomatoes, wine, bay leaf, salt and pepper.
- Place sauce in a casserole dish with the fish on top.
- Mix the prosciutto, cheese, and breadcrumbs together and sprinkle on top of the filets.
- Break up the butter and put on top of the fish.
- Bake for 20 minutes at 375 degrees.

339. John Dory Baked Fillets Recipe

Serving: 3 | Prep: | Cook: 20mins | Ready in:

Ingredients

- 3 John Dory fillets

- butter to grease Pyrex dish + 2 Tbsp to dot fish tops
- 1/2 lemon's juice
- Salt
- Pepper
- Garlic Powder
- 1/2 c chopped fresh parsley
- 4 Tbsp capers, rinsed

Direction

- Preheat oven to 375 degrees
- Grease a Pyrex dish large enough to lay the fillets out
- Season with salt, pepper, and garlic powder.
- Sprinkle on the chopped parsley and capers
- Squeeze on the juice of the 1/2 lemon
- Dot with the butter
- Bake, uncovered, fifteen minutes.

340. Lemon Sole In Cornmeal With Tomato Caper Relish Recipe

Serving: 4 | Prep: | Cook: 20mins | Ready in:

Ingredients

- 1/2 cup plain yogurt
- 2 tablespoons chopped fresh basil leaves
- 1/4 cup cornmeal
- 1/2 teaspoon salt
- 1/4 teaspoon freshly ground black pepper
- 1-1/2 pounds lemon sole cut in 40 pieces
- 2 tablespoons extra virgin olive oil
- Tomato caper Relish:
- 1 cup fresh tomatoes seeded peeled and diced
- 1/4 cup red onion diced
- 1/4 cup capers
- 1 tablespoon chives finely sliced
- 1 tablespoon olive oil
- 1 clove fresh garlic minced
- 1/4 teaspoon salt
- 1/4 teaspoon freshly ground white pepper

- juice of 1/2 lemon

Direction

- Turn the oven to broil and lightly grease a broiler pan.
- Stir together the yogurt and chopped basil then set aside.
- Blend cornmeal, salt and pepper together.
- Brush the sole with olive oil and dredge in the cornmeal mixture.
- Arrange fillets on the broiler pan and broil them without turning for 4 minutes.
- Pull the pan out from under the broiler and spread a thick layer of the basil yogurt mixture over the top of each piece.
- Put the pan back under the broiler for 30 more seconds.
- To make relish, combine all ingredients and serve over fish.

---

341. Macadamia Parmesan Sole Recipe

Serving: 4 | Prep: | Cook: 12mins | Ready in:

Ingredients

- 2 large eggs
- 3/4 cup freshly grated parmesan cheese
- 2 tablespoons all-purpose flour
- 4 sole fillets (4 to 6 oz. each)
- 3 tablespoons salad oil
- 3 tablespoons butter or margarine
- 1/2 cup finely chopped roasted salted macadamia nuts

Direction

- Put a 10-by 15 inch rimmed baking pan in oven as it preheats to 425 degrees.
- In a 9- or 10-inch-wide pan, beat eggs to blend. On a piece of wax paper, mix cheese and flour.
- Rinse fish and pat dry.

- Dip in egg to coat; drain off excess, then coat fish in cheese mixture. Set fish in a single layer on wax paper.
- Remove heated pan from oven; add oil and butter and swirl until butter is melted. Lay a piece of fish in pan; turn to coat with butter. Repeat with remaining fish, arranging pieces slightly apart in pan. Sprinkle fish evenly with nuts.
- Bake, uncovered, in a 425 degree oven until fish is just opaque in thickest part (cut to test), 7-10 minutes. With a wide spatula, transfer fish to a platter. Garnish with watercress and lemon halves.

---

342. OLIVE DIPPER N SOLE Recipe

Serving: 4 | Prep: | Cook: 5mins | Ready in:

Ingredients

- Olive Cream Sauce:
- 1/4 cup. plain yogurt
- 1/4 cup. mayonaise
- 1/2 tsp. grated lime zest
- 2 tsp. lime juice
- 1 tsp olive juice
- 2 tbsp. minced green olives
- 1 tbsp. chopped mixed fresh herbs (such as dill, oregano, thyme)
- 1 1/2 lbs.sole
- flour for dusting
- vegetable oil, for deep frying
- salt and pepper to taste
- Batter:
- 3/4 cup flour
- 1/4 cup grated parmesan cheese
- 1 tsp. baking soda
- 1 egg, separated
- 2/3 cup buttermilk
- 1/2 cup water
- salt & pepper to taste

Direction

- To make the Cream Sauce:
- Mix yogurt, mayonnaise, lime zest, lime & olive juice, olives, and herbs together.
- Place in the fridge to chill.
- To make the batter:
- Mix the flour, Parmesan, soda and a pinch of salt.
- Whisk in the egg yolk and buttermilk in to the batter to make it thick, but smooth.
- Gradually whisk in the water.
- Season with salt and pepper.
- Whisk the egg white until stiff in a separate bowl.
- Gently fold it into the batter until just blended.
- Skin the fish and cut it into strips.
- Place the flour in a large shallow plate and season it with salt and pepper.
- Dredge the fish in the seasoned flour, shaking off any excess.
- Heat a deep fryer to about 350F. Dip the floured fish into batter, then drop gently into the hot oil.
- Cook fish for about 4-5 minutes, turning once.
- Cook in batches to prevent the oil from cooling down and to keep the strips from sticking to each other.
- When the batter is golden brown, and crisp, remove the fish and drain on paper towels.
- Serve hot, accompanied by the Olive Cream Sauce.

343. Pan Seared Lemon Sole Recipe

Serving: 4 | Prep: | Cook: 20mins | Ready in:

Ingredients

- 1/4 cup all-purpose flour
- 4 sole fillets
- 1/2 teaspoon kosher salt
- 4 1/2 tablespoons unsalted butter

- 1 lemon, ends trimmed
- 2 tablespoons capers, rinsed and drained

Direction

- Place the flour on a plate.
- Season the sole with the salt and then coat it in the flour, shaking to remove any excess; set aside.
- Melt 1 tablespoon of the butter in a large skillet over medium heat. Slice the lemon into 12 thin circles and add them to the skillet. Cook until the lemon is lightly browned, about 2 minutes.
- Push the lemon to the side of the skillet and add the sole. (You may need to cook it in batches.) Cook until the sole is the same color throughout and flakes easily, about 2 minutes per side.
- Add the remaining butter and the capers to the skillet. Remove from heat and tilt the skillet to swirl the butter until it melts.
- Transfer the sole and lemon to individual plates and spoon the capers and butter over the top.

344. Parmesan Crusted Sole W Lemon Capers Recipe

Serving: 2 | Prep: | Cook: 7mins | Ready in:

Ingredients

- 2 5-6oz sole fillet
- flour for dredging
- egg, slightly beaten
- Parmesan Flour:
- 1/2 cup flour
- 1-1/2 cups parmesan cheese, grated
- Mixed well
- 1 Tbsp olive oil
- 1 tsp garlic, chopped
- 1-1/2 tsp capers, drained
- juice of 1/2 lemon
- 3 Tbsp white wine

- 1/4 cup chicken stock
- salt and pepper
- 1 Tbsp unsalted butter

Direction

- Prepare Parmesan flour in shallow pan, set aside.
- Dredge fish in plain flour, shaking off excess flour.
- Dip in egg wash.
- Coat in parmesan flour mixture.
- Heat non-stick frying pan with olive oil (must be fairly hot).
- Brown fish on both sides, remove from pan and keep warm.
- In the same pan add more oil if needed, and sauté garlic.
- Add capers, lemon juice, wine, stock, and pinch of salt and pepper.
- Reduce by half. Remove from heat and add whole butter.
- Plate fish and spoon sauce over.
- Serving suggestion: Serve with pasta, Caesar salad.

345.   Poached Dover Sole Recipe

Serving: 1 | Prep: | Cook: 5mins | Ready in:

Ingredients

- 1 Dover sole fillet (bones removed) A good white fish would work haddock, cod, Tilapia or similar
- white wine, enough to cover fish slightly
- 1/4 juice of a lemon
- A small bunch of parsley
- I tbs. unsalted butter
- salt and white pepper to taste

Direction

- We used to do a sauce for poached fish that was a reduction of white wine, a little fresh lemon juice, chopped parsley, unsalted butter, white pepper and salt to taste.
- Take a small pan long enough to hold fish, salt and pepper, melt butter, add fish, add lemon juice and wine, and cover. Let simmer till fish is flaky; add parsley. You can freshen with a little fresh lemon juice.
- You can garish with a lemon twist on the Sole or use two twists together and make a pinwheel.
- You can take this a little further and add some heavy cream and some fish stock and reduce, for a white sauce. Please use a good white wine.
- If you are poaching a white burgundy or its equal is best to serve.
- If using the cream sauce a sharp dry wine is best to serve.

346.   Rolled Sole Fillets With A Tomato Sauce Recipe

Serving: 4 | Prep: | Cook: 35mins | Ready in:

Ingredients

- 1/3 cup olive oil, plus extra to drizzle on fish rolls
- 2 cloves garlic, minced
- 1/4 cup white wine
- 1 cup canned diced tomatoes
- salt and pepper to taste
- 4 tbsp fresh Italian parsley, chopped
- 4 tsp olive paste* see note below
- 4 sole fillets
- *Olive paste a spread made with pureed olives and olive oil. Available at gourmet and specialty stores. The homemade version is made by finely chopping, crushing or blending good quality pitted olives (e.g. Kalamata), then adding olive oil until the mixture becomes a paste.

Direction

- Preheat the oven to 205°C/400°F.
- Heat half of the oil in a saucepan over medium heat. Add the garlic and sauté, with stirring, 1-2 min, until it softens and becomes fragrant. Pour in the wine, bring to a boil and cook until it has reduced by half, about 1-2 min. Add the tomatoes and gently simmer until they have thickened, 5-6 min. Season with salt and pepper, then transfer the sauce to a baking dish.
- Place parsley in a small bowl. Add the olive paste and remaining oil, then mix well. Lay the sole fillets flat, skin side (light grey-colored) down on a working surface. Season the fish with pepper. Divide the prepared filling among the fillets and spread evenly. Beginning at the narrow end, roll up each fillet. May be secure with a toothpick.
- Arrange the fish rolls, seam side down, on the tomato sauce in the baking dish. Drizzle each roll with the a little olive oil and bake, uncovered, in the middle of the oven, until the fish is just cooked through, about 15 min. Since the cooking time depends on the thickness of the fillets and the actual temperature of your oven, it is important to check them with a fork to see if they are cooked through.
- Remove toothpicks, place the fillets on plates, spoon the sauce on top and serve immediately.

---

347.   Saute Sole With Caper And Lemon Recipe

Serving: 2 | Prep: | Cook: 5mins | Ready in:

Ingredients

- 1 pound fresh sole dredged in seasoned flour (salt, pepper, garlic)
- 3 Tablespoons olive oil
- 1 Tablespoon chopped fresh parsley
- 2 Tablespoon capers
- 2 Tablespoons whole butter
- 1/2 of a lemon

Direction

- Heat sauté pan till hot, and I mean hot.
- Add olive oil and immediately add dredged sole before oil smokes.
- Sauté 2 minutes.
- Gently flip, sauté until sole flakes maybe another minute.
- Add whole butter, let melt a bit.
- Add parsley, capers and adjust seasoning if needed.
- Transfer to serving plates and pour sauce over fish.

---

348.   Seafood Risotto Saffron With Lemon Grass Sauce Recipe

Serving: 2 | Prep: | Cook: 45mins | Ready in:

Ingredients

- 1 box of pre-packaged 250gm Risotto Ponto saffron (I like to use the brand: GALLO)
- 1 250gm packet of frozen mixed seafood.
- 300 gm sole fillet
- 1 tb olive oil
- 3 cheery tomato
- 2 pieces sliced lemon rind
- Ingredients for lemon grass sauce:
- 6 shallots
- ½ head garlic
- 1 stalk lemon grass (serai)
- 1/2 ts oysters sauce
- 1/2 ts sugar
- 1/4 cube chicken bullion

Direction

- Preparation for sauce:
- Dice lemon grass, sliced shallots and garlic and pound till very fine in pastel and mortar.

Add oyster sauce, chicken stock and sugar and mix well. Scoop up 1 table spoon to marinate the sole fillet for about 15 mins. Heat sauce pan with oil and add balance of mixture and sauté till fragrant. Turn off heat. Side the pan aside.

- Preparation of the Risotto Ponto Saffron:
- Just follow the instructions on the box. Have the risotto cooked and set aside.
- Preparation of the Sole fillet and seafood:
- Cut Sole into 1 in. by 2 in. and 2 cm thick pieces. Brush small amount of butter on frying pan and brown each side about 3 mins a side and put them aside on a plate. Heat olive oil and add lemon grass sauce, add mixed seafood and stir fry for 3 mins. Add in cooked risotto and mix well. Finally add the cooked sole fillet and transfer to serving plate and decorate the plate with cherry tomato and lemon rind. I serve this with a bowl of mints leave and egg soup and freshly baked baguettes.

349. Simple Sole Recipe

Serving: 4 | Prep: | Cook: 6mins | Ready in:

Ingredients

- 2 lbs sole fillets (or any other mild white fish)
- 1 teaspoon Penzey's Northwoods seasoning (or any other seasoning mix you like)
- 1/4 cup white wine

Direction

- Lay fish fillets in microwavable dish with lid.
- Sprinkle with seasoning mix.
- Microwave on high for 4 minutes and check doneness.
- Cook for 2 minutes more.
- These times will depend on the strength of your microwave, so check it to make sure!

350. Sole Coconut Curry Recipe

Serving: 4 | Prep: | Cook: 30mins | Ready in:

Ingredients

- 1 onion, diced
- 1 cup tomato, diced (I used grape because it was what I had on hand)
- 1/2 cup carrots, diced
- 1 bunch spinach, chopped
- 1 cup chicken stock
- 2 tbs. curry paste
- 1 tbs. lime juice
- 1 can coconut milk
- 6-8 sole filets (or any other white light fish)

Direction

- In a large frying pan, sauté onion and carrots in olive oil (about 3-4 minutes) over medium high heat. Add tomatoes and sauté a few more minutes. Add two tablespoons of curry paste and stir into veg and cook out a few minutes. Add 1 cup chicken stock and 1 tbs. lime juice, increase heat and simmer about 5 minutes to reduce. Add 1 can coconut milk and combine with sauce. Stir in spinach and, nestle fish into liquid. Reduce to medium high heat and, simmer until cooked (depending on filet size about 3-5 minutes).
- Serve over white basmati rice.

351. Sole Edward VII Recipe

Serving: 2 | Prep: | Cook: 20mins | Ready in:

Ingredients

- 1/2 pound unsalted butter
- 3 oz chopped salted almonds
- 1/4 pound chopped fresh mushrooms

- 1 Tbsp chopped fresh parsley
- juice of 1 lemon
- salt
- pepper
- 1 tsp nutmeg
- 2 sole fillets
- white wine

Direction

- Mix butter, almonds, mushrooms, parsley, lemon juice, salt, pepper, and nutmeg.
- Salt and pepper the sole fillets, and spread the butter over the fish.
- Pour 2 or 3 ounces of white wine in the bottom of the pan with the fillets.
- Bake at 375 for 20 minutes, or until fish is done.

352. Sole Filets In Lemon Parsley Butter Recipe

Serving: 4 | Prep: | Cook: 20mins | Ready in:

Ingredients

- 1/2 cup butter melted
- 2 tablespoons cornstarch
- 3 tablespoons lemon juice
- 1 tablespoon chopped fresh parsley
- 2 pounds sole filets
- 1/2 teaspoon celery salt
- 1 teaspoon freshly ground black pepper

Direction

- Melt butter in a large glass baking dish.
- Add cornstarch, lemon juice and parsley then stir to blend well.
- Dip each filet in butter sauce then arrange in baking dish butter sauce side up.
- Sprinkle filets with celery, salt and pepper.
- Cover loosely with clear plastic wrap and heat in microwave for 7 minutes.

- Let stand covered for 2 minutes to finish cooking then spoon sauce over each serving.

353. Sole Fillets Baked With Mushrooms Recipe

Serving: 2 | Prep: | Cook: 10mins | Ready in:

Ingredients

- olive oil spray
- 3/4 pound sole fillets
- 1 teaspoon olive oil
- 4 ounces sliced mushrooms
- 1 tablespoon chopped fresh thyme
- 1/2 teaspoon salt
- 1 teaspoon freshly ground black pepper
- 1/4 cup white wine

Direction

- Preheat the oven to 450.
- Line baking tray with foil and spray with olive oil spray.
- Place tray in the oven while oven preheats.
- Rinse fish and pat dry.
- Remove tray from oven and place fish on it.
- Brush fillets with olive oil then spoon mushrooms over top.
- Sprinkle with thyme, salt and pepper.
- Pour wine over fish and cover tray with foil then bake 10 minutes.
- Place fish on plates and spoon mushrooms and sauce over top.

354. Sole Fillets In Marsala Cream Recipe

Serving: 4 | Prep: | Cook: 20mins | Ready in:

Ingredients

- 2/3 cup fish stock - See note below
- 8 sole fillets
- 1 Tblsp olive oil
- 1Tbsp butter
- 4 shallots - finely chopped
- 3 1/2 oz baby button mushrooms - cleaned & halved
- 1 Tblsp peppercorns - lightly crushed
- 1/3 cup marsala
- 2/3 pint heavy cream

Direction

- Heat oil & butter in a large skillet.
- Add the shallots & cook for 2 - 3 mins until softened.
- Add the mushrooms & cook for a further 2 - 3 mins until they are just beginning to brown.
- Add the peppercorns & fish to the skillet.
- Fry the fish for 3 - 4 mins on each side or until lightly golden.
- Pour the wine & fish stock over the fish & simmer for 3 mins.
- Carefully remove fish & set aside - keep warm.
- Increase heat & boil mixture in the skillet for about 5 mins or until the sauce has reduced & thickened.
- Stir in the cream.
- Return the fish to the skillet & heat through.
- .
- NOTE:-
- In a pinch, if I didn't have ingredients to make the fish stock, I have used an instant fish/seafood stock mixed with water & had great results.

355.   Sole Le Duc Recipe

Serving: 6 | Prep: | Cook: 15mins |Ready in:

Ingredients

- 4 tbsp butter
- 3 Tbsp minced shallots or green onion
- 3/4 tsp.curry powder

- 2 pounds sole fillets, cut crosswise into 1 1/2 wide strips
- 1 Tbsp canned green peppercorns, drained
- 1 Tbsp lemon juice
- 1 cup whipping cream
- salt to taste

Direction

- In wide frying pan over medium heat, melt butter.
- Add shallots, curry, and fish; cook over high heat, shaking pan or pushing fish with a wide spatula to turn(taking care not to break up fish)until fish flakes readily when prodded in thickest portion with a fork(3 to 5 minutes)
- Gently lift fish from pan to serving dish.
- Place peppercorns in a small strainer, rinse with cold water and drain.
- Add to pan with lemon juice and whipping cream.
- Bring to a boil over high heat and cook, stirring, until shiny bubbles form (6 to 8 minutes)
- Drain any juice from fish into pan.
- Return fish to pan, shaking gently to mix with sauce, and heat through.
- Wonderful served with rice and a good... Chablis!

356.   Sole Matanzas Recipe

Serving: 6 | Prep: | Cook: 10mins |Ready in:

Ingredients

- 6 sole fillets
- 2 beaten eggs
- 4 ounces crabmeat
- 1/4 cup softened butter
- 1 tablespoon lemon juice
- 1 tablespoon oil
- 1/8 teaspoon hot pepper sauce
- 1/8 teaspoon salt

Direction

- Add lemon juice, pepper sauce and salt to softened butter and whip until smooth.
- Add oil to a sauté pan and bring to medium high heat.
- Dip each fillet in egg and sauté for 2 minutes on each side.
- Place fillet on plate and top with 1 ounce crabmeat and a dollop of lemon butter sauce.
- Place under broiler for 1 minute then serve immediately.

---

357.   Sole Meunire Recipe

Serving: 4 | Prep: | Cook: 5mins | Ready in:

Ingredients

- Sole Meuniére
- Serves 4
- Cooking Technique = Saute
- INGREDIENTS
- 1 lemon
- 4 fillets of Dover Sole, 6 to 7 ounces each
- salt and freshly ground pepper to taste
- flour for dredging
- 5 tablespoons unsalted butter
- 2 tablespoons olive oil
- 4 tablespoons fresh parsley, chopped

Direction

- PREP WORK
- The prep is easy for this one. Get all your ingredients together and chop the parsley and you are ready to go.
- HOW TO MAKE AT HOME
- 1. Cut the lemon into quarters lengthwise. Then slice each quarter wedge crosswise into paper-thin slices. Remove any seeds and set aside.
- 2. Season the fillets with salt and pepper and dredge them thoroughly in flour. I suggests putting the flour in a paper bag, adding a fish

filet and shaking it. Kind of like the Shake N Bake idea for those of you old enough to remember. Shake off any excess flour.
- 3. Heat 4 tablespoons of butter and oil in a large sauté pan (fry pan, skillet) over medium high heat. When the butter stops foaming, add the fillets. Cook, turning once, until golden and cooked through. Should take about 5 minutes.
- 4. Lower the heat and swirl in the remaining tablespoon of butter and the lemon slices. Sprinkle with parsley and season lightly with salt and pepper. Spoon the sauce over the fillets and server immediately.

---

358.   Sole With Garlic Lemon And Olives Recipe

Serving: 4 | Prep: | Cook: 20mins | Ready in:

Ingredients

- 4 (1/4 -lb.) sole fillets
- 1/2 cup flour
- 3 Tablespoons olive oil
- 2 large cloves garlic, crushed
- 2 Tablespoons lemon juice
- 10 flavored (marinated) black olives, pitted and chopped
- Pinch crushed red pepper
- 1/4 tsp. salt to taste
- 2 Tablespoons chopped fresh parsley

Direction

- Rinse the fish, then dry them on a paper towels.
- Spread the flour on a plate.
- Warm the oil and garlic in a large skillet.
- Sauté gently till the garlic is golden, then discard it.
- Dust the fish with flour, slip them into the hot oil.
- Sauté until golden, about 1 minute for each filet.

- Transfer to warm plate.
- Reduce heat, stir the lemon juice and 2 tablespoons of water into the pan.
- When the liquid begins to bubble, add the olives, red pepper, salt and parsley.
- Heat briefly, then pour over the fish and serve.

359.   Sole With Mushroom Sauce Recipe

Serving: 6 | Prep: | Cook: 30mins | Ready in:

Ingredients

- 1 1/2 lb (750 g) fresh sole fillets
- 1 can (10 oz/284 mL) Campbell's condensed cream of mushroom soup or 50% Less Fat Cream of Mushroom Soup
- 1/2 cup (125 mL) grated cheddar cheese
- 1/4 cup (50 mL) dry sherry
- 3 tbsp (50 mL) dry bread crumbs
- 1 tbsp (15 mL) margarine or butter, melted
- 6 cups (1.5 L) oven-baked potato wedges

Direction

- Place fillets in a lightly greased 2 qt. (2 L) shallow baking dish.
- Combine soup, cheese and sherry; spread evenly over fillets. Mix bread crumbs and margarine and sprinkle over fillets.
- Bake in preheated 350°F (180° C) oven until fish is cooked through – about 30 minutes. Serve with potato wedges or rice.

360.   Sole With Parsley And Mint Recipe

Serving: 4 | Prep: | Cook: 20mins | Ready in:

Ingredients

- 1 pound sole
- 2 tablespoons minced fresh parsley
- 1 tablespoon chopped fresh mint
- 2 teaspoons vegetable oil
- 1 medium clove garlic chopped
- 1 teaspoon margarine
- 1 green onion chopped
- 1/2 cup dry white wine
- 1/4 cup water
- 1/4 teaspoon white pepper

Direction

- Preheat broiler then lightly spray a broiler pan and rack with vegetable oil spray.
- Rinse fish and pat dry with paper towels then put fish on rack.
- Combine parsley, mint, oil and garlic then rub mixture on fish.
- Broil 4" from heat 8 minutes.
- Melt margarine in nonstick skillet over medium high heat then sauté onion 2 minutes.
- Add juices from fish and remaining sauce ingredients then heat thoroughly and pour over fish.

361.   Sole With Shrimp And Mussels Recipe

Serving: 4 | Prep: | Cook: 20mins | Ready in:

Ingredients

- 2 pounds filet of sole
- 6 tablespoons butter
- 2 tablespoons shallots finely chopped
- 1/2 teaspoon salt
- 1/8 teaspoon white pepper
- 2 tablespoons lemon juice
- 2 cups white wine
- 16 mussels well scrubbed and drained
- 20 baby shrimp boiled
- 1/4 pound fresh mushrooms sliced thin

Direction

- Preheat oven to 400.
- Melt 4 tablespoons butter in pan and lightly sauté shallots.
- Fold each filet of sole over twice and place in pan large enough to hold sole comfortably.
- Season with salt and pepper then sprinkle with lemon juice and l cup wine.
- Cover barely with water then place in oven and cook 10 minutes.
- Remove from oven then remove liquid from pan and place liquid in saucepan.
- Cover with foil and reduce liquid for 5 minutes over moderately high heat.
- While sole is cooking heat other cup of wine in pot until boiling.
- Add mussels then cover and cook until mussels open about 5 minutes then turn off heat.
- Remove mussels from their shells and return mussels to broth.
- Add baby shrimp.
- Sauté mushrooms in 2 tablespoons butter over low heat until lightly brown.
- Place sole on large platter and garnish with mussels, shrimp and mushrooms.
- Cover with white wine sauce.

---

362.   Spice Sole In White Wine Sauce Recipe

Serving: 6 | Prep: | Cook: 25mins | Ready in:

Ingredients

- 8 fillets of sole
- 5 TBS butter
- 2 TBS chopped shallots
- salt and pepper to taste
- 2 TBS chopped dill
- 1/2 cup dry white wine
- 1/2 LB cleaned raw shrimp cut into 1 in pieces
- 1 1/2 cup heavy cream
- 1 tsp cayenne
- 1 tsp lemon juice

Direction

- Preheat oven to 400. Take a baking dish large enough to lay the fish in it with one layer. Grease the dish with 1 tbsp butter. Lay the fish in it, sprinkle with salt and pepper, scatter shallots over the fish dot with remaining butter, sprinkle dill over, pour wine over then place on top of stove and bring to a boil. Place dish immediately in the oven. Bake 5 minutes. Drain the liquid from the dish into a medium skillet. Add the shrimp and a dash of Tabasco, simmer 1 minute. Remove shrimp with slotted spoon and scatter over the fish that are still in the dish. Reduce the cooking liquid for 2 minutes add the cream, cayenne and reduce it on high heat for about 10 minutes or until thick. Add the lemon juice to the sauce and pour over fish.

---

363.   Spinach Stuffed Sole With Lemon Chive Sauce Recipe

Serving: 4 | Prep: | Cook: 30mins | Ready in:

Ingredients

- 4 4-ounce fresh or frozen skinless sole, flounder, or other fish fillets, about 1/4 inch thick
- salt and black pepper
- 1 10-ounce package frozen chopped spinach, thawed
- 1 beaten egg
- 1 cup herb-seasoned stuffing mix, slightly crushed
- 2 tablespoons slivered almonds, toasted (see tip below)
- 1/3 cup dairy sour cream
- 1/3 cup mayonnaise or salad dressing
- 1 tablespoon snipped fresh thyme or 1 teaspoon dried thyme, crushed
- 1 teaspoon finely shredded lemon peel
- 1/2 teaspoon prepared mustard
- 1/4 cup whipping cream

- 1 tablespoon snipped fresh chives
- Snipped fresh chives or thinly sliced green onion (optional)

Direction

- Thaw fish, if frozen. Rinse fish; pat dry with paper towels. Season with salt and pepper; set aside. For filling, drain spinach; squeeze out excess liquid. In a medium bowl combine spinach, egg, stuffing mix, and almonds.
- Spoon one-fourth of the filling onto the widest end of each fillet. Roll up, securing rolls with wooden toothpicks. Place fish in a greased 2-quart square baking dish. Bake, covered, in a 350 degree F oven for 30 to 35 minutes or until fish flakes easily when tested with a fork and filling is heated through.
- Meanwhile, for sauce, in a small saucepan combine sour cream, mayonnaise, thyme, lemon peel, and mustard. Cook and stir over low heat until heated through (do not boil). Remove from heat. In a medium mixing bowl beat whipping cream with an electric mixer on low speed until soft peaks form (tips curl). Fold whipped cream and the 1 tablespoon chives into sour cream mixture. Serve immediately over fish. If desired, sprinkle with additional snipped chives or thinly sliced green onions.

364. Stuffed Sole With Sauce Newberg Recipe

Serving: 8 | Prep: | Cook: 30mins | Ready in:

Ingredients

- 1-1/4 cup finely minced celery
- 1-1/4 cup finely minced onion
- 1 green pepper cored seeded and finely minced
- 12 tablespoons butter
- 3 teaspoons paprika
- 1 teaspoon salt
- 1 teaspoon freshly ground black pepper
- 12 raw shrimp shelled and deveined
- 1-1/2 cup fresh bread crumbs
- 16 small sole fillets
- Sauce Newburg:
- 4 tablespoons butter
- 1 tablespoon flour
- 1/4 teaspoon paprika
- 2-1/4 cups heavy cream
- 1/2 teaspoon salt
- 1 teaspoon freshly ground black pepper
- 3 egg yolks
- 1/4 cup dry sherry

Direction

- Preheat oven to 450.
- Combine celery, onion and green pepper.
- Melt 8 tablespoons butter in a saucepan and add vegetables.
- Sprinkle with 1 teaspoon paprika, salt and pepper and cook stirring 5 minutes.
- Do not overcook.
- The vegetables must remain crunchy.
- Finely chop shrimp then add to vegetables.
- Cook 30 seconds stirring then remove from heat.
- Add bread crumbs and stir to blend then cool.
- Place 8 fillets skinned side up on a flat surface and sprinkle lightly with salt and pepper.
- Spoon equal amounts of filling on each and pat filling to shape it to the fillets.
- Cover each with another fillet skinned side down.
- Butter a baking dish large enough to hold the stuffed fish in one layer.
- Arrange fish and brush with 4 tablespoons of melted butter.
- Sprinkle remaining paprika through a small sieve over fish.
- Bake 15 minutes or until fish flakes easily.
- Serve with sauce.
- To make sauce melt butter in a saucepan then add flour stirring with a wire whisk.
- Add paprika and stir.
- Add two cups of the cream stirring rapidly with the whisk.

- Cook stirring until well blended then add salt and pepper.
- Beat yolks lightly and add remaining cream then stir to blend.
- Add yolk mixture to sauce stirring rapidly.
- Remove from heat immediately and continue stirring.
- Add sherry and stir then heat through but do not boil.

365. Twin Oaks Stuffed Fillet Of Sole Florentine Recipe

Serving: 18 | Prep: | Cook: 20mins | Ready in:

Ingredients

- 10 sole fillets (3 ounces each)
- 1 pound cooked or frozen spinach
- 30 sliced black olives
- 6 ounces cheddar cheese (chopped)
- 18 slices mozzarella cheese (1 inch wide)
- 1 cup olive oil
- 1 clove of garlic
- salt and red pepper seeds to taste

Direction

- In saucepan, brown garlic clove in oil. Remove garlic. Add spinach to oil for flavor then remove spinach and put in mixing bowl. Add chopped Cheddar cheese and olives. Mix thoroughly.
- Lay out fillets. Add one slice of mozzarella cheese to each fillet. Then add a heaping tablespoon of spinach mixture. Roll up fillets and place in oiled baking pan. Brush with a mixture of melted butter and lemon juice then sprinkle with a mixture of crushed Ritz crackers and bread crumbs.
- Bake in preheated 425-degree oven for 20 minutes.

Index

Conclusion

Thank you again for downloading this book!

I hope you enjoyed reading about my book!

If you enjoyed this book, please take the time to share your thoughts and post a review on Amazon. It'd be greatly appreciated!

Write me an honest review about the book – I truly value your opinion and thoughts and I will incorporate them into my next book, which is already underway.

Thank you!

If you have any questions, **feel free to contact at:** _author@cuminrecipes.com_

Jennifer Wilson

cuminrecipes.com

Printed in Great Britain
by Amazon

76534625R00106